Women
Discover Orgasm

Women
Discover Orgasm

A Therapist's Guide to
a New Treatment Approach

Lonnie Barbach

THE FREE PRESS
A Division of Macmillan Publishing Co., Inc.
NEW YORK

This book is not intended as a substitute for medical advice of
physicians. The reader should regularly consult a physician in mat-
ters relating to her health and particularly in respect of any symp-
toms which may require diagnosis or medical attention.

The Free Press
A Division of Macmillan Publishing Co., Inc.
866 Third Avenue, New York, N. Y. 10022

Library of Congress Catalog Card Number: 79-7847

Printed in the United States of America

printing number

1 2 3 4 5 6 7 8 9 10

Library of Congress Cataloging in Publication Data

Barbach, Lonnie
    Women discover orgasm.

    Bibliography: p.
    Includes index.
    1. Anorgasmy. 2. Orgasm, Female. 3. Sex therapy.
I. Title.
RC560.A56B37   618.1'7   79-7847
ISBN 0-02-901800-5

To my mother and father, for everything.

Contents

Preface

THIS BOOK had its genesis in 1972, when, as a graduate student in psychology at the University of California, Berkeley, I was hired by the university's student health service to work with Bob Cantor in Masters and Johnson style couple sex therapy. When the time came to begin work, Bob was unavailable, and there was a backlog of requests for therapy from female students and faculty members who had never experienced orgasm and who did not fit the couple treatment format. Some of these women had no regular sexual partner, some had a partner who refused to participate in couple therapy, and some did not wish their partners to know that they were seeking therapy. I felt strongly that a program should be available for these women and, with Nancy Carlsen, another sex therapist, used this situation as an opportunity to design a new form of treatment.

Nancy and I were familiar with the important supportive aspects of women's consciousness-raising groups and reasoned that the group process would prove similarly helpful for women with sexual problems. We also believed that these problems could and should be treated through a behaviorally oriented psychotherapeutic approach. We therefore instituted an experimental program, treating anorgasmic women in groups of six or seven members in a ten-session series.

The group process, and the specific techniques we developed (described in detail in the chapters to follow), proved remarkably successful from the start. While conducting the research for my doctoral dissertation (1974), I discovered that all 17 of the women comprising three experimental groups were orgasmic with masturbation by the end of the ten sessions. Not all the women had regular sex partners, but still, at the eight-month follow-up, 14 women were orgasmic in partner-related activities—11 of them more than 50 percent of the time. Furthermore, responses to my research questionnaires postgroup indicated greater happiness, relaxation, and partner communication, as well as increased self-acceptance in certain physiological areas that are sex related (e.g., overall health, appetite, excretion, weight).*

Since these first tentative efforts, I have conducted numerous therapy groups, alone or with a co-therapist, and supervised many additional groups led by therapists in training, accounting for the treatment of some 250 American and foreign born women with a variety of sexual problems. I have also held more than 35 workshops designed to train group leaders. In 1973, I decided to make the techniques available to women who were unable to attend a therapy group. *For Yourself: The Fulfillment of Female Sexuality* (1975) has been used by thousands of such women, and many of them have reported their success to me. For example, a married woman from the South wrote, "I used your book *For Yourself* in a program of self-therapy and am now a happily orgasmic woman. . . . One famous Thursday I had two orgasms in the same day . . . and we celebrated with wine and roses." A graduate student wrote, "Thank you! I'm still shaking from my first orgasm. It was fantastic! I received your book yesterday, finished it this morning, and had my first orgasm this afternoon."

Despite these successes, however, there are many cases in which a trained therapist is essential to deal with resistance, to circumvent or resolve dynamic and interpersonal issues that appear to be related to orgasm, to handle crisis situations or problems growing from a woman's sexual progress in the group, and, most important, to individualize the homework assignments, which are the heart of the process, taking into account each woman's specific problems, per-

*Similar findings were reported by other therapists using the method we developed. See Heinrich (1976), Kuriansky et al. (1976), and Ersner-Hershfield (1978).

sonality, physiology, and sexual value system. More therapists are needed, and requests for training workshops have increased to the point that I am unable to meet more than a small fraction of the demand. I am therefore delighted to have this opportunity to write a book for sex therapists.

This book, then, is intended as a guide for therapists in practice or in training who seek a better understanding of women's sexual problems and a proven technique for dealing with them. The first few chapters describe the evolution of the group treatment technique as compared with traditional methods as well as a presentation of my conceptualization of the etiology of anorgasmia. The rationale for certain choices (for example, whether to include situationally orgasmic and preorgasmic women in the same group) is presented, along with certain limitations of the group program. Subsequent chapters carry the reader through a session-by-session analysis of the process, illustrated by case examples and transcripts of taped sessions. The information contained herein can also be applied to women with orgasmic problems who are treated in individual therapy.

I make no claim that the method I describe is the only effective way of treating anorgasmia in women or that it is wholly original with me. As a matter of fact, during the 1940s Stone and Levine (both gynecologists) held group marriage-counseling discussions with women having sexual response problems.

> The reports of the groups revealed a significant change in attitude on the part of many wives and husbands. An awareness that they were not alone with their problem proved highly reassuring to most of them. Some also observed a marked improvement in their sexual adjustments and a few of the wives stated that since participating in the discussion they had for the first time actually achieved an orgasm during sexual relations [1950: 201].

My debt to other therapists is specifically acknowledged in the pages that follow. I do contend, however, that the group sex therapy described in this book has been and can be a successful mode of treatment. It helps women to achieve orgasm, alone or with a partner, and its ancillary benefits in improved self-image are no less important.

Acknowledgments

I could not have written this book without the assistance of the following friends and colleagues: Nancy Carlsen, who developed the preorgasmic group process with me; Robert Cantor and David Geisinger, who worked relentlessly tidying up the final draft; my editors at The Free Press; Rhoda Weyr, my agent; Kathy Adams, Karen Schanche, Dianne Cooper, and Sheila Dekel, who all helped to type the manuscript at one point or another; Bernie Zilbergeld, Karen Jacobs, Jay Mann, Brandy Engel, Lewis Engel, Rebecca Black, Harvey Caplan, Jane Lehman, Susan Campbell, Barry McWaters, and Ed Brecher for their comments, guidance, and help; and my dearest friends, Alberto Villoldo, Caroline Fromm, Linda Levine, and Drummond Pike, without whose support I would have been lost. I cannot thank these people enough.

Women
Discover Orgasm

CHAPTER 1

Causes of Orgasmic Dysfunction

ACCORDING TO MASTERS AND JOHNSON, orgasm is defined as: "a psychophysiologic experience occurring within, and made meaningful by a context of psychosocial influence. Physiologically, it is a brief episode of physical release from the vasocongestive and myotonic increment developed in response to sexual stimuli. Psychologically, it is subjective perception of a peak of physical reaction to sexual stimuli [1966: 127]." Since no two people are physiologically or psychologically alike, the experience of orgasm is unique to each person. Women vary not only in the type of stimulation they require for orgasm, but in the intensity of the experience, and the number of orgasms necessary for satisfaction; a wide range of factors, including diverse relationship and environmental influences, affect each orgasmic response. Women in my therapy groups have described orgasm as a "rush," a "mint-flavored heat wave," "like one heartbeat all over," a "misty cloud that envelops me." One woman said, "I feel this buildup, then there is this feeling after it that's different, that's distinct. I don't feel contractions, but I don't feel like going on anymore. And I feel relaxed."

Through the years, many competing theories have been offered as to the causes of anorgasmia in women. The factors cited range from simple lack of information and misinformation to negative sexual attitudes and pervasive psychological disturbance. Each theory adds bits of information to a complex puzzle. The current understanding seems to be that in most cases there is no one single cause of a woman's inability to experience orgasm, but, rather, a number of interacting factors are responsible.

Lack of Information and Negative Attitudes

A popular viewpoint that appears to explain those cases of orgasmic dysfunction that can be reversed with minimal intervention, attributes the absence of orgasm to either lack of information or negative sexual attitudes. The psychoanalytic writings of Caprio (1953), Fenichel (1945), Lorand (1966) and the work of Kaplan (1974) cite sexual ignorance, prudishness, misinformation about normal sex, and inadequate understanding of stimulation techniques as creating orgasmic dysfunction. The behaviorists (Lazarus, 1963; Wolpe, 1973) blame sexual problems on faulty attitudes and sexual practices; Masters and Johnson (1966) add that negative attitudes on the part of one's parents and their failure to transmit information greatly contribute to anorgasmia.

Women who are not orgasmic commonly report that they learned nothing at all about sex from their parents or at school. Many have no idea of what is involved in having sex, do not know that women can and do masturbate or that women experience orgasm, or have a false expectation of what an orgasm is like. Generally, these women had done very little self-exploration. Possibly because, as Mead (1949) claimed, the female genitals are not readily visible and thus receive less touching than the male genitals, many little girls fail to discover the erotic sensations that can be aroused there. More likely however, this lack of interest is the result of trained inhibition. We have seen that when given even minimal information, many women with this history seem to be able to stimulate themselves to orgasm almost immediately.

Lack of information is just one contribution to female sexual problems. False notions that women are not supposed to enjoy sex still prevail; for example, until the early part of this century it was generally believed in our society that a "good woman" had little or no sex drive; she was virtuous and chaste (Bullough and Bullough, 1977). Sex was a wifely duty, nothing more, and any indication of sexual appetite was a clear sign of immorality. (This perspective is not wholly dead; a woman in one of my therapy groups reported that she had been told by her mother always to make it clear to her husband that intercourse caused her pain.)

Strict sexually disapproving religious environments have been found to affect sexual responsiveness adversely as well (Kinsey, et al., 1953; Masters and Johnson, 1970). Religious teachings may lead women to feel that they are bad or abnormal if they experience strong sexual urges. Feelings of shame and sometimes disgust toward the genitals and sexual functioning often result from exposure to religious orthodoxy. In these cases, the woman must first overcome the negative messages by receiving considerable support and permission from others. Once this task has been accomplished, she is generally able to achieve orgasm easily.

The Elusive Vaginal Orgasm

Without accurate anatomical and physiological information, many women expect that the one "right" way to be sexual is to have orgasms as the result of the penis's thrusting in and out of the vagina. If they have other experiences, and especially if these are enjoyable, they feel that they are abnormal. This very common misunderstanding arises in large part from Freud's distinction between vaginal and clitoral orgasms.

Freud presented a theory of psychosexual development that described sexuality as a life drive in both men and women, from birth onward. Although his work was the foundation and framework for contemporary psychotherapy, his view of female sexual inadequacy has had many harmful repercussions. Lacking accurate scientific data and writing from the perspective of a middle-class Viennese male, Freud developed the notion that there are two types of orgasm experienced by females—an immature (clitoral) orgasm and a mature (vaginal) orgasm. He argued that the development of healthy sexuality in women is complicated by the need to renounce the clitoris, originally the principal genital zone, in favor of a new zone, the vagina: "In the phallic phase of girls the clitoris is the leading eroto-

3

genic zone. But it is not, of course, going to remain so—with the change to femininity the clitoris should wholly or in part hand over its sensitivity, and at the same time its importance to the vagina [1965: 118]." Freud's work had a powerful impact upon Western society: with few facts to go on, many psychoanalysts (e.g., Fenichel, 1945; Horney, 1967) have continued to assert that even though a woman experiences orgasm with clitoral stimulation, failure to achieve a peak sexual response from the thrusting of the penis during intercourse indicates fixation at an earlier stage of psychosexual development and is symptomatic of an underlying conflict warranting psychiatric assistance.

These conceptions of female sexuality are rooted in the Victorian view that sexual activity is permissible only within rather narrowly defined limits: between married people and principally for the purpose of procreation. Sexual activity as a source of healthy pleasure and a way of expressing intimacy was not popularly encouraged, especially for women.

The modern scientific position, as expressed by Masters and Johnson, is that "from an anatomic point of view, there is absolutely no difference in the responses of the pelvic viscera to effective stimulation, regardless of whether the stimulation occurs as a result of clitoral-body or mons area manipulation, natural or artificial coition, or for that matter, specific stimulation of any other erogenous area of the female body [1966: 66]." Yet the influence of Freud persists. Although Hite (1976) found that 70 percent of her sample of women required direct clitoral stimulation in order for orgasm to occur, most of them continued to feel abnormal if the so-called vaginal orgasm was not within their grasp. Sherfey amplified this psychocultural observation: "More and more women (and men) accept the equation: vaginal orgasms equal normalcy. Hence, there is an ever-growing incidence of guilt, fear, and resentment in otherwise healthy women who find themselves unable to achieve the elusive prize [1972: 26]."

The repercussions of this viewpoint cannot be overemphasized.

> Not just the couples with sexual problems and most of the educated public, but almost all psychiatrists and physicians (excepting gynecologists and endocrinologists) are still committed to the belief in the existence of the vaginal orgasm as distinct from the infantile clitoral orgasm and consider the vaginal orgasm to be a vital sign of normal feminine development. . . . Could many of the sexual neur-

4

oses which seem to be almost endemic to women today be, in part, induced by doctors attempting to treat them [Sherfey, 1972: 27–28]?

Meanwhile, convincing women about the normalcy of clitoral stimulation requires considerable attitudinal change, a process that generally takes time to solidify.

Belief in a Standard Sexual Response

We all admit that each of us in unique in many ways—in the jobs we choose, the hobbies we enjoy, and the people we find attractive. Some women are great athletes, others have fine manual dexterity, some are musically inclined, and some have a sophisticated palate. Likewise, each woman's sexual responsiveness is unique. Kinsey noted that whereas "considerable variation occurs among males, the range of variation in almost every type of sexual activity seems to be far greater among females [1953: 146]." Masters and Johnson also cautioned: "It always should be borne in mind that there is wide individual variation in the duration and intensity of every specific physiologic response to sexual stimulation [1966: 7]." Accordingly, Lazarus (1963) found that a low threshold of distractibility can interfere with orgasmic responsiveness in some women; Masters and Johnson found a history of low sexual tension to be correlated with anorgasmia; and Kaplan (1974) and Hite (1976) found that lovemaking techniques that are not suited to the needs of the individual woman are frequently responsible for the inability to climax.

Yet much of the public remains unconvinced by the documentation produced by these and other researchers and adheres to a fixed notion of sexual normality. In addition, since so little information is available about how others respond to sex, many myths continue to circulate, creating a variety of sexual problems. Thus, if a woman learns that multiple orgasm is possible, she feels somehow deficient if she has only one orgasm at a time. If she learns that some people make love for an hour, she thinks she must lack sexual energy if she prefers shorter episodes. If she finds anal sex painful, she wonders what is wrong with her. Some women become sexually aroused very quickly; others respond slowly. Some women require intense and direct clitoral stimulation to reach orgasm whereas others react to subtle pressure and indirect clitoral stimulation. Lack of acceptance of the physiological differences among women (as well as men) creates a personal sexual olympics: there is no other human activity in which everyone expects to be a gold medal winner or regard herself as a total failure.

The physiological issues become more complex when a woman strives to adapt her unique physiological requirements to the anatomical and physiological uniqueness of her partner. He may like hard and rapid thrusting though she prefers a slower and more sensual movement; she may require a protruding pubic bone for sufficient clitoral stimulation during intercourse whereas his pubic bone recedes. If she has been taught to believe that there is only one right way to function sexually, she will try to fit herself into a mold she assumes is normal and thus will not attempt to develop lovemaking techniques that meet her own needs and enhance her sexual pleasure.

Orgasm Is Learned

The need to learn to be sexual, that is, to learn appropriate techniques for deriving sexual satisfaction, is a revolutionary concept, especially for women who grew up thinking that sex should be a totally spontaneous and natural activity. However, since nearly everything we do is learned, it should come as no surprise that Kinsey found that more highly educated women, who were more likely to be sophisticated and liberal and hence not to accept wholesale the views of parents or clergy, were also more likely to experience orgasm; that women who experienced premarital orgasm by any means were three times more likely to experience orgasm in marital sex than were those without such a history; and that the ability to experience orgasm increased with the length of the marriage. Kinsey wrote, "It is doubtful if any type of therapy has ever been as effective as early experience in orgasm in reducing the incidence of unresponsiveness in marital coitus, and in increasing the frequency of response to orgasm in that coitus [1953: 385–386]."

Kinsey's data, therefore, laid the foundation for the important assumption that orgasm can be considered a learned response and that failure to achieve it is not necessarily a sign of neurosis but, rather, a possible result of faulty or inadequate learning. Furthermore, a learned response reflects certain cultural definitions. Mead pointed out that "there seems to be a reasonable basis for assuming that the human female's capacity for orgasm is to be viewed much more as a potentiality that may or may not be developed by a given culture [1949: 217].'' Thus, women who have sexual problems because they define as normal only certain responses within the confines of certain limited activities are frequently demonstrating inadequate or inappropriate sexual learning.

Female Role Scripting

It is extremely difficult to change women's perceptions about normal female sexual functioning in a way that makes them more accepting of both the need for clitoral stimulation and their own physiological uniqueness. Their resistance appears to be based on the female role scripting in this culture, which teaches women, among other things, not to be assertive.

In our society, both men and women are taught that men are the authorities on sex. With no instruction, each man is somehow expected to understand each woman's unique sexuality. This, of course, is supposed to occur without any input from the woman herself, who, if she is decent and respectable, is expected to be innocent of sexual knowledge and experience. The man cannot ask his partner for information: not to be omniscient would make him appear less masculine. Likewise, the woman cannot tell her partner what would bring her pleasure because first, she is not supposed to know and second, because she fears she may hurt his ego by implying that he is inadequate or insufficiently knowledgeable. Some women subscribe to the romantic expectation that if a man "really" loves her he will know specifically what she would most enjoy at every point in lovemaking.

Submerged in the mystical vision of sex that arises out of this mutual lack of information, many women do not learn about themselves sexually and do not accept responsibility for their sexuality but, rather, expect the man to awaken them.

Nelson (1974) found that women fall into two categories regarding their sexual attitudes. They are either "romantics," whose attitudes reflect an idealistic, mystified vision of romantic love, or "realists," who show a rational understanding of conscious sexual cooperation. Realistic women were discriminating about their sexual activity and able to tell their partners what they liked and did not like; they were active in initiating sex; they concentrated primarily on themselves during lovemaking, and tended to direct lovemaking overtly in order to get what they wanted. Romantic women, by contrast, did not talk about sex, rarely initiated sex, focused selflessly on the partner in an attempt to please him, and amiably followed their lover's direction during lovemaking. It is interesting to note that Nelson's subjects' self-reports indicated that 77.3 percent of the romantic women were low-orgasmic whereas 70 percent of the realistic women were high-orgasmic. Nelson's research thus gives credence to the popular theory that the way women are trained to behave may in itself contribute to the lack of female orgasm.

The sex-role training of American girls establishes passivity and dependence as desirable female attributes. As they are prepared for their future roles as wives and mothers, girls are taught to provide the nurturance their husbands and children will require. They are trained to serve selflessly but are not adequately provided with the skill or the confidence to manage their own lives and achieve a sense of independence. Since they are taught to be dependent, they learn to approach life from a powerless position. They are trained, above all, to seek love. If they are attractive, charming, and not so intelligent as to threaten the man's self-esteem, they can get a man to take care of them for the rest of their lives. Their security lies in being loved. If they are loved, they will be cared for and will not be abandoned. Their position in life is therefore determined by how good their choice of a partner has been. They feel no sense of positive power to attain things for themselves. Their only power is to make requests of (or to manipulate) their husbands and, when they do not like what they get, to withhold.

A woman trained to be passive may relinquish control over her life to others—to a spouse, for example, or to the fates. When she does attempt control, it often takes the form of resistance, or negative control. Her behavior is a way of saying that even though she cannot attain what she wants, no one can force her to do what she does not want to do. Such a woman may deprive herself of the experience of orgasm as a way of punishing her partner for her dissatisfaction with their relationship by making him feel inadequate sexually. This response is understandable in a society that views sex as an activity engaged in for the man's and not the woman's pleasure. Since women can use sex as a way to catch a man, they can withhold sex when they are angry. The case of Maria illustrates this point.

MARIA: In my relationship with Greg I don't have orgasms all the time and I want to have them all the time.

THERAPIST: Do you ever have them with him?

MARIA: Yeah, but I want to have them all the time. When I don't, I feel really left out and I feel real cheated and I feel anger, too. Greg said, "Why don't we keep a record every time you have an orgasm?" I felt that was not the right attitude either. He has an orgasm every time we have sex, so why shouldn't I? Why should I be deprived of having an orgasm every time?

THERAPIST: It's probably not possible every single time. Aren't there some times when you're exhausted and it's too much effort?

MARIA: Yeah.

THERAPIST: That happens to me every once in a while, too. Sometimes I feel like having sex but I don't feel like putting in the effort to have an orgasm. But, meanwhile, what's the difference between the times when you do have an orgasm and the times when you don't?

MARIA: I probably go into it thinking, "I'd better have an orgasm or I'm going to be mad."

THERAPIST: And then you do or you don't?

MARIA: And then I don't.

THERAPIST: Okay, so you set it up. Anything else you notice about the times you don't have orgasms?

MARIA: How can I say it? Like if I felt in the day that I was hassled with cleaning or cooking or something. He comes and he's reading. How dare he sit and read when I've been doing all these things! I feel that that is my way of getting even. And then the days when he helps me with the dishes or something everything's fine. It's all very simple.

THERAPIST: So when you're angry enough, instead of just being angry, you just don't have an orgasm. And then you can really be angry, right? A good, legitimate reason.

MARIA: Yeah, except I'm hurting myself.

THERAPIST: In addition, he doesn't know what you're angry about.

MARIA: That puts a lot of pressure on him. That's the other thing I was thinking about. When I don't have an orgasm he feels that I don't love him. And then he gets more desperately into pleasing me.

THERAPIST: That's a great payoff in addition.

MARIA: Yeah.

Fear of Losing Control

The lack of control that women feel over their lives can be pervasive. Kaplan (1974) noted that the fear of losing control over feelings and behavior is very common among women who are preorgasmic and that the resulting defense mechanisms of holding back and overcontrolling are crucial in the genesis of this disorder. At the intrapsychic level, a feeling of control is intimately related to the degree to which a woman experiences herself as separate and differentiated from others. Having well-defined ego boundaries affords a person a certain sense of control; she feels the power and security of being whole and autonomous. Since most women sense a loss of control at the point of climax, relinquishing conscious control when experiencing the orgasmic state can be extremely anxiety producing for a woman with little or no initial sense of control. These women often express the fear that they will dissolve or merge with the partner as sexual sensations become intense.

Fear of loss of control appears to be the fundamental problem of women who require more than simple permission and information in order to reach orgasm. These women need to experience sexual arousal gradually so that they can slowly become familiar with sexual intensity and thus feel more in control. If arousal mounts too rapidly, they can be overwhelmed by the strength of their sexual feelings and experience fears of exploding or even having epileptic fits. The compensatory overcontrol, which limits sexual expression, frequently also encompasses the expression of other feelings, such as anger and caring. Women who fit this pattern are often incapable of showing feelings to a limited degree. They experience the world and their options as either black or white, with no gradations between the extremes. They are thus unable to set limits and find themselves either immobilized and unable to approach something new, or overwhelmed because they jump in too quickly.

MARIA: That's what I do, okay? I have a vibrator, and if I can't take it anymore, then I move the vibrator on other parts. And when it builds up again and it's great, then it comes to pain again. I'm getting better at it, so I can take more. I feel something coming. It's getting so intense. And I say, "Oh! Time out!"

BEVERLY: The pain is getting intense or the feeling?

MARIA: The feeling, something, the orgasm. It's just when it's coming. My lover says that I always stop the orgasm when we're making love. Just before I'm coming, I'm just some-where. I just start going into space and I'm afraid.

JOSEPHINE: I caught myself doing that, stopping myself.

MARIA: Just after I was eighteen and I wasn't a virgin anymore, I asked this older woman, "How does it feel to have an or-gasm?" And she said, "Oh, it's like an explosion. Your whole body explodes." And I think that must've made an impression on me 'cause I think something's going to happen to me. I'm going to explode. And I'm scared of that.

PAMELA: I'm afraid I'll die if it happens. I'll lose such control and that'll be the end of it.

ABBY: I'm scared of shaking and looking like I'm in an epileptic fit. That's what I'm scared of. I'm also scared of not being able to hold my urine at a certain point.

The process of learning to reach orgasm by approaching new sex-ual situations in carefully graduated steps helps such women to de-velop a sense of internal control thereby eliminating the need to overcontrol. To become orgasmic, a woman must test levels of sex-ual intensity slowly and over time until her security is built up by the knowledge that indeed she can control these feelings. She finds that she can stop the stimulation if she wants to or she can continue with it and gradually experience more and more intense feeling. Slowly, she can learn to trust her sense of control to the extent that she can allow the sensations to build to orgasm and still expect to survive the experience, first while alone, then with a partner. When that is achieved, she learns to assume control by asserting her needs and communicating her sexual likes and dislikes to her partner in order to insure that the sexual encounter will be satisfying.

A change in the woman's sense of control has been documented through testing before and after participation in a preorgasmic group, using the Rotter Internal-External Locus of Control Inven-tory (Rotter, 1966). Heinrich found a "significant difference in the direction of internal locus of control indicating an increase in the subjects' belief in their personal control of events [1976: 102]." She explained the finding thus: "The treatment for primary orgasmic dysfunction rests heavily on the notion that people should take re-sponsibility for their own sexuality. The [research results] suggest that this notion may have generalized to other areas of life for those subjects in the study [p. 98]."

This analysis of the role of control in anorgasmia is somewhat simplified, but I hope the point is clear: young girls are trained to be passive and to relinquish control over their lives. The sense of insufficient control leads to other problems: absence of differentiated ego boundaries, inability to express feelings, and lack of orgasm. Consequently, if girls are trained to be more assertive and independent, one would expect that the incidence of anorgasmia would be greatly reduced in situations in which these dynamics come into play. This premise is substantiated by the findings of anthropologists Ford and Beach.

> The societies that severely restrict adolescent and preadolescent sex play, those that enjoin girls to be modest, retiring, and submissive, appear to produce adult women that are incapable or at least unwilling to be sexually aggressive. The feminine products of such cultural training are likely to remain relatively inactive even during marital intercourse. And, quite often, they do not experience clearcut orgasm. In contrast, the societies which permit or encourage early sex play usually allow females a greater degree of freedom in seeking sexual contacts. Under such circumstances, the sexual performance of the mature woman seems to be characterized by a certain degree of aggression, to include definite and vigorous sexual activity, and to result regularly in complete and satisfactory orgasm [1951: 266].

Other Psychological Factors

Psychoanalysts used to believe that a number of other situations resulted in anorgasmia. Most of these theories have been either dismissed or reinterpreted. The idea that "excessive" masturbation localizes the woman's sexual feelings in the clitoris for example, was dismissed when Masters and Johnson (1966) discovered that in masturbation women stimulate the clitoris rather than the vagina because of the already existing density of nerve endings in that area. The incestuous wishes resulting from an unresolved Electra complex—the little girl's desire for sexual union with her father and the implied wish for the death or disappearance of her mother in order to make this union possible—are believed by many psychoanalysts to produce severe conflict in the young girl, frequently manifested in anorgasmia and/or fear of injury to the genitals. Kaplan (1974) asserted that if the young female abandons herself totally to her sexual

12

feelings, she fears being deserted or destroyed by her jealous mother, particularly if the daughter is very dependent. Thus, she reinterpreted the Electra complex to place less emphasis on an unresolved relationship with the father and more on issues of dependency and vulnerability if control is lost. Finally, Thompson (1971), Moulton (1973), and others have attributed penis envy—the belief that aggressive women are anorgasmic because they have an unconscious wish for a penis and feel cheated or deprived because they lack one—to the woman's craving for the societal status and freedom experienced by the possessor of a penis rather than to the wish for the male organ itself.

Although in some rare cases it may be true that deep-seated problems cause orgasmic dysfunction, women who do not respond to short-term behaviorally oriented treatment and require intensive psychotherapy to experience orgasm have been few and far between. Fisher's research seems to indicate that for the most part lack of orgasm and psychological disturbance are not correlated: "There are so many things with which orgasm consistently is *not* linked. Particularly noteworthy is the fact that it does not seem related to maladjustment or psychological disturbance. . . . There does not appear to be a relationship between the 'mental health' of a woman and her ability to attain orgasm [1973:275]." Age, religious affiliation or religiosity, characteristics of the husband, or measures of femininity (e.g., use of cosmetics or adornments and attention to dress) were also found not to correlate with ability to achieve orgasm.

Both Fisher and I did find, however, that the inability to experience orgasm correlated with having grown up with a physically or emotionally absent father (Barbach, 1974; Fisher, 1973). Fisher interpreted these findings psychoanalytically to mean that the father's absence creates fears of love-object loss in the young girl. However, anorgasmia resulting from this situation can also be ascribed to the woman's abandoned mother unintentionally teaching her that men are unreliable and likely to desert her. In this situation, the mother, through her own insecurity, may transmit to her daughter the need to control her emotions and maintain separateness.

It appears that although a woman's overall mental health may not be called into question because of her lack of orgasm, many psychological concerns can be linked to the issue of orgasm. Fears of pregnancy, childbirth, and venereal disease, among others, may affect a woman's anxiety level and hence her responsiveness during sex; so may her concern about problems involving children, illness, or money, particularly when these worries are chronic. Deeper fears, however, frequently surface once the woman becomes actively aroused sexually. Some women feel overly vulnerable to their partners as sexual tension mounts. The fear of losing the partner becomes exaggerated as they anticipate the intense intimacy that might occur with orgasm. Other women fear they will not find the partner attractive , or that their partner will find them unappealing once they become orgasmic and hence will have to face the possibility of separation or divorce. Many women fear that by becoming orgasmic they will have to behave more maturely or that their lives or personalities will change dramatically. These anxieties tend to be associated dynamically with the fear of losing control. In order for orgasm to occur in these cases, it appears to be less important to resolve the underlying issue than to disconnect it from the experience of orgasm. Work on these other issues can be resumed if they remain problematic after the simpler task of learning to become orgasmic has been achieved. (The question of psychological issues is explored further in Chapter 6.)

CHAPTER 2

Treatment of Orgasmic Dysfunction

DESPITE THE SO-CALLED sexual revolution, little progress has been made in the reduction of orgasmic dysfunction. Kinsey and his colleagues (1953:513) reported that approximately 10 percent of married American women and 30 percent of sexually active unmarried women never experienced orgasm. Only 40 percent of married women were orgasmic in 90–100 percent of their coital experiences (p. 403). Roughly the same figures were obtained twenty years later in a survey sponsored by the Playboy Foundation (Hunt, 1974) and even more recently by Hite (1976). The apparent stability of these figures for more than two decades testifies to the perseverance of antiquated ideas and the unavailability of effective treatment.

Psychoanalytically Oriented Therapy

In the past, if a woman sought help for anorgasmia, she was generally referred to a therapist who was psychoanalytically oriented. The therapist would treat the anorgasmia as a symptom of underlying problems or conflicts and would propose years of psychoanalysis as a solution (Lorand, 1939). After spending considerable time and money (Bergler, 1947), she might end treatment happier with some aspects of her life but often still not experiencing orgasm. In a study of 61 partially or totally "frigid" women treated four times a week for a minimum of two years, O'Connor and Stern (1972) found that 25 percent of the cases were cured and an additional 35 percent showed some improvement.

The relative ineffectiveness of early analytic treatment may have resulted from a number of factors, including the false distinction made by Freud and his followers between clitoral and vaginal orgasms. Also, by its very nature psychoanalytic therapy puts the woman in an inferior position vis-à-vis the therapist-authority. According to Chesler, "For most women the psychotherapeutic encounter is just one more instance of an unequal relationship, just one more opportunity to be rewarded for expressing distress and to be 'helped' by being (expertly) dominated [1972:373]." This situation makes it even more difficult for a woman to learn to assert herself and to recognize her own sexual needs. However, it must be kept in mind that no other form of therapy available before the 1960s was any more successful in reversing female orgasmic dysfunction.

Behavior Therapy

As I have noted, Kinsey laid the groundwork for the important assumption that orgasm is a learned response and that failure to achieve it may be the result of inadequate learning. The behavioral approach to treatment, with its foundation in learning theory, is based on this notion. It argues that some women have learned to feel intense anxiety during sex. Thus, therapy must help the woman unlearn the primary stimulus configuration and relearn a more appropriate configuration. (see Brady, 1966; Lazarus, 1963; Madsen and Ullman, 1967; Wolpe, 1969). This goal is generally accomplished through systematic desensitization and vicarious learning.

Vicarious learning is the process of learning through modeling or through the reports of another. Desensitization is a therapeutic process that involves relaxing the client and, once he or she is relaxed, gradually introducing the phobic stimulus. Self-relaxation is the technique generally used, but drugs such as Brevital, meprobamate, and chlorpromazine (Brady, 1966; Wolpe, 1961)—in fact any stimulus that competes with or is antithetical to the anxiety response can be used. For example, vaginismus, the involuntary, spasmodic contraction of the pelvic musculature prohibiting intercourse, is one reaction to anxiety during sex. To have the woman bear down in the pelvic area as if she were pushing out a tampon is a behavior antithetical to the muscular contractions that produce vaginismus. While she is bearing down, she cannot involuntarily contract.

The technique of desensitization consists first of determining a hierarchy of anxiety-producing behavioral situations. Next, the antithetical response (say, relaxation) is paired with each item in order, beginning with the one producing the least anxiety. Once this item can be presented without arousing anxiety, an item of slightly greater anxiety-producing potential is presented with the antithetical response. The hierarchy is gone through in small, discrete steps until the most anxiety-producing stimulus has been presented. The nine-step masturbation desensitization format developed by Lobitz and LoPiccolo (1972; described on pp. 19–20 of this chapter) is an example of such a program designed to dissipate anxiety related to sexual behavior. A desensitization program can be conducted either by using real-life situations (in vivo) or by having the client imagine the appropriate circumstances.

For example, an exercise generally used early in conjoint sex therapy (see pp. 189–192) is sensate focus (a localized massage or body rub) because a nonsexual massage is generally less anxiety producing than an explicitly sexual exercise for a couple having sexual problems. If this step appears to be too anxiety producing, the partners may be asked to imagine that they are massaging, or being massaged, by each other before they actually do it.

The Masters and Johnson hierarchy of homework assignments is an example of in vivo desensitization. If the homework assignments are fulfilled only in fantasy, this would represent imaginal desensitization. Both methods can be successfully employed in the treatment of female orgasmic problems. Frequently, the client is encouraged to imagine a particular situation a number of times until she can do so without anxiety; then she attempts to complete the assignment in real life.

Behavioral therapists Lazarus (1963), Brady (1966), Madsen and Ullman (1967), and Wolpe (1969) have reported 86–100 percent success in the treatment of female orgasmic dysfunction. Unfortunately, since the numbers of cases reported were small and procedures varied considerably, rigorous evaluative research was difficult

17

and generalization almost impossible. Lazarus (1963) considered his results (nine successes in a sample of 16) more encouraging than those of any other therapeutic approach at that time, particularly since all of his patients had received some form of treatment for orgasmic problems prior to consulting with him.

While behavior therapy may be effective in cases wherein the manipulation of the behavior is sufficient by itself, it sometimes ignores important intrapsychic conflicts. Also, behavior modification techniques used alone often fail to resolve the anorgasmic symptom in the woman who is experiencing hostility toward her husband.

Conjoint Sex Therapy

Although Masters and Johnson do not call themselves behavioral therapists, their treatment incorporates fundamental behavioral principles. The homework they prescribe is a basic desensitization program to extinguish performance anxiety, and their male-female team of therapists provides vicarious learning through modeling behavior for the clients—a couple—to imitate. Each member of the couple is given a same-sex ally on the co-therapy team, and the therapists model communication behavior, which can be used by the clients to reinforce each other's positive changes. The dual-sex team also focuses on correcting irrational attitudes and beliefs in an educational and nonjudgmental manner. Conjoint therapy has the additional advantage of permitting the therapists to observe the couple's interactional and communication system directly and to intervene as necessary.

Masters and Johnson reported that of a sample of 193 women who had never experienced orgasm 16.6 percent totally failed to become orgasmic after two weeks of treatment; 22.8 percent of 149 women who were either anorgasmic with masturbation or with coitus, or infrequently or inconsistently orgasmic by these means, also totally failed to become orgasmic. The remainder of the women were successful to some degree (1970:314). Couples with serious marital or psychological difficulties in addition to the sexual problem were not accepted for treatment. Though this screening procedure probably increased positive results, this is offset by the fact that their goal of coital orgasm is now beginning to be viewed as not physiologically realistic for many women. As Kaplan noted, and as my research has corroborated: "The woman who does not reach orgasm on coitus, but is otherwise responsive . . . may represent a normal variant of female sexuality [1974:374]."

Though conjoint therapy provides important information regarding the couple's relationship, information not easily acquired by seeing only one member, there are obvious limitations with the Masters and Johnson approach. It precludes the treatment of women without regular sexual partners and of women whose partners are unwilling to participate in treatment. Also, because two therapists are required, this form of treatment is very costly in terms of therapist time and monetary expense to the clients.

Masturbation Desensitization

Although Masters and Johnson do not rely on masturbation as a learning technique, others have adapted their methods to include masturbation as a way for a woman to experience her first orgasm before having her partner control the stimulation. Lobitz and LoPiccolo (1972) developed a nine-step masturbation desensitization program for women who had never experienced orgasm by any means. The women practice each step until they have successfully completed it before proceeding to the next step.

Step 1: Nude bath examination; genital examination; Kegel exercises (Kegel, 1952).

Step 2: Tactile as well as visual genital exploration with no expectation of arousal.

Step 3: Tactile and visual genital exploration with the object of locating areas that produce pleasurable feelings when stimulated.

Step 4: Manual masturbation of the areas identified as pleasurable.

Step 5: Increased duration and intensity of the masturbation if no orgasm occurred in step 4.

Step 6: Masturbation with a vibrator if no orgasm occurred as the result of step 5.

Step 7: After orgasm has occurred through masturbation, the husband observes the wife masturbating.

Step 8: The husband stimulates the wife in the manner she demonstrated in step 7.

Step 9: Once orgasm occurs in step 8, the husband stimulates his wife's genitals manually or with a vibrator during intercourse.

Lobitz and LoPiccolo developed a coordinated program of working with the woman individually on masturbation while working with the couple conjointly on related sexual and communication issues. They reported 100 percent success in a sample of three women, the slowest of whom required three months to achieve orgasm through masturbation. This program appeared to have considerable potential; however, they did not make it available to unattached females, and it was as costly as more traditional sex therapy.

The Preorgasmic Group Process

A new approach to the treatment of the anorgasmic woman seemed to be needed—one that would be available to women regardless of their relationship status; one that was short-term, relatively inexpensive, and economical in regard to therapist time so that a large number of women could benefit; yet one that could be tailored to the unique needs of each woman. The preorgasmic* group process accomplishes these goals and others by first encouraging changes in behavior, allowing changes in attitude and insight to follow at a pace which is comfortable for each woman.

The program involves groups of six or seven women who meet together for 10 sessions of about two hours each. Generally, the sessions are held once or twice weekly. Each woman is required to do an hour a day of assigned sexual and nonsexual tasks at home and to report to the group at the next meeting on how her "homework" and other relevant concerns are progressing. The initial assignments, described in detail in later chapters, follow the Lobitz and LoPiccolo nine-step masturbation program. As the women progress, the assignments are modified to meet each woman's distinctive needs. The

*The word "preorgasmic," coined by a woman in one of the first treatment groups, reflects the optimistic attitude that women who do not experience orgasm are not psychologically disturbed but, rather, lack the necessary information and experience for orgasm to take place. Every female is at some point in her life preorgasmic. The rapidity with which this term has been accepted by professional and lay audiences seems to indicate a change in the perception of female orgasmic dysfunction.

therapist* works with each woman on an individual basis to design, with her help, assignments that fit her unique problem, personality, and sexual value system.

The overall concept is to approach new goals through small behavioral steps. By gradual stages, the woman learns to gain control over and feel good about her body; then she learns to take responsibility for her own orgasm through masturbation; finally she learns to ask for or to do what feels best with her partner.

As I embarked on designing the program, I had to confront some of the major tenets of sex therapy, particularly the basic concept of Masters and Johnson that a sexual problem is a relationship problem and that consequently the partners must be treated conjointly. I felt that although sexual dysfunction in some cases results from relationship dynamics (and in other cases causes problems in the relationship), it seemed reasonable that more often it results from some aspect of the individual's sexual history, values, or expectations—especially if the dysfunction has occurred with every partner. Consequently, for women who had rarely experienced orgasm with any partner and not with masturbation, it seemed that orgasm might be an issue to be resolved by the individual woman first and worked into a relationship after she had become comfortable with the experience of orgasm on her own. Later, women who were already orgasmic with masturbation but who were not orgasmic with a partner were included.

I had some concern about the transferability of the orgasm from masturbation to the partner sexual relationship but was encouraged by the results reported by Lobitz and LoPiccolo (1972), as well as by Kinsey's finding that "there are very few instances among our several thousand histories of females who were able to masturbate to orgasm without becoming capable of similar responses in coitus [Kinsey et al. 1953:391]."

The theory behind the women's group treatment model, then, combines the premises of various other treatment modalities. It is behaviorally oriented in using a graduated desensitization program, and it incorporates the methods of other body oriented therapies by providing a way for women to explore and learn to be more comfortable with their bodies. This exploration often leads to the uncovering of fears, conflicts, and relationship problems, which are examined through individual inquiry within the context of the group. Negative cultural attitudes and role scripting regarding women's feelings

---

*Ideally, the process involves two therapists working together (see pp. 54–57).

about their sexuality are overcome by giving the explicit message that each woman is unique and therefore is the authority on her own sexuality. The women learn that they are deserving of pleasure—including sexual pleasure—but that it is their responsibility to obtain such pleasure if and when they desire it.

Preorgasmic groups are therapy groups and skilled therapists are required to run them. Each woman is different and requires specialized interventions that suit her physiological and psychological needs. The therapist must be trained in handling a broad range of psychological problems. The preorgasmic process is no better than the skill of the therapists who run the groups.

The therapists use clinical techniques for dealing with resistance, and the group process itself often aids in resolving or bypassing resistance by providing a supportive environment in which to experiment. Although only half of the couple is being treated, the communication and interactional system of the partnership is not ignored, although whenever possible the woman's responsibility for relationship problems and conflicts is pointed out and explored.

The etiology of a woman's sexual problem affects both the therapeutic approach and the issues explored during the therapy. However, I try to circumvent dynamic and interpersonal issues that do not appear to be intimately related to orgasm, relying instead on a more behavioral approach. This is not always possible, and short-term but dynamic therapeutic intervention is frequently also required.

Women's groups are not only easier to conduct than individual therapy but are often more successful in terms of outcome. The group process eliminates feelings of isolation and abnormality as each woman works with and learns from others like herself. This approach seems as fruitful with women who grew up in an era of sexual inhibition as it does with younger women, reared in an era of sexual coercion. The same basic group process can also be adapted as an educational program for women who have no particular sexual problem but wish to enhance their relationships by becoming more comfortable and accepting of their sexuality.

SOME RESULTS OF TREATMENT

The achievement of orgasm is the expressed goal of the women who come to the group, but the ancillary benefits appear to be at least as noteworthy. Considerable research (Barbach, 1974; Heinrich, 1976; Kuriansky, Sharpe, and O'Connor, 1976) has indicated that women who participate in these preorgasmic groups feel far better about their bodies and feel that they have better control over their lives after the therapy has successfully concluded.

In Heinrich's study, for example, 100 percent of the 15 preorgasmic women attending the treatment group became orgasmic with masturbation within ten sessions. At her two-month follow-up, 13 of these women were orgasmic in partner related activities and seven during coitus. These results were corroborated by responses from a male partner questionnaire. Heinrich also found significant postgroup increases in the frequency of sexual activity among the women, as well as significantly more reported pleasure in sexual activity. In addition, there was a significant increase in the women's sense of internal control as measured by the Rotter Internal-External Locus of Control Scale (Rotter, 1966). This is an important finding since the control issue is central to overcoming orgasmic dysfunction. The women also showed increased satisfaction with their clitoris, sex activities, sex drive, and weight as measured by the Body Cathexis Scale (Secord and Jourard, 1953).*

The preliminary results of research by Kuriansky, Sharpe, and O'Connor (1976) at New York Medical College, using the Structured and Scaled Interview to Assess Maladjustment (SSIAM), indicated that women who sought preorgasmic group treatment had higher than normal levels of maladjustment in all life areas. The highest level of maladjustment was found in the sexual area, the next highest in family relationships, and the lowest in work. At the one-year posttreatment evaluation the SSIAM indicated a decrease in maladjustment in all areas, particularly in sex and work. The changes on the Derogatis Sexual Functioning Inventory were less dramatic. Changes in sex-role identification and attitude were marked: the women expressed more liberal attitudes toward sex and rated them-

---

*The Locke-Wallace Marital Adjustment Test showed no major effects for the total score; the subjects had generally good relationships with their partners both before and after treatment. However, at follow-up there was a significant decrease on an item assessing the woman's belief that she would marry the same person if she had her life to live over. The partners of the women, on a similar question, were less likely to wish they had not married the same person. This reappraisal of the relationship "may be an outcome of a re-evaluation of the women's own needs and values in light of their newly acquired sex education and orgasmic response [Heinrich, 1976:131]."

The responses to another questionnaire item indicated that an increase in the female's sexual authority and assertion did not have a deleterious effect on the male's sexual response.

selves as having more "masculine" traits, that is, as being more assertive, aggressive, and strong as opposed to sentimental, dependent, and domestic.

Most women become orgasmic with masturbation through the preorgasmic therapy process. Though relatively few transfer their orgasmic ability to the relationship before the end of the group, most do so within seven or eight months after the sessions have ended, without any further therapy. This result suggests that the women do more than solve a narrowly focused problem; they learn concepts and tools for approaching a broad range of problems, and can utilize these techniques at a later date.

In a group of 26 women who were reliably orgasmic with masturbation before entering therapy 22 were orgasmic with a partner less than 25 percent of the time pregroup. At the 12–24-month postgroup follow-up, 14 were orgasmic with a partner 100 percent of the time and three others were orgasmic with a partner more than 50 percent of the time. In addition, 82 percent of the women felt that the group had had a positive effect on their experience of orgasm, 90 percent felt it had had a positive effect on their enjoyment of sex, and 50 percent felt it had had a positive effect on their feelings about themselves (Barbach and Flaherty, in press). A similar study by Price and Heinrich (1977) at the University of California, Los Angeles, indicated that 10 of 13 participants had learned to have orgasms with a partner in new ways.*

The question of whether treatment effects last is always of concern. Although the preorgasmic process is too young to have had any long term follow-up, the results of women two years posttreatment indicates not only that the effects of the therapy last, but that most women continue making positive sexual changes beyond the end of the group. Judging from the fact that it is relatively rare for a woman who has once been orgasmic to seek treatment because of having lost this ability, it seems unlikely, barring new relationship problems, that many women will lose their new-found ability to experience orgasm.†

---

*In both the Barbach and Flaherty and the Price and Heinrich studies, the goal of orgasm with a partner covered any sexual activity engaged in with a partner during which orgasm occurred.

†Masters and Johnson (1970) reported at a five-year follow-up only two treatment reversals of 161 nonfailures treated for primary orgasmic dysfunction and only three treatment reversals of 115 nonfailures treated for situational orgasmic dysfunction.

LIMITATIONS OF THE PROGRAM

Effects on the Relationship

Like any other therapeutic approach, the preorgasmic group treatment program has its limitations and for some women another approach may be advisable. The women's group program is an excellent way of giving a woman back the power that is innately hers, teaching her that she is an authority on her own sexuality, and reinforcing her right to pleasure and her worth as an individual. But it may not in and of itself help to bring about sufficient change either in her partner's attitudes about sex or in her sexual interaction with a partner.

When the preorgasmic model is used alone, the woman is responsible for educating her partner. This task is difficult since men grow up in the same culture as women do and receive the same misinformation about sex. Additionally, many men are threatened by having a partner teach them about sexuality: they experience this as a role reversal of sorts that may interfere with their seeing themselves as the powerful or knowing one in the relationship. To ameliorate these problems, I include the partner, when he is willing, in a private pre-group screening session, and I work with the couple in 2-12 conjoint or group sessions after the women's group ends. Of course, if the partner is unwilling to attend any therapy program concerned with sexuality or to accept therapy for whatever reason, the sexual prognosis for the couple is poor. Yet participation in the preorgasmic group process at least gives the woman the opportunity to become more comfortable with her own sexuality and to educate her partner to her needs at a pace he can handle.

When the couple's relationship is seriously disturbed by poor communication, unexpressed or indirectly expressed anger, unresolved power struggles, or any other problems that are reflected in the bedroom, treating the woman alone may not be sufficient; such problems may interfere with the woman's ability to transfer the orgasm to the relationship with her partner. However, in a few cases couple sex therapy with competent therapists proved unsuccessful whereas success was later attained when the woman participated in a women's treatment group. It appears that these women had so little self-esteem and feeling of control over their lives that they needed to gain a sense of their own identity before they could effectively work out the sexual problem with the partner.

Research by Ersner-Hershfield (1978) on the group treatment of anorgasmia revealed no significant differences in outcome between all-women and all-couple formats in the majority of the measures used, including the Locke-Wallace Marital Adjustment Test. Of the 22 women in the two groups 91 percent became orgasmic with self-stimulation. Seventy-three percent were orgasmic in couple activities at the conclusion of the group and 82 percent at the 10-week follow-up. The only significant difference concerned maintenance of outcome at follow-up; the women's group was found to be superior on two measures and the couple's group on one.

Payn (1976) researched preorgasmic women's groups to determine the effect of the treatment on couple relationships. She found that the outcome varied with individual partners' levels of ego development as well as with the nature of the interactional system between the pair.* All the women became orgasmic with masturbation as a result of the therapy, but not all were able to transfer orgasm to sex with a partner.

Although Payn's sample was small—only 11 couples were included—she described three distinct types of couple interactional systems.

> *Bridge* couples [3] were psychologically well-differentiated individuals who responded postively to the treatment. Female orgasm was integrated smoothly into partner sex.
> *Barrier* couples [2] had many ego characteristics associated with "borderline personalities" and interacted with each other "pseudo-mutually." Female partners abruptly and unilaterally terminated their relationships shortly after the group treatment ended. Male partners, while hurt and confused, were unable to confront the women's defiant behavior.
> *Separate-but-Equal* couples [6] were developmentally closer to Bridge couples, but competition and fears of vulnerability pervaded all aspects of their relationships, especially the sexual aspects. Female orgasm was integrated into partner sex either partially or not at all [1976:3].

Kuriansky, Sharpe, and O'Connor (1976) found that some women who improved on the sex subscale of the SSIAM also improved

*Nearly all the participants in Payn's study scored below 100 on the Locke-Wallace Short Marital Adjustment Test (Locke and Wallace, 1959), indicating mild to serious dissatisfaction with their relationships prior to treatment. These couples would have been screened out of most sex therapy research projects.

on the SSIAM marital relationship subscale. Others who regressed on the sex subscale also regressed on the marriage relationship subscale. However, they did find a very small number of women who improved on sex but whose relationships worsened.

In research on situationally orgasmic women, Barbach and Flaherty (1978) found that four out of 19 women who were in committed relationships pregroup had ended their relationships at the 12–24-month follow-up. These four women were in relationships of less than a year's duration when the group began. Interestingly, these women were unanimously pleased with the treatment results. At the follow-up, none felt she still had sexual problems, and two of these women were involved in very serious relationships with new partners.

The research reviewed raises the important issue that in certain types of relationships treatment of only one member may unbalance the system in such a way that the relationship will suffer if the therapist does not take these dynamics into careful consideration. As is true in other forms of sex therapy, the probability of treatment success is far greater when couples with serious relationship problems are screened out (Lobitz and LoPiccolo, 1972; Masters and Johnson, 1970). If effective screening procedures were developed, it might be possible to identify high-risk couples and to determine whether another mode of therapy would be more beneficial than the preorgasmic women's group. In the absence of such discriminating procedures, it is reasonable to forewarn couples entering any type of sex therapy program that the therapy process may exacerbate some of their conflicts and that the relationship could break up as a result of the therapy.

Dealing with Individual Crises

The preorgasmic women's group treatment program is limited in its ability to deal effectively with crises that occur during the course of therapy; for example, if a woman needs an abortion, if a parent dies, if she discovers that her husband or lover is having an affair, or if her husband, who has been on the verge of separation, finally decides to leave. Working on orgasm may be inappropriate in such periods, and although most women experiencing crises remain in the group for the support it provides, only a few are emotionally capable of concentrating on the sexual homework. Many choose to join another group at a later, more auspicious time. Of course, a crisis may be a form of resistance, and the therapist must distinguish between a genuine crisis and one that is disguised resistance.

Integrating Changes

Sometimes the brief-term treatment process creates problems in that the woman makes major changes too rapidly to integrate them fully. Such women may require individual or group therapy to support them while the changes are stabilizing during the period following the preorgasmic group.

Because the preorgasmic process operates on such a central dynamic, that of sexuality, it affords the possibility for broad and far-reaching changes. For the same reason, it may exacerbate certain problems if careful attention is not paid to the client's process of change. The more structured the therapy, the greater the attention that must be paid to the client to keep the structure from overriding her individual needs.

CHAPTER 3

Major Elements in the Preorgasmic Group Process

THE BASIC ELEMENTS accounting for the success of the preorgasmic treatment program are the group process, the behavioral approach, and the role of the leader.

The Group Process

By far the most important aspect of the preorgasmic group process is the format of a small group of women meeting to discuss the intimate details of their sex lives and sexual dissatisfactions and working together to overcome their orgasmic difficulties. Research by Berzon, Pious, and Parson (1963) showed that the main curative mechanism of their short-term therapy was the interaction among group members. They found that the influence of the therapist was less important than the interpersonal feedback, which enabled patients to restructure their self-images in part because they realized that their problems were not unique.

FEELINGS OF ISOLATION AND ABNORMALITY

Entering a group with women like herself who have a similar complaint enables a woman with orgasmic problems to feel less isolated, less like a freak. She no longer needs to consider herself psychologically maladjusted but is now a member of a group joined together against the cultural forces that taught them how not to be sexual. The group members can relate to one another, sympathize, and, most important, accept one another. According to Yalom, "It is not only the discovery of others' problems similar to our own and the ensuing disconfirmation of our wretched uniqueness that is important; it is the effective sharing of one's inner world and *then* the acceptance by others that seems of paramount importance [1970:38]."

Though some people feel more at ease discussing sexual problems privately with a therapist, that same privacy can act to maintain a sense of shame and isolation. Without the physical presence of other women who share her difficulty, the client may believe intellectually that her problem is not unique but deep down continue to feel that it is a mark of horrendous personality and social deficiency. Such a woman is directly reassured when she sees that at least five other women share her problem—and that they are attractive, intelligent people who seem well adjusted in other respects. These two messages—you are not alone and you are normal—provide enormous relief and are communicated quite easily in the initial sessions just by having the women discuss some of their feelings and experiences with sex, as shown in the following excerpt from the first session of a group.

PAMELA: I feel uncomfortable. Why am I here? Why do I have to be here? I really don't want to talk about it.

MARIA: I feel nervous. I am a pretty nervous person anyway.

JENNY: What's funny is that I was feeling all those things you're talking about before I came. When I came in to the waiting room and saw you were all people, I relaxed a little. I am not feeling relaxed to the point where I could strip away everything and get down to the nitty-gritty, but I am much more relaxed now than I was when I was in my car looking at my watch wondering whether I should come or not. I don't know what I expected, but it wasn't real people.

The women confront their sense of shame about sex by revealing their doubts and fears not only to a therapist, who is expected to be understanding and accepting, but also to a group of peers, whose responses are less predictable. The experience of sharing negative feelings and still being accepted by other group members helps free the woman from these feelings.

SUPPORT AND COHESIVENESS

Awareness of having common sexual problems and sexual histories as well as sharing some of their deepest and most shameful feelings of sexual inadequacy, and having these disclosures met by acceptance and understanding by the other group members seems to establish trust and cohesiveness among members almost immediately. According to Yalom, group cohesiveness is a necessary precondition for effective group therapy. "Members of cohesive groups are more accepting of each other, more supportive, more inclined to form meaningful relationships in the group [1970:56]." This support system is essential in order for the women in preorgasmic groups to make changes. Indeed, Dickoff and Lakin (1963) found that patients experienced social support as the chief therapeutic factor. The support in the preorgasmic groups comes from a shared sense of attempting to cope with the same feelings and fears. One woman said to her husband as she was about to do her homework, "At least I know there are five other gals in the Bay Area who are masturbating tonight." Women frequently mention how the other members of the group helped them. For example, one woman claimed that she had her first orgasm because she imagined the whole group telling her it was all right to do so. Another imagined a group member telling her it would happen if she could just let go.

The support sometimes includes interactions outside the group. Women telephone each other to exchange information or to seek sympathy if one has had a particularly difficult day or problems in her relationship. Members meet for lunch, see another couple for dinner, or meet as a group with their partners for a party. This support system may continue long after the group ends.

When a group is cohesive, peer pressure and group reinforcement make it infinitely easier to cut through individual resistance to doing the masturbation homework and experiencing orgasm than is the

31

case in individual or couple therapy. As an individual develops, she learns to regard and value herself according to how she perceives that others regard and value her—just as a child, in the quest for security, develops those traits and aspects of herself that elicit approval and represses those that meet with disapproval. And experiencing high levels of sexual arousal and orgasm are met by strong approval in the group.

GROUP PRESSURE

In order for the group members to have influence on one another, they must have a sense of solidarity, of we-ness. If a woman feels herself to be an integral member of the group, she is likely to take suggestions seriously and follow directions conscientiously. When she does not, the group tends to put pressure on her. This pressure can be both supportive and coercive.

THERAPIST: How are other people feeling listening to Beverly?
ABBY: I'm feeling partly strained with you. I feel like you are making a lot of excuses. You don't say the noes that need to be said. A lot of them have been around having people in your house.
BEVERLY: Houseguests.
ABBY: See, it's like I'm trying to say something to you and you interrupt right in the middle with something like an excuse. I would just like you to take time for *you*. Just stop. Slow down. You're healthy and a lovely person and I'm sure you'll be hanging around on this earth for many more years. You need to take time for yourself.

Beverly would be likely to resist such prodding if it came from a sexually functional therapist who she felt could not possibly understand her feelings, but it is more difficult to resist when it comes from a woman who is like herself.

Group pressure is probably most important in the early stages of therapy, when a woman who has never masturbated seeks ways to avoid doing the homework. She may say that she cannot find the time to do it—that her children, friends, husband, or job command all her time and energy. But then one of the group members who has done the homework reports a positive response, and this functions as an incentive to others. Each woman's progress reinforces the idea that the participants will get out of the group only as much as they are willing to put into it and that the women who are doing the homework are enthusiastic and seem to be progressing. In this way, a mini-society with sexually positive messages is created to offset the attitudes held by the larger society that sex is bad, dirty, basically for the man's enjoyment, and so on. The group process also enables the leader to step back from a resistant client who is fighting her authority and let the other group members do the bulk of the therapeutic work, as is illustrated in the following transcript.

PAMELA: I just wish I could have a real physical feeling.

ABBY: I want to say to you, maybe because I'm trying to say it to myself, "Do it, do it. Don't put a ceiling on what you can experience." I don't want to feel that you can't have an orgasm. That's a bummer.

PAMELA: Well, that's something that may be a reality.

ABBY: It doesn't matter how many workshops you go to. There is nothing wrong with your body. It might just be necessary to find the right timing.

Later in the group, the first person to have an orgasm in effect gives permission to all the other women to overcome their fears and experience orgasm also. Each member realizes that if a woman like herself can enjoy orgasm—a woman with whom she can identify, a woman who is in no way more deserving of the experience than she, no better adjusted, no freer of problems than herself—there is every reason *she* can, too. And one by one, each woman has her first orgasm and receives tremendous positive reinforcement from all the other group members and the leader.

RESPONSIBILITY AND EQUALITY

Another advantage of group treatment is that it assists in returning the responsibility for change to its rightful owner—the client. When a woman is treated individually, she often sees the therapist as the authority and diminishes her own ability and authority. This unfortunate imbalance is exacerbated in couple therapy, for the therapist (or therapists) and the more functional partner are often perceived by the woman as having greater experience and knowledge.

Such a perception can magnify the preorgasmic woman's feeling of inadequacy and her belief that everyone else knows better when it comes to sex.

In the mini-society of the group, the women are equals. Although to some extent the leaders remain authority figures, they teach their clients to assume responsibility for themselves, and this teaching is greatly facilitated by the fact that the group members help one another to solve problems. Women have the opportunity to become authorities, and this experience must not be underestimated: it both reinforces the women in being responsible and enhances their growing sense of self-worth. In the following transcript Maria explains to Jenny how to attract a sexual partner.

MARIA: Just try looking around, making a game out of it to see who's attractive. It's a different kind of looking. Instead of waiting for someone to be obvious.

B.J.: It's not easy.

JENNY: Under certain circumstances, I can make the first move. I can't call up somebody and say, "I met you at a party and I'd like to take you out to dinner," and pay for the check as some of the nice young things that are growing up now can do. No, I can't do that. But I can let somebody know I'm interested.

MARIA: Just stare at them. That works. That's how I met Bill.
   [Laughter]
   It was at an audition and I was teaching dance. He came with a friend and it was the third time I saw him. And, I must say, I had a drink or two and I felt very comfortable. And I was dressed nice, and I felt confident and sexy, and I stared at him just like that and he got so nervous and so flustered, he said to me, "Why are you staring at me?" And I said, "You know why I'm staring at you." He practically dropped his drink, he was so nervous. And then I whispered in his ear—I wasn't going to let him get away this time—I mean, three times was luck. And I whispered in his ear that I wanted to be with him as soon as possible. I don't know what I said exactly, but something to that effect. He could hardly talk. He was really nervous. The next step was to write my number very sensually, not on paper, but on his hand, and then dramatically disappear and wait for the call. He called me the next night and then he came over. I thought it would be a one-night or two-night thing, but here we are. And that was the first time that I was

34

aggressive, but I cared about him and he didn't even notice me.

In the next transcript, the other group members help in finding a solution to Pamela's problem of lack of arousal.

PAMELA: No, I wasn't feeling turned on at all. It was almost like I should be doing this even though I don't really want to be doing it. There's some feeling. I can touch my hand and it feels okay. And so I was touching my clit and it felt okay. But it wasn't anything. No feeling of excitement. Nothing built up. I bought the other book, Nancy Friday's other book, brought it home, I read it and it was just like reading the newspaper. It didn't turn me on. And I'm beginning to wonder if I should just get myself in places and in situations that are a little bizarre and it might get me a little bit excited because a physical touch does not do anything. When I use the vibrator I feel nothing, then I feel the pain. And with my finger, I don't feel any pain. I cannot comprehend how someone could have an orgasm masturbating. I don't understand. My body is not allowing it. And so it is just continual frustration.

THERAPIST: Anybody have any ideas?

BEVERLY: The other day you brought up slower touching, when you had more sensation.

PAMELA: Yeah, I do like a slow movement. I like it. It is a nice feeling. That's all it is. It's no more pleasure than touching myself anywhere else. It's just there. I just happen to be touching it, that's all.

JOSEPHINE: When you went to that bookstore and were reading that book, what was different about that?

PAMELA: It was an excitement, a tingle. I felt it in my arms.

In ordinary circumstances women rarely talk to other women explicitly about sex. Deliberately sharing in a group situation makes it obvious that although women have some similarities, each is unique. The idea that there are individual differences in sexuality is often greeted with surprise. Listening to others replaces the notion that there is one supposedly normal sexual mold with the understanding that there are numerous normal sexual patterns and that therapy is designed to help each woman discover and be more accepting of her own pattern. For example, some women are turned on by fantasy

35

whereas others do not fantasize. Some women respond dramatically to the use of a vibrator; others find the same sensations irritating. Realizing that there is no one right way to be sexual enables the women to try techniques that others suggest and yet feel free to discard them if they do not prove helpful.

VICARIOUS LEARNING

The group process enables the women to learn from each other's mistakes and successes. As one member discusses her guilty or shameful feelings about sex in depth, the others merely listen or share peripherally; yet each benefits from the reported experiences. The time-consuming process of having each woman deal with the same issues often becomes unnecessary. One woman can provide the therapeutic experience for the rest of the group.

For example, in session five, Pamela had been lying fully clothed in the center of the room on the floor while all the other group members simultaneously massaged her. Accepting so much caring was painful for Pamela, who has spent most of her energy until this point keeping her emotions inside. She alternately cried and screamed while the others continued to massage her in a caring manner. After a while, I asked them to stop. As Pamela was composing herself, it was obvious that all the other women were moved by her experience and most had been crying.

THERAPIST: How are you feeling?

PAMELA: I feel like I opened up, but I feel like I'm going to block again. It's like all this good feeling I have been receiving is dying right now, just after it is over.

BEVERLY: I get the feeling that she was really experiencing the caring and warmth that we were all feeling about her, and that feels good, but then she gets that scared feeling when she is not around us and this is making her afraid.

THERAPIST: How did her experience make you feel, Beverly?

BEVERLY: I was very moved by it. I realize how much I give to other people and how difficult it is for me to receive from others. I just don't let myself receive. I think maybe others would give, but I don't give them the opportunity.

THERAPIST: Pamela, would you like to know how the others felt during this experience?

[Pamela nods assent]

ABBY: I though you were incredibly brave and beautiful.

THERAPIST: What did you feel while it was happening?

ABBY: A lot of respect for her. There was so much pain and she was willing to go into it anyway. It made me feel that I could be that brave, too.

JENNY: As I was doing the massage I realized just how much I want from people and how alone I feel sometimes. Maybe I have more friends than you do, but I feel just as alone. I want to be close to someone so badly that it is hard to face it. I'm feeling very sad now, too.

JOSEPHINE: [through tears] I can't say what I feel. I feel close to you. Do you known what I mean? I can't express it now.

B.J.: I can't cope either sometimes and it's not so terrible to cry. I wish I could have done what you did.

PAMELA: But I didn't want to.

B.J.: I know, but it was beautiful.

A FORUM FOR PRACTICE

The group provides a perfect situation for the women to experiment with and practice taking risks, communicating feelings, and sharing information regarding the specifics of sexual touching.

A fundamental purpose of therapy is to replace self-defeating behavioral patterns with patterns that are more self-serving. In order to make these changes, new and unfamiliar behavioral patterns must be tried out. Although old, self-defeating patterns cause problems, they are at least predictable and familiar. Experimenting with a new behavior initially requires taking risks and consequently produces anxiety. It makes sense, therefore, to begin the process by taking small risks under circumstances that are likely to bring success. Frequently, the safest place to experiment is with the other group members during the sessions. Sometimes I encourage this activity and sometimes the women initiate it themselves. In the following transcript, Josephine experiments with being more assertive and expressive.

THERAPIST: How shy and unaggressive do you feel in here?

JOSEPHINE: The same as always.

THERAPIST: I would like you to say a sentence describing how you feel about each of us.

JOSEPHINE: [Unclear]

THERAPIST: It's hard, I know. So's having orgasms.

JOSEPHINE: I feel something different about everybody.

THERAPIST: Well, try.

JOSEPHINE: I admire you, Beverly, because you are older and you're still so nice. I'm glad you keep on telling me to keep at it. I need that.

BEVERLY: Thank you.

JOSEPHINE: Jenny, I'm glad you're here. I've learned a lot from you about being good to myself.

JENNY: Thank you.

JOSEPHINE: I admire you, B.J., because of your ability to keep at it even when you're frustrated.

B.J.: Thank you.

THERAPIST: How are you feeling now?

JOSEPHINE: I feel really, still feel nervous.

THERAPIST: Because you skipped two people. It's almost like with masturbation. You go almost all the way, then, just before the end, you give up.

JOSEPHINE: Do I have to do the rest?

THERAPIST: It might be nice for you to follow it to the end; give you some practice at it.

[She continues with the last two women.]

In the following homework session Josephine experienced her first orgasm.

One area of risk taking that arises in every group is the willingness to check out assumptions. Most people see implicit messages in the statements or acts of others and then respond as if their assumptions were correct. Martha, for example, on two occasions had asked other women in the group to go out for drinks after the session was over. Both times she was refused. A few sessions later, as she shared some of her hurt feelings, she struggled against concluding that the others were not interested in getting to know her better. She made the assumption explicit by stating that she would ask one more time before giving up. The other women were surprised; their refusals had been based on circumstance and prior commitments. In fact, one woman had intended to ask Martha to go out for a drink after the session that evening and was delighted that Martha was still interested. The incident illustrated to all the women how easily they tended to interpret a refusal as a rejection and showed the value of checking out their assumptions since so often assumptions of this kind are incorrect.

Sometimes it is necessary for the therapist to facilitate the checking out process within the safe context of the group. It had been very difficult for Doris to tell the group that she had female as well as male lovers. Following this disclosure, she became concerned that some of the group members might be upset or might feel differently about her. I urged her to use her concern as an opportunity and suggested that she ask some of the group members directly how they felt about her revelation. She asked three women and discovered to her astonishment that their feelings about her remained unchanged. Feeling secure enough to take risks in nonsexual situations better enables the women to check out their perceptions and assumptions during lovemaking.

GROUP NORMS

Every group takes on a life that is distinctly its own. Part of the uniqueness of each group stems from implicit group norms that evolve out of the interaction among group members. These norms, rarely articulated, can enhance or jeopardize the success of the therapy. If the group develops an esprit de corps in which there is support for success rather than protection from failure the probability is increased that the members will attain their goals. However, some groups develop negative group norms that validate fearfulness and lack of success and interfere with the attainment of individual goals. When all or most of the women in a group seem unable to progress, it is frequently the result of a negative group norm. This can present a serious problem, particularly for leaders lacking experience with groups or understanding of group process. (For a detailed discussion of group norms see Chapter 6).

GOAL ORIENTED, TIME-LIMITED, WOMEN'S GROUPS

Certain characteristics of preorgasmic groups that are less common in general therapy groups may contribute to the effectiveness of this treatment format. For instance, women in preorgasmic groups are seeking a clearly defined goal and can perceive that they are indeed moving closer to that goal. The contract that is established in behavior therapy—one of the key components in the success of this approach—sets a reasonable objective toward which progress can be measured.

The relative brevity of the preorgasmic group, in addition to affording the prospect of more immediate gratification than longer term groups provide, helps keep enthusiasm high and is especially advantageous for women who are resistant. As the end of the group approaches, an eleventh hour effect frequently is seen. These women realize that they must do something to overcome their problem now or never and the imminence of the end of therapy causes them to work harder to realize this goal. Limiting the length of treatment affords other advantages. A certain stability emerges because the group is closed to new members once it begins. And since members rarely drop out, it allows for the creation of a group of optimal size.

That the group is composed exclusively of women is an additional factor promoting cohesiveness and support for changes in addition to the experience of orgasm. In our society women have been conditioned to expect men to wield power and make decisions. Having no males present in the group requires the women to make their own decisions, to look to other women as authorities, and to respect other women and hence themselves: "In a group without men, women have more freedom to examine themselves in terms of their role expectations and their relationship to other women [Meador et al., 1972:345]." It also frequently enhances the women's ability to relate to other women.

Sharing a symptom, as well as experiences and role expectations, increases the members' ability to understand and support one another as they make changes. It also reinforces each woman's awareness that she is an individiual who has rights; that she is deserving of pleasure; and that she can competently govern her life to a degree she never before considered possible.

The Behavioral Approach

The preorgasmic group is a behaviorally oriented psychotherapeutic approach to the treatment of orgasm problems. It structures direct behavioral change which often works more rapidly to eliminate a symptom than does intrapsychic understanding. However, understanding and behavior are intimately connected. Some people require the sense of safety achieved through a deeper understanding of themselves in order to begin the process of change. If a client understands her characteristic way of interacting and can trace it back to its source, if she can see the secondary gains it currently produces or the unreality of some of her fears, that particular behavior begins to lose a certain survival value. Armed with this understanding, such an individual may be better prepared to take carefully calculated risks in order to change her behavior.

Nevertheless, mere understanding with no concomitant change in attitude or behavior is virtually useless, and full understanding is not necessarily required in order for change to take place. Behavioral approaches attempt to institute behavioral change directly. A client tries out the new behavior, with or without insight into the purposes the old behavior served. The new behavior brings positive reactions from the therapist and perhaps from others, which reinforce the new behavior and give the client a new perspective on herself. This simplified framework can produce the same long-lasting behavioral changes as in-depth therapies and in a much shorter period of time.

Preorgasmic women's groups put primary emphasis on specific sexual tasks, or homework assignments, tailored to the individual's attitudes, interaction patterns, or sense of self, which are integrally related to her sexual functioning. However, even in behavioral approaches, one never really deals with the sexual symptom in isolation. Thus, in preorgasmic groups an understanding of the woman, her background, her relationships, and her sense of ego boundaries determines the pace and the nature of the homework assigned. And without conscientious participation in the homework assignments, the woman cannot expect to make progress in overcoming her sexual problem.

During the first three sessions of the preorgasmic group homework is predetermined and is given to all group members with minimal individual variation. Assignments thereafter are tailored to meet each woman's needs. (The designing of individual homework is described in Chapter 6.) Every new assignment is built upon the outcome of the previous exercise. In most cases this means a progression of assignments leading toward higher levels of arousal until orgasm is attained.

Masturbation is the major sexual learning tool. It allows the woman to maintain complete control over her level of sexual excitation. Should she become uncomfortable with the intensity of her sensations, she can reduce or stop the stimulation. The experience of control is essential. It enables the woman to progress slowly, increasing the intensity of the experience as she feels able to tolerate it. Experiencing control over her sexual response also gives the woman a sense of control over other aspects of her life.

Masturbation is demystified and a great deal of anxiety is alleviated through the step-by-step format of the homework assignments combined with the use of a film showing a woman masturbating. The homework begins with looking before touching and progresses to body touching before genital touching, to orgasm through masturbation while alone before orgasm through masturbation while with a partner, and to orgasm achieved by self-stimulation while with a partner before orgasm achieved by partner stimulation. This procedure allows each woman to approach the goal at her own pace and to experience a number of reinforcing successes along the way until finally she can experience orgasm with a partner. (The orgasm need not occur through stimulation by the penis alone for the therapy to be considered successful.)

The Leader's Role

Preorgasmic women's groups are therapy groups, not educational groups, and require skilled clinical therapists to run them. Although some women will become orgasmic merely by participating in a group, regardless of what the therapist does, the majority will not. Each woman requires specialized interventions that fit her particular personality dynamics, form of resistance, and set of values. Accordingly, the therapist may adopt a different interactional style in relation to each woman. She may be supportive with some and confrontational with others, while maintaining a nonauthoritative and paradoxical relationship with women for whom this style is appropriate. The therapist must also have the requisite training to handle a broad range of psychological problems, particularly when working with very resistant or seriously disturbed women who want to become orgasmic.

As in every therapeutic relationship, the interaction between therapist and client will affect the outcome of the therapy. Each therapist has her own basic approach, but within that approach there is considerable room for variation. Determining exactly which qualities and skills are most helpful, however, is complicated by the dynamics of each group and the fact that other group members and the group as a whole have therapeutic qualities of their own.

What follows, then, is not a prescription but rather a description of the clinical skills, therapeutic techniques, and personality qualities that characterize successful group leaders. Specific interactional styles will not be discussed here, but in Chapter 6 in relation to particular situations occurring in groups. This presentation on general leadership attributes is based on my experience as both a leader, and a trainer, an objective assessment of a series of tapes made by other group leaders, feedback from group members, and an analysis of successful groups as well as those in which members dropped out and in which few if any members achieved orgasm during the treatment program.

TECHNICAL EXPERTISE

The leader's ability to convey her expertise at the beginning, to impart information, and to instill hope is very important in the establishment of group cohesiveness. The group leader is responsible for giving out information on sexuality and correcting misinformation and myths. Therefore, every leader should master the literature on the anatomy and physiology of male and female sexuality. *The New Sex Therapy* by Kaplan (1974), *Human Sexual Response* by Masters and Johnson (1966), *For Yourself* by Barbach (1975), and a basic human sexuality text such as *Understanding Sexual Interaction* by DeLora and Warren (1976) will provide most of the relevant information. However, this is a new field and there are both conflicting theories and gaps in our knowledge.

MODELING AND PERSONAL DISCLOSURE

A group leader in any type of therapy is a role model whether she intends to be or not. Her status as leader makes modeling implicit. Therefore, the more "real" the therapist is, the more easily the group members can identify with her.

Self-disclosure by the leader is a disputed subject. Psychoanalytic therapy is based on the assumption that resolution of the patient-therapist transference is the primary curative factor. However, group therapy is significantly different from individual therapy. According to Yalom (1970), the therapist who is self-disclosing increases the therapeutic power of the group because of her ability to determine group norms. She becomes a model for open, honest, direct, and uninhibited communication. By being honest and direct in her attitude and in her approach to the discussion, she promotes honesty in group members. By sharing information about herself and her sexual history she encourages similar sharing among the participants. By demonstrating that she is comfortable with her sexuality, she serves as a model for group members to look to as a possibility for themselves.

If the therapist appears to have no current or past sexual difficulties, the group members may have difficulty identifying with her and may feel that they can never reach her level of sexual competence. I frequently relate traumatic experiences or situations I bungled to illustrate that I, too, have had sexual problems to overcome.

> PAMELA: What if you have a person who says everything feels good? I find it's just nicer to have feedback.
> MARIA: Yeah.
> THERAPIST: I used to kiss my boyfriend's ears a lot. The more I kissed his ears, the less he'd kiss my ears, so I kissed his ears more. Then one day we talked about it and I said, "I really like it when you kiss my ears." And he said, "I hate it."
> [Laughter]
> So we were both doing to the other what neither wanted and until we sat and talked about it, we didn't know. Because you do to the other person what feels good to you. But the other person may not like it.

A therapist with no negative sexual experiences may reinforce the members' expectation that sexual responsiveness either comes easily or is hopeless; the women may think that if only they were as "together" as the leader their problems would be over. Obviously, I do not fabricate incidents, but I capitalize on any unfortunate sexual experiences I have had. When a group member is encountering a problem that reminds me of an episode in my own life, I share it. The message I thereby convey is that one can have negative sexual experiences and overcome them, that I can understand members' difficulties, and that their situation is not hopeless. The therapist's ability to disclose can promote group norms of sharing and nonjudgmental disclosure. It demonstrates that the group is not divided into those who are "sick" (members) and those who are "well" (leaders). Berger advocated this type of disclosure: "It is at times very helpful for the therapist to share some past or current real-life problem and to afford a model for identification through his capacity to come through such a problem period constructively [1967; quoted in Yalom, 1970: 103]." (Of course, the leader should not use the group as a place to deal with her own current problems.)

A leader who has the self-confidence to admit her own mistakes gives the women the powerful message that one does not have to be perfect to be a competent person. Nor does one have to be free of all problems in order to enjoy sex and have orgasms.

I easily share my worst experiences in bed and my past difficulties in not saying no to someone for fear of hurting his or her feelings. I received virtually no information about sex while growing up and can always find an occasion to share this fact along with the many misconceptions I developed as a result. Women in my groups frequently mention that they would like to have me recount even more stories about myself. They feel they gain a lot from hearing about how I got myself into and out of some very uncomfortable situations. This degree of sharing puts us on an equal plane. Seeing parts of themselves in someone for whom they have a great deal of respect enables group members to have greater respect for themselves.

I try to do this sharing with humor. When things are not so deadly serious, it becomes easier to take risks, to make errors in judgment, and even to "blow it" completely sometimes. One's experiences may be painful, but being able to look back and laugh helps keep them in perspective.

It is particularly important to use humor when working in the area of sexuality. When sex becomes too serious it ceases to be fun. And if it is not fun and pleasurable, there seems little reason to participate. Being able to laugh at our awkwardness or at our resistance can relieve anxiety and tension. Being able to do so in the group is the first step in this direction. The following exchange occurred in the second session of a group after the body looking and body touching homework assignments had been completed.

BEVERLY: I found my back appears very stocky and there are a lot of fatty deposits all over and it doesn't look pretty at all. It's like a blob of fat and I just wasn't happy with it. So, I don't know if it's exercise that would do it or rolfing or whatever to get rid of the fatty deposits.

THERAPIST: I wonder what it would be like if you just started thinking about that part of your body and noticing it?

BEVERLY: Well, my immediate reaction was, I'm finished with it."

45

[Laughter]
THERAPIST: Out of sight, out of mind.
BEVERLY: I don't want anything to do with it.
THERAPIST: Well, the nice thing about it is that it's behind you.
[Laughter]

The therapist is in a position to set standards that are different from the "sex is dirty—don't talk about sex even if you're doing it—good girls don't like sex" model the women's mothers are likely to have provided. A therapist who is sexual and yet respectable can be a healthy identification figure. However, it is important not to go overboard. The leader who proselytizes her individual values, particularly if her experiences depart significantly from the norm, can have a negative effect on the group. For example, the therapist who has maintained a sexually open marriage for years, who easily relates sexually to both men and women, enjoys group sex, and can have orgasms in 60 different ways may unintentionally be transmitting the message that one has to be like her to be sexually satisfied. Furthermore, group members will have difficulty identifying with her.

The group leader should be aware of the danger that the information she discloses about her own sexuality and how she discloses it may make the group members feel inadequate if their sexual value system differs considerably from hers. Likewise, it is essential that the therapist be accepting and nonjudgmental in regard to the values and sexual activities of her clients. I have found that respecting a client's perception of a situation, as well as her evaluation of the best approach to attaining her goals, before disclosing my own concerns or attitudes enables me to be more effective in helping her design an approach well suited to her individual circumstances.

For example, I used to believe that a woman who had been faking orgasm should reveal that fact to her partner. Otherwise, I felt, she was only encouraging him to continue ineffective methods of stimulation. I believed that open discussion would bring the couple closer together so that they could begin to learn appropriate techniques. A woman in my first group made me reexamine my thinking. She insisted that her partner would be devastated to learn that she had been faking orgasm. I encouraged her to tell him, but she maintained that he would be terribly hurt. I finally concluded that unless this decision proved to be an obstacle in later sessions she should follow her own judgment. The woman became orgasmic on her own by the end of the program and soon thereafter during oral sex with her partner. She must have done a convincing job of faking because he never knew the difference. This situation and others have taught me that a woman's knowledge of her own situation is frequently better than mine and that I need to trust her perceptions.

SUPPORT RATHER THAN HELP

Although modeling and personal disclosure remain somewhat constant throughout the course of the group, other modes of interaction frequently change.

Permission giving and support from the leader are necessary initially, but as the group develops, the role of the leader must change accordingly. In the early sessions, her job is to replace myths and misinformation with accurate information about female sexuality. While fulfilling this function, the leader is supportive, validating, and permission giving.

Truax and Carkhuff (1967), Heine (1953), Fiedler (1951), and Lieberman (1972) have argued that the effective therapist is one who develops a warm, accepting, understanding, and empathetic relationship with patients. Acceptance by a respected person heightens the client's self-esteem. Support and positive reinforcement are sometimes necessary to help women in preorgasmic groups make the difficult changes necessary to become orgasmic. Consequently, the therapist must attempt to understand and validate each group member's perspective on her past and present sexuality. In some cases she must give women permission to push on and explore further; in others she must give permission not to try so hard but rather to slow down and relax.

The general therapeutic process entails joining in rather than fighting the women's defenses. If a woman feels that something is too difficult for her to attempt at the time, I support her stance and then ask her to help me figure out what she *would* feel capable of doing. It is important not to confuse being supportive and validating with solving group members' problems or being responsible for their progress. A supportive and validating therapist can aid the women in self-acceptance; "doing for" them frequently engenders resistance.

As I noted earlier, the average woman in our society is trained to be dependent and helpless. She is taught not how to go after and get what she wants but, rather, how to charm and cajole someone else into doing things for her. Lacking a sense of positive power, many women develop negative power—at least no one can make them feel what they do not want to feel.

Lack of a sense of positive power over her life can lead a woman to withhold in many areas in which she feels pressured, especially when she feels pressured sexually. This withholding is not necessarily on a conscious level. It is frequently an automatic response to the sense that the power lies in the hands of another, usually her partner. Sometimes, however, the women regard the therapist as having power over them and resist what they perceive as the therapist's attempts to make them have orgasms. Even though orgasm was their initial goal in the process they may begin to feel that if they succeed and have an orgasm the leader will win; therefore, they withhold. A leader who plays the authority role—who tries to tell group members what to do and how to do it—can foster this tendency and thereby create resistance.

An excellent illustration of the line between supportiveness and helpfulness comes to mind. After I had been running groups for about two years I received a call from some therapists I had trained. They wanted to consult with me because, they said, "preorgasmic women were getting harder to treat." They felt that the availability of information on sexuality had enabled women who merely needed a little basic information to learn to become orgasmic without therapy. They needed new strategies to deal with the more difficult patients currently seeking treatment. However, the problem became obvious as I later listened to the leaders express their concerns. With running many groups, the leaders had become so proficient and knowledgeable that they had also become overly helpful and were taking responsibility away from group members. When a woman had a problem or felt stuck, the leader had a solution in the form of an already devised homework exercise. The women were left with no way to assert themselves; they could either follow orders or resist. So they resisted solutions made to seem too easy and proved that they as individuals were indeed too complex to be "fixed" so readily.

One way for the leader to remain supportive without being overly helpful is to use group members as authorities. When questions or issues are raised, the group members themselves offer a variety of opinions and experiences from which others in the group can pick and choose, dispelling the notion that there is only one right answer or one authority.

FOCUSING AND FACILITATION

The therapist must be able to keep each woman focused on the details of her homework and to maintain the group's focus on the central dynamics that affect their sexual responsiveness. A group discussion of sexuality usually touches off an exchange of autobiographical information and a discussion of relationship problems, work problems, and numerous other topics that may be peripherally related to sex but may not require further exploration in order to reverse the orgasmic dysfunction. Being able to separate the relevant from the irrelevant issues is one of the most important skills of the leader.

Once the therapist determines that an issue is not relevant, she must be able to refocus the group without making the woman who is speaking feel devalued. Picking out the essential aspect of the discussion and tossing it back to the group members or making a transition by relating an aspect of one woman's account to a more relevant issue raised by another woman are two ways to refocus the group. If the leader concentrates on facilitating positive group interaction, the women learn to take responsibility for their own progress, and fewer serious resistance problems develop.

A major role of the group leader is to obtain a detailed account of the homework from each woman in order to determine the next assignment. The therapist must be able to visualize the sequence of events as clearly as if she were watching a film of the homework session so she can determine exactly where the woman is encountering difficulties. Also, by having to relate the homework experience precisely, the women learn to attend to relevant details. Both physical and emotional details must be elicited.

ABBY: I found out that I can get right up to the point of orgasm in minutes, which I was delighted over, but it doesn't matter what I do. I try turning on my stomach, sideways. I tried all these other positions, and they are great. I had gotten locked into thinking I somehow had to be on my back with my legs apart, which is okay, but I like to do other things and so I tried all kinds of other things but I got up to a point and it started hurting. The sensation became unpleasurable and this is what I realized I've experienced over and over. I can masturbate, but

I get to this point where it doesn't feel good so I want to stop. And so I stop. I thought, "Okay, I'll just let the tension drop a little bit." So I'd do that and then it would build up and then I'd stop again and it would build up and it wasn't a pleasurable experience doing that. And my clitoris is a little sore. I didn't mutilate it, but it just seems sore.

THERAPIST: Now, it's pleasurable up to a point, right? And you are enjoying it. What's the difference in quality between when it feels good and when it doesn't? I know that's hard to explain.

ABBY: The difference in quality is a physical sensation, of physically not feeling stimulated. It's hard to tell you. Not burning, but something along that line, something like burning.

THERAPIST: Where? Where is the burning?

ABBY: Over my clitoris or inside under there. You know, the sensation sends tingles throughout my body. I feel myself more excited and then it changes.

THERAPIST: Does it change in a second or does it change gradually?

ABBY: That I can't say. It seems like it's a little more gradually. But it's always getting up to that point. I have to back off from it because of that. And I had another kind of odd thing, of getting way up and then suddenly going dead. Or else there was some kind of release that I didn't know about. All of a sudden, all interest for me was gone. But then I started masturbating again about four minutes later. I could feel that rise again, so it felt like I hadn't completed this thing. But, yet, I don't know what that deadness was either. And so I tried to get into that place and feel what that was like and I couldn't get in touch with it. I didn't know if it was a mental turn-off on my part or a plateau that I needed to hang out with and just do something else. But, the thing that I'm complaining about is that I don't like having that rise in pleasure and it turning to pain because it makes me not want to masturbate.

THERAPIST: It sounds to me like intensity, not pain.

ABBY: It's not a burning like a yeast infection. It's an intensity that's unpleasurable. Is it too much direct stimulation?

THERAPIST: See, it could be any number of things. I'll tell you what's going through my mind. I've heard before, many times from women, that as they get highly aroused, the intensity of that feeling is foreign and uncomfortable and they don't like

50

it. And it takes a while to get used to it. That's possible. The other possibility is that something's happening when the feelings suddenly go. So, in either case, I want you to really focus on how that change takes place.

ABBY: Okay, so is it a split second before it starts feeling bad or is it a gradual process?

THERAPIST: Right.

ABBY: And then, if it's a gradual process, take it easy and if I start feeling that coming, lay off. Is that what you're saying?

THERAPIST: Yeah, and to move back down to get used to it. Just like you were doing. The other thing is that I'm not exactly sure what the quality of that tenderness is. In other words, if you move your hands, do you still feel it? Or is it only in certain places that you touch that you feel that intensity?

ABBY: No. If I take my hands away from there I can still feel it, sort of a buzzing. It's not pleasurable.

THERAPIST: What happens if you leave your hand resting there?

ABBY: That would be okay.

THERAPIST: Would that feel arousing?

ABBY: It would be neutralizing.

THERAPIST: Neutralizing?

ABBY: Yeah, And probably, if anything, lower the intensity just a little bit.

In the middle sessions, the leader's primary role is to facilitate the group process rather than to answer questions or design homework assignments. At this point, the leader who involves herself in identifying issues rather than devising solutions will teach the women to focus on themselves and to learn the process of moving from point A to point B by the appropriate steps. The leader can describe various issues that seem to be interfering with the attainment of orgasm, but each woman must decide for herself what issues are relevant to her situation. She can then discuss her plans for doing something about them in terms of a homework assignment.

If the leader is too laissez-faire she runs the risk of seriously deemphasizing the importance of the homework. If she assumes too much responsibility for the women's success, they may experience her as taking over their orgasms and will resist. The appropriate therapeutic stance for the leader grows out of the realization that she does not have the power to make anyone have an orgasm; the women themselves control what they will or will not allow their bodies to experience. The most the therapist can do is to evaluate the homework assignments carefully, anticipate problems that might develop in carrying them out, and lend encouragement and support in the face of inevitable difficulties.

INTERPRETATION

The therapist does not address the symptom in isolation, although the homework desensitization exercises may make it appear that she does. In reality, the deeper issues that frequently accompany orgasmic dysfunction are indirectly being affected by the process.

As in any therapeutic role, the leader must be able to interpret the behavior, fantasies, and conflicts of the clients when appropriate. In general, however, interpreting the blocks to progress is less crucial than directly helping the women to surmount the blocks.

Interpretations, to be useful, must be expressed to the client in language she can understand, that is, in words that use her own concept of reality. Often, important work can be accomplished merely by reframing the facts and circumstances in such a way as to change their meaning and open up options: "To reframe . . . means to change the conceptual and/or emotional setting or viewpoint in relation to which a situation is experienced and to place it in another frame which fits the 'facts' of the same concrete situation equally well or even better, and thereby changes the entire meaning [Watzlawick et al., 1974:95]." The following transcript demonstrates the use of reframing.

PAMELA: I watch T.V. That doesn't help.
THERAPIST: Some things don't help.
PAMELA: I think perhaps if they put me under, you know, like when you go for an operation, you get a needle. And then maybe someone could do it to me. I wonder if that would work. I certainly wouldn't have my head to say no.
THERAPIST: My feeling is that if you have the power to get your head to turn off like that, you've got a lot of strength in your head to do other things with. It's a matter of figuring out how to do that. The beginning is just to figure out how you can turn off. You have a good, strong head and that can be really positive. I wouldn't want you to lose that ability in the process of

learning how to do other things with it as well. It's important that you don't lose that ability. Keep your head in control.

GROUP MEMBER CONFLICTS

Negative communication patterns sometimes develop within the group. However, preorgasmic groups are not encounter groups or T-groups, so it is essential to deal effectively with group member conflicts or process problems without devoting substantial time and energy to them. In most situations, I find that focusing on the feelings of the woman who complains about another's behavior is more fruitful than working with the woman who is perceived as offensive. The woman who complains about another's behavior has more at stake in changing things. For example, in one group, Janice, a quiet member, was very annoyed with Alice, who rarely reported any personal information but readily related numerous examples from the histories of her friends and relatives. When Janice confronted Alice with her behavior, I asked why it upset her so. She replied that to talk is to take risks and whereas she was trying to muster up her courage to risk, she felt that Alice was not. I then asked Janice whether her lack of participation in the group was a result of anxiety or disinterest. "Anxiety," she replied. To which Alice said, "I'm anxious, too, and when I'm anxious, I talk a lot." Thus, it became clear that each woman handled anxiety differently. Janice did not like Alice any better after that interaction, but both women learned something from each other, and the group continued with its task without being bogged down in a personality clash.

SUMMARY

In the preceding pages I have described some of the qualities and skills necessary in leading preorgasmic groups effectively: the expertise of the leader; her ability to be a role model and to set positive group norms; her capaicty to support group members while allowing them to develop their independence; her awareness of individual, interpersonal, and group processes; her skill in making appropriate interpretations; and her ability to keep group members focused on developing their sexual arousal until the natural outcome of orgasm is reached. The groups are complex and difficult to run because of the intensity and rapid pace of the process. At no time can any woman be taken for granted. Finally, as in all group therapy, outcome depends not only on the leader but also on the attributes of the group members, group cohesiveness, and group norms; accordingly, groups differ in the amount of change they promote.

Co-Therapy

Preorgasmic groups are generally led by two female co-therapists. Although co-therapy has a number of advantages, it may not be a feasible option for many practioners, and a lot of therapists who run groups successfully prefer working alone. But a team of co-therapists can offer the group members a greater variety of skills and experiences than one therapist alone can provide. With only 10 sessions in which to reverse a lifelong sexual problem, the co-therapy team is often able to focus more quickly and precisely on the dynamics and blocks that prevent orgasmic release for each of the group members.

The presence of two therapists facilitates interaction in the group. With one therapist leading the group, the process is naturally focused on that one person. Dividing the leadership promotes interaction among members and helps reduce the resistance that commonly develops toward the authority figure.

Between sessions the leaders discuss the obstacles to growth of the group members and plan strategies to work with each woman. During the sessions they can discuss aloud, in front of the entire group, their specific concerns about any of the members. Since the woman is not being *directly* addressed by the therapists this technique relieves her of the need to respond. Consequently, rather than formulating a defense, she can focus all her attention on the dialogue the two therapists are having about her.

Finally, co-therapy allows the leaders to separate or alternate supportive and confrontational roles. It is naturally more difficult for one therapist to wear these two hats. The following case is a good example of a problem whose solution was facilitated by the presence of a second therapist.

Carole came to the group ostensibly to make sex better for her husband. He was very demanding sexually and she felt that accommodating him sexually would make her life easier. We agreed to help her do precisely that although we detected some resentment in her tone. Carole denied any resentment, insisting that whereas she might have been able to make her husband less selfish and more attentive sexually and in other ways when they were married 25 years earlier it was now too late for him to change.

Carole rarely did homework and never volunteered any feedback. Since she was quite unassertive, my co-therapist and I agreed after the third session to respond to her only when she initiated a discussion. After two sessions of nonparticipation Carole began volunteering reports of minor successes with her homework. I continued to help her do more things to please her husband. Finally, she got mildly angry and said she felt that I was "needling" her. My co-therapist helped her express her annoyance with me. At first, Carole discounted her anger: "I don't like what you're saying, but I'm sure you didn't mean it and you're probably right anyway." However, with support from my co-therapist, Carole was able to say, "I *really* don't like what you said." I told her I appreciated hearing her feelings and that she had made me realize that I was pushing her because I could never get a feeling response from her. I then wondered aloud whether maybe that was what her husband was doing as well. This session proved to be a turning point for Carole. She began to see sexual participation as being for her own enjoyment rather than just for her husband's benefit. This breakthrough would have been much more difficult without a co-therapist.

CO-THERAPY DIFFICULTIES

Co-therapy has unique complexities, and numerous issues must be resolved before two therapists can work together harmoniously. Conflicts can arise as the result of different therapeutic approaches, different assessments of the group members and their needs, personality clashes, power struggles, or lack of mutual respect. The co-therapists may feel that they are handling their difficulties well by discussing them outside the group; even so, their problems frequently have a negative influence on the group process. However, if properly handled, disagreement between the therapists can provide the group with a model that reinforces the notion that just as there is no one right way to run a group, there is no one right way to have an orgasm. Of course, leaders must be aware of the danger of setting up a competitive situation between themselves, thereby confusing group members.

When there is friction between leaders, I generally try to determine where the conflict is greatest and attempt to change the process in order to sidestep the conflict. For example, in one group, the co-therapists clashed most noticeably over assigning homework. Though they respected each other, they had very different styles and consequently were unable to interact comfortably. Roz preferred to work out the next homework assignment as each woman completed her report of the previous week whereas Betty preferred to make the individual assignments at the end of the group session. To resolve the problem, each therapist took responsibility for the homework on alternate sessions.

In another group, the two therapists differed in approach, style of doing therapy, and conceptualization of individual needs. They sought supervision because there seemed to be no way for them to work constructively together without confusing the group members and complicating the process. A consultation helped them decide to divide the group, with each co-therapist having major responsibility for the three women with whom she worked most comfortably. This solution did not mean that they were to have no interactions with the other women, but they were to do so only after the co-therapist had finished working with them for that session.

MALE CO-THERAPISTS

To date, most preorgasmic groups have been led by female co-therapists although I have successfully run groups of situationally orgasmic women with a male co-therapist. The presence of a man is bound to affect the process of an all-female group. Meador, Solomon and Bowen found that "women together talk differently from the way they do in the presence of men. The cultural conditioning which most women have assimilated rises to the fore if only one man is present [1972:338]."

If men are to run preorgasmic groups, they must be keenly aware of women's tendency to disclaim responsibility and place the man in the position of authority, particularly when he is vested with the authority of the leadership role. The male therapist must be aware also of his own social scripting, which inclines him to accept this authority role and assume the stance of an expert who will solve the women's problems. A combination of these two tendencies contains the seeds of failure, for resistance is frequently engendered in such circumstances.

CHAPTER 4

Setting Up a Group

THE FIRST STEP in setting up a group is to decide whether to limit it to either preorgasmic women or situationally orgasmic women or to combine these categories in a single treatment unit. Another issue is whether to restrict the group to women only or to include the partners of those women who are involved in relationships.

Types of Orgasmic Dysfunction

Masters and Johnson broke new ground in describing and categorizing orgasmic dysfunction. Before their research, frigidity was defined as any response short of the "mature vaginal orgasm." Masters and Johnson developed two categories of orgasmic dysfunction. They defined a woman with primary orgasmic dysfunction as one who has never attained orgasm by any means: "Every possible physical approach to sexual stimulation initiated by self or received from any partner has been totally unsuccessful in developing an orgasmic experience for the particular woman diagnosed as primary nonorgasmic [1970: 227].'' Their second category, "situational orgasmic dysfunction," is composed of three subgroups—masturbatory, coital, and random orgasmic inadequacy. The common denominator is that all women so classified must have experienced at least one orgasm regardless of how it was produced. A woman with masturbatory orgasmic inadequacy can experience orgasm only through coitus and not by self or partner manipulation.* Coital orgasmic inadequacy indicates an inability to experience orgasm during coitus, although orgasm can be attained by either manual stimulation or oral-genital contact with a partner. A woman suffering from random orgasmic inadequacy has had at least one orgasm through coitus as well as through manipulative techniques but experiences orgasm rarely and unexpectedly and generally has little desire for sexual expression.

Kaplan, though roughly following the Masters and Johnson scheme, also defines a third category, "general sexual dysfunction," or "frigidity": "The woman suffers from primary orgastic dysfunction if she has never experienced an orgasm; if, on the other hand, the disorder developed after a period of being able to reach orgasm, it is considered a secondary orgastic dysfunction [1974:374].'' Women with general sexual dysfunction derive little or no erotic pleasure from sexual stimulation and may go to great lengths to avoid sex. Frequently, these women are anorgastic as well.

Being primarily a clinician and not a theoretician, I define orgasmic concerns operationally. I consider a woman preorgasmic if she is unable reliably to masturbate to orgasm using her hands. A woman who is irregularly orgasmic with intercourse but cannot masturbate manually to orgasm is considered preorgasmic for treatment purposes since she needs a better understanding of her own arousal process before she can experience orgasm whenever she desires to do so, either alone or with a partner. This would also be true of women who are orgasmic only with vibrator stimulation, since stimulation produced by a machine is substantially different from that provided by a person, and the ability to respond to more subtle stimulation is generally a prerequisite to experiencing orgasm with a partner. I define situationally orgasmic women as those who are currently reliably orgasmic with manual masturbation and possibly in some situa-

---

*That Masters and Johnson considered inability to achieve orgasm through masturbation a problem rather than condemning those who masturbate is in itself an indication of changing cultural attitudes toward sexuality.

tions with a partner but who still have concerns about attaining orgasm with a partner. This division is based on the premise that until a preorgasmic woman knows what kind of stimulation is most pleasurable to her and most likely to lead to orgasm, she has very little information to communicate to her partner. A situationally orgasmic woman needs to learn to create in additional situations that which already produced orgasm in some situations.

Objectives

Preorgasmic and situationally orgasmic women differ somewhat in the objectives they hope to achieve through treatment, and this will necessarily affect the focus of the treatment program.

Note that inability to experience orgasm, with or without a partner, is not a sexual dysfunction unless the woman herself defines it as such. I do not consider a woman to have a sexual problem unless *she* feels she has one, whether or not she has orgasms. Orgasms are nice, and many women prefer their sexual interactions to include them, but enjoyment of sex is not limited to the experience of orgasm. Many women have a satisfying sex life without ever reaching orgasm. Hite's (1976) research, though difficult to interpret because of the open-ended nature of her questions, suggests that 13–33 percent of her respondents felt that orgasm is not always necessary and that sex would be enjoyable if orgasm sometimes did not occur (pp. 434–435).

Masters and Johnson's criterion of success for treatment of female orgasmic dysfunction is achievement of orgasm in 50 percent of one's coital experiences. I do not agree that orgasm 50 percent of the time is a fair measure of success for a woman who desires orgasm 95 percent of the time. (How many men would be satisfied with this criterion of success?) However, many women do not wish to expend the physical and emotional energy necessary to experience orgasm every time they have sex and feel satisfied having orgasms, 70, 50, or 20 percent of the time as long as they are confident that they can have an orgasm when they want one. Orgasms 100 percent of the time would be an inappropriate goal for these women. I believe that women seeking treatment for sexual dysfunctions should help set their own goals; thus, I integrate goal setting into the preorgasmic group process. During the third session, the group members determine their individual goals in behavioral terms (see Chapter 5, for a discussion of goal setting).

The basic goal of the preorgasmic participants is orgasm and the program is designed to teach them to have orgasms through self-stimulation. Once the preorgasmic woman has learned to gain control over and feel good about her own orgasm through masturbation, she learns to ask for or to do what feels best with a partner.

The goals of situationally orgasmic women are far more diverse. The general goal I offer them is to increase their options for having orgasms with a partner by "one new way." This objective is obviously inappropriate for women who are without a partner or who are in an unsatisfactory relationship. However, the goal of orgasm in "one new way" is consistent with the view that there is no one right way to have an orgasm. Once a woman learns the process for experiencing orgasm in one new way, she can apply the process used to learn to have orgasms in other ways. My overall objective is for the woman to leave the program no longer feeling sexually inadequate but knowing that it is within her power to experience orgasm if she is willing to communicate certain information to a partner or to initiate certain behaviors. Learning to be comfortable with these changes may take time and may have to be developed anew with each partner, but there is a considerable difference between feeling that there is something basically wrong with oneself and knowing that the route to attaining one's goals is open if the requisite changes are made. Many situationally orgasmic women in casual or unsatisfying relationships who terminate the group without having had orgasms with a partner consider themselves successful because they no longer feel inadequate and realize that attaining orgasm is not beyond their control. They have a clear understanding of what they need to do to experience orgasm but choose not to practice the necessary techniques with the current partner or at the current time. At a later date, such women may decide to work on orgasm with different goals in mind.

Issues in Treatment

Preorgasmic and situationally orgasmic women differ in terms of the issues that must be dealt with. Preorgasmic women spend most of the sessions discussing the masturbation homework. A lesser amount of time is devoted to the partner work that is assigned after orgasm is reliably experienced through masturbation. Transfer of the orgasm to the partner relationship is fairly easy for most women who become orgasmic during the sessions. These women initially have little idea of what produces an orgasm. After they learn, they readily accept that what they are doing is normal, and all they have to do is teach a partner what they have learned about themselves sexually.

Most women who are situationally orgasmic can masturbate to orgasm but feel guilty and ashamed about it. As a result, they masturbate very quickly and only to relieve tension. Masturbation is seen as distinct from "real" sex, and most of the women feel uncomfortable about requiring clitoral stimulation to reach orgasm. Hence, they do not expect or ask a partner to engage in the kind of touching that produces orgasm for them when they masturbate. Many of these women even believe that masturbation is responsible for their lack of orgasm during intercourse.

Moreover, situationally orgasmic women often have a fixed manner of masturbating: they use only one position and only one type of stimulation. Generally, their technique was accidentally discovered. Since it worked, they rarely deviated from it. By contrast, a woman who discovers orgasm as the result of her participation in a group is encouraged to try new positions and different types of stroking, which can result in her being less rigid about how she attains orgasm.

With both preorgasmic and situationally orgasmic women, it is necessary first to make masturbation a more sensual and valid experience in order to enhance the women's feelings about themselves as sexual beings. Once a woman feels more accepting of her sexual responses she may be more at ease communicating her needs to a partner. However, the situationally orgasmic woman's negative early conditioning seems somewhat more difficult to overcome than the preorgasmic woman's lack of initial learning. Furthermore, since general relationship problems which directly affect sexual response are more prevalent with situationally orgasmic than with preorgasmic women, intervention in the relationship system may be required in order to resolve the sexual problem.

Although some of the issues differ, a similar process is used to treat both sexual dysfunctions. Preorgasmic as well as situationally orgasmic women must have the information, support, and permission necessary to enjoy sex. Whether the client is preorgasmic or situationally orgasmic, it is essential to begin with the woman's feelings about herself, her own sexuality, and masturbation. Once we establish a firm foundation in this area, we can proceed to partner exercises or exploring relationship problems. All of these women must develop assertiveness, acquire skills in relating to others and learn to approach their goals through safe, small steps.

Homogeneous versus Mixed Groups

I have run three types of groups: preorgasmic women only, situationally orgasmic women only, and mixed groups with a variety of sexual problems. Within certain limitations, I have found that the mixed group offers the best results. Not only are mixed groups the most practical for the therapist, who may not have a large enough pool of applicants to draw from in order to form a homogeneous group, but since the treatment process for preorgasmic and situationally orgasmic women is virtually identical, group members who are at various levels of sexual self-discovery can assist one another.

Preorgasmic women must begin by taking the time to give themselves sexual pleasure and, in order to learn what an orgasm is, must attend to the minute details of the masturbation process. Consequently, they help the situationally orgasmic women attend to the stimulation techniques they already use during masturbation and thereby prevent them from prematurely moving into partner related activities. Situationally orgasmic women provide preorgasmic members with a variety of self-stimulation techniques and with descriptions of orgasm that are more diverse than those the leader alone could provide. Also, the preorgasmic women have the benefit of observing the situationally orgasmic women's progress with couple assignments. This modeling better enables them to integrate their orgasms into a partner relationship, which is especially significant should attainment of the first orgasm take most of the group sessions, leaving little time during the course of the treatment to concentrate on couple activities.

The drawbacks of a mixed group are the greater number and diversity of the issues discussed. Since the process is a rapid treatment program, the fewer issues requiring attention, the more time available to delve into the most relevant ones. If none of the women can have orgasms with masturbation, the therapist can focus on the fear of loss of control, disgust about masturbation and women's genitals, and other common concerns, at the beginning, leaving time for relationship issues after a number of the women have learned to experience orgasm on their own. A mixed group requires the therapist to divide her attention between self-sexuality issues and issues involving partners from the start. This two-pronged approach tends to diffuse the focus of the group, particularly when women suffering from vaginismus or lack of interest in sex are included in the mixed group.

In mixed groups that include only one or two preorgasmic women, the identification process and the domino effect of one orgasm leading to another may never have the opportunity to develop. In fact, the preorgasmic women may become discouraged and feel that they are too far behind the situationally orgasmic women ever to catch up. Hence, although these women may benefit in the same nonsexual ways as the situationally orgasmic women, they may receive insufficient support to experience their first orgasm. Including a minimum of three preorgasmic women in a mixed group of six or seven aids in alleviating this drawback.

Including Partners

A number of formats exist for directly including partners in the therapy program. One format consists of inviting partners to attend the second group session, which contains the majority of the educational information, and the seventh or eighth session, which focuses on couple issues raised during the course of therapy. Unfortunately, this approach can have a divisive effect on the group unless all the women have partners who are willing to participate. Therefore, women without partners or those whose partners are unwilling to attend the sessions must be in a separate group so that all group members feel they are receiving comparable treatment.

But homogeneity also has its drawbacks: it gives the women only limited exposure to significantly different kinds of relationships. Single women do not gain perspective on the range of relationship problems that can develop over time, and married women forget about the anxieties and difficulties being single entails. Such sharing may make it clear that neither acquiring nor discarding a partner in itself holds the solution to their problems.

The advantage of homogeneous groups is that more time can be devoted to relevant issues. Groups with women who have willing partners can spend time extensively exploring the issues involved in changing the ingrained patterns that develop in an old relationship. Groups for women without partners can focus on issues relevant to finding new partners and beginning new sexual relationships that are healthy and rewarding. In general, the prognosis for women whose partners are unwilling to participate in the therapy program is limited at best.

Another way to include partners in the treatment process is to run a men's group concurrently with the women's group. Although this format has not been fully evaluated, it appears to have a major drawback: many men are unwilling to attend such a group because they see the woman as the one with the problem.

The best approach is to mix women with and without partners in the initial ten-session group and then to add another two to four sessions for those women with partners willing to participate. This series may include only three or four couples. I have found that preparing the partner by including him in the initial interview and then following up the women's group with some couple sessions generally provides a framework for handling common sexual and relationship issues adequately. Most partners are receptive to the couples' sessions and participate actively. They seem to benefit from talking with other couples in much the same way that the women benefit from talking with other women. Another alternative is to offer conjoint sessions to couples who want them or to couples with extensive problems. As has been noted previously, a ten-session couples' group for women and their partners is another workable alternative to the women's group program (Ersner-Hershfield, 1978).

Group Size and Scheduling

Groups with fewer than five members cease to operate as a group because each woman has an insufficient number of other women with whom to identify and interact. In addition, when there are few participants, the group members generally feel pressure to contribute. Consequently, they may look more to the therapist for leadership and direction, which encourages both resistance and a tendency to assign authority to others rather than to assume responsibility themselves. These problems have been reported by most leaders who have started groups with fewer than five women.

Two hours per session is an optimal time for a group of six or seven women. Since each woman is expected to report her homework progress at every session, a larger group would require too much time. And the longer the session, the greater the opportunity to waste time. Keeping the session short enhances the sense that every moment is important.

It is desirable to select the participants so that each shares significant external characteristics with at least one other woman. For example, if there is one woman over 50 years of age, there should be another who is also over 50; likewise, there should be two married women, or two gay women, or two women of an ethnic or racial minority. If a woman sees herself as too different from all the other members she may isolate herself and benefit less from the group. When such balancing is not possible, the therapist should be aware of this problem and promote a sense of shared experience.

Originally, the preorgasmic groups met twice weekly for five weeks. This schedule was established to accommodate students, who were the initial clients. We later discovered that the intensified process that developed by meeting twice weekly added to the therapy's effectiveness. It is natural to avoid doing something that causes discomfort or anxiety, and in therapy groups that meet only once a week, clients tend to put off doing the homework until a day or two before the next session. Holding sessions at four- and three- day intervals (Monday and Thursday, Tuesday and Friday) provides continuous positive reinforcement and increases the likelihood that the women will complete the homework assignments daily. Completing the assignments in turn maximizes the likelihood of orgasmic release.

However, a five-week program did not provide sufficient time for progress with partner homework since it was more difficult for the women to set aside an hour a day with a partner than it was to do so alone. A schedule of twice weekly meetings for three weeks followed by weekly meetings for four weeks for a total of ten sessions seems to combine the positive aspects of both programs. Ersner-Hershfield (1978) compared twice weekly and once weekly sessions, and found both schedules to be adequate, although she suggested that a mixture of the two is most beneficial.

Selecting Participants

The first therapeutic contact is usually made over the telephone. Most women are shy, embarrassed, and ambivalent about asking for help with a sexual problem. A concerned but straightforward approach on the part of the therapist is desirable. If the therapist is uncomfortable asking explicit questions about sex, the client most certainly will feel ill at ease.

An initial office interview is important for a number of reasons. Given that the woman has probably always had a problem with orgasm, talking with her and setting up an individual session immediately will capitalize on her motivation to seek therapy at this particular time. It will help alleviate her initial anxiety and insure that she will remain interested until a group can be formed. Otherwise the therapist may find that when she thinks she finally has enough women to form a group, her waiting list has dwindled.

The initial interview not only provides the woman with the opportunity to talk with the therapist, see who she is, and evaluate her skills and attitudes, but also enables the therapist to determine whether group treatment is appropriate for this client. If the woman is in a stable relationship, I include the partner, whenever possible, in the second half of the initial interview to help me determine whether couple therapy might not be more appropriate. The initial interview also gives the therapist a chance to formulate a strategy by which to approach a particular woman and her situation and an opportunity to explain the group process in detail and to ascertain whether the woman is willing to make the necessary commitment. This preparation allays the woman's anxiety and increases the probability that she will show up for the first group session.

In the initial interview I try to elicit specific information in a number of areas. How does the woman see her problem? Does she experience it as a problem for her alone, for her partner, or for both of them? Does she now have orgasms? Has she ever had them? If she says she has never had an orgasm, I ask whether she ever has orgasms with masturbation. Many women who are orgasmic with masturbation do not consider the experience they have alone as having anything to do with sex. If I mention masturbation first and do so directly, without embarrassment, I am likely to get a straightforward answer, as well as a sigh of relief, especially if the woman has never talked about masturbation to anyone before. If the therapist is vague—asking the woman whether she experiences "fulfilling sex," whether she is "satisfied" by her partner, whether she has orgasms in "any other way"—the woman may feel too insecure and anxious to state explicitly what she does sexually for fear that it is outside the realm of the "normal."

If a woman says she has never had an orgasm either with a partner or with masturbation, I may inquire as to her expectations of orgasm. Sometimes women are having orgasms but do not know it because they expect the experience to be different from what it is. In one group, a woman described sensations in the sixth session that clearly sounded like orgasm to me. When I told her so, she was disappointed—she had been having these feelings for years. She was expecting the earth to move and to be at one with the universe when she had an orgasm.

If a woman has had orgasms in the past or currently has them with masturbation, obtaining the specifics of the experience is important in determining the choice of treatment. If she has been orgasmic with masturbation in the past but has not masturbated in years, the interview may provide an opportunity for her to get a head start by masturbating during the interim between the initial interview and the first group meeting. Few women lose their ability to have orgasms with masturbation. If she is orgasmic with masturbation, oral sex, or manual stimulation by a partner but not with intercourse alone, an educational program that stresses the role of direct clitoral stimulation in attaining orgasm might be a more appropriate initial intervention, with group treatment a possibility if education alone proves insufficient.

If a woman is orgasmic with masturbation but has not been orgasmic or only irregularly orgasmic with partners, preorgasmic group treatment may be most appropriate. However, if she is orgasmic with masturbation and once was orgasmic with her current partner but is no longer, I would press for further details about when the orgasms stopped and what important events occurred at that time. Frequently this situation indicates a relationship problem and may be dealt with more appropriately in conjoint therapy. Only the therapist's experience and intuition can help here. If there appear to be serious relationship problems in addition to the sexual concerns, I may decide that couple therapy should precede or run concomitantly with a preorgasmic group. When the partner also has a sexual problem, conjoint sex therapy alone, simultaneous conjoint sex therapy and preorgasmic women's group therapy, or conjoint sex therapy following completion of the preorgasmic group may be beneficial.

Women who are turned off to sex are frequently the most challenging cases for sex therapists. Power struggles within the relationship are the most common cause of this problem, especially when the woman has been attracted to her current partner in the past and is seeking therapy mainly at his request. In these situations, the initial contract with the woman is crucial. To agree, explicitly or implicitly to help her feel more sexual with her partner—translated into the woman's language as "for" her partner—will almost always produce resistance. However, success usually results from following a basically paradoxical approach; that is, being skeptical about whether any progress can be made and accepting as a goal the woman's being able to experience sexual feelings *just for herself* regardless of whether or not she chooses to act on these feelings.

Eleanor is an example of such a woman. She had been married twice and in both cases enjoyed sex while dating but gradually lost interest in sex after marriage. Once married, she experienced sex as a duty and either rebelled or submitted resentfully although she continued to experience orgasm during sex.

I refused to help Eleanor to enjoy sex more with her husband since that would have placed me on his side and she would have fought me as well. Instead, I agreed to work on her getting turned on sexually for her own pleasure if and when she wanted to feel aroused again. At some future date she could determine whether she wanted to share those feelings with a partner. She agreed, and having completed certain body looking and touching exercises, some assertiveness training, and several assignments to practice flirting with other men, Eleanor began to have more intense orgasms with her husband and to feel better about herself sexually. Moreover, Eleanor and I made it clear to her husband that he did not have the power to alter her level of sexual interest since it was totally in *her* head. This interpretation served to reduce the pressure he had been feeling to do something to arouse her. He could then stop pressuring her to enjoy sex, which in turn reduced her need to resist. Eventually Eleanor began to feel more aroused and was enjoying intercourse a few times a week, which made her and her husband happy.

Regardless of whether the woman is situationally orgasmic or preorgasmic, I like to know how she accounts for not having orgasms. Everyone has reasons to explain the unexplainable. Answers like "My mother never talked to me about sex" or "I didn't know until recently that women could have orgasms" do not provide much information. But answers that include a history of childhood molestation, an incestuous relationship, or fear of growing up and assuming responsibility can yield very important psychodynamic clues to the absence of orgasm. (These "psychological hooks" are explored in greater depth in Chapter 6.)

Ascertaining whether the woman has any physical or medical problems that might affect her sexual functioning as well as obtaining information about the type of contraception she uses and her comfort with that method can sometimes provide invaluable information. In one case, all the woman required to experience orgasm was a change from a diaphragm alone to a diaphragm plus a condom to enable her to feel safe enough from pregnancy to relax during sex.

Including the partner in the second half of the initial interview has advantages and disadvantages. The chief disadvantage is that it may give the woman the message that her orgasm is her partner's responsibility or that she must have a partner to be sexual. Either of these messages may be corrected once the group begins. On the positive side, meeting with the couple reassures the partner about the process and provides the therapist with a better picture of the relationship.

Leading a group composed of only half a partnership requires skill in understanding relationship dynamics. Both partners will have equally self-serving interpretations of events, and thus the woman's perspective on the relationship and on certain incidents inevitably will be biased. However, there are rarely pure villains and victims in relationships. Both people play a part in maintaining the system in its current state even though neither is satisfied with the way things stand. As the group progresses, I need to know how the woman can best present the couple exercises to her partner. Meeting the partner before the group begins gives me some sense of both his personality and the dynamics of the relationship and a better idea of how to proceed.

No adequate screening procedures have been established for eliminating women who cannot work constructively in a group situation, whose relationship would not benefit from this form of treatment, or for whom a rapid treatment program would be insufficient to meet current life needs or personality structure. Until further research in this area has clarified the salient issues, I recommend that the therapist not work with a client with whom she is very uncomfortable. For some therapists, this might entail screening out psychotic women. However, if the therapist is comfortable working with seriously disturbed women, it is entirely possible for these women to realize their goal of orgasm within a group setting. Surprisingly, sexual therapy seems to help the reality testing of psychotic women and the exercises seem to enhance their ability to concentrate.

However, possible negative reactions from other group members present a drawback to including these women in a group. If a noticeably disturbed woman is avoided by other members or is treated differently, she may fail to benefit from the group process. This places an added burden on the therapist to make sure that the woman feels a part of the group and is given a chance to join in interchanges. Women who are depressed, however, appear to pose no problem to the group. As a matter of fact, many women commence group treatment in a somewhat depressed state since helplessness and loss of control are characteristic of women who do not have orgasms.

A final consideration in the selection process is whether a woman is currently involved in any other form of psychotherapy. If a woman is currently in therapy, I want to know whether she is in it for her sexual problem and whether her therapist knows of her intention to join a preorgasmic group. If the therapist has referred her, I assume that he or she knows about the process and has confidence in it. Some therapists like to discontinue individual therapy until the group ends; others prefer to continue the individual treatment in order to work on nonsexual issues. My concern here is that the woman not bring up issues in her individual sessions that concern the group because if she works out group related issues elsewhere, she limits her participation in the group and deprives other group members of her insights. Refraining from discussing the group in her individual therapy also minimizes the chances of eliciting contradictory meassages from the different therapists involved and thereby minimizes the possibility of her playing one therapist off against the other.

It is not uncommon (especially if the individual therapist is a male) for the woman to be uncomfortable discussing sex with her therapist and hence not to inform her therapist of her wish to be involved in a preorgasmic group. In this situation I inquire as to how participating in a group might pose problems. If the woman can imagine no potential problems, I suggest some; for example, how she feels about withholding important information from her therapist or how she feels about being caught between two therapeutic modalities. I usually suggest that she discuss the group with her therapist. However, I am less concerned about her talking to her therapist than I am about her own clarity regarding the process. Women who refuse to talk to their therapists about the group but who clearly separate the two therapeutic experiences in fact experience no difficulties. Those who are more confused or for whom seeking additional therapy may represent an important issue in individual therapy generally will be better off if before joining a group they are helped to come to terms with the possible conflicts.

The most complicated situation arises when a woman who is already working on sexual issues with her therapist or whose therapist advises her against a group joins anyway. This decision can easily lead to competition between the two forms of therapy and between the two therapists involved. If the group is successful, does this somehow prove her other therapist inadequate? Will she feel she has to discontinue individual therapy, even though it has been helpful with other problems? If she thinks so, she may find herself thwarting her sexual goals in order to maintain her relationship with her individual therapist. Discovering these issues mid-group can complicate the sex therapy considerably and in some instances markedly interfere with the woman's attaining her goals. Therefore, it is imperative to clarify these issues before the group has started.

Explaining Details

Once I determine that a client is appropriate for women's group sex therapy, I explain the details of the process. The topic of masturbation should be broached gently with women who have never masturbated since many of them have strong inhibitions against it. Most women accept the idea if I tell them, "We have found that women in your particular situation are generally out of touch with their own bodies. Does that fit for you? The easiest way to get back in touch with your body is through self-stimulation. Consequently, each woman in the group first focuses on learning to have orgasms on her own through masturbation and then learns how to communicate what she has discovered about herself to her partner." For situationally orgasmic women this message can be modified: "Now that we know that you work, that you're not broken, what we have to find

72

out is why what works for you on your own is not happening when you have sex with your partner." In both cases, it is important to stress that since the woman's partner is not in the group, she will have the responsibility to teach him what she learns from the sessions.

It is necessary to explain that agreeing to participate in the program means that the woman is willing and able to attend all the group sessions and to do an hour of homework a day. The group will be a place to discuss the homework and related issues. Pointing out that all the sexual assignments are done at home will relieve many women who are concerned that they might have to disrobe or masturbate in the group.

After I have explained the process, I want to be sure that the program is acceptable to the woman. If I detect even a hint of hesitancy, I encourage her to take time to think it over before she accepts a place in the group. I want her to be certain that she wants to do it for herself and not because I am pressuring her. In this way, I am assured that the woman is highly motivated. If a woman is unsure and I try to convince her that she should join the group for her own sake, I am taking on more responsibility then I should, and once the group begins she may resist me or drop out.

In my experience, any manifestation of ambivalence such as frequent telephone calls before the first group meeting or unusual fee-setting difficulties warrants postponing the decision to include the woman in a group; she can join a group at a later date when she feels less unsure. One woman called me three times prior to the first session to get further details. First she was concerned that her problem might be too different from that of the other group members; then she feared that external pressures might make this an inappropriate time to begin. When she called a third time, I told her that she had so many reasonable concerns that *I* did not think she should join the group. She then became very quiet and her voice began to quaver. The fear that came up immediately when she realized she might not be included assured her of how important this therapy was to her, and her ambivalence vanished. The tactic proved to be very successful. She was a woman whose power came from withholding and she most likely would have tried to defeat the therapist had she not felt in charge when the group began.

Once it seems clear that a woman does want to join a group and is willing to commit herself to the group sessions and the requisite hours of homework, I ask her how she thinks she will try to sabotage getting what she now says she wants; for example, by not doing the homework, by procrastinating, or by getting ill. I ask this question because it both gives the client insight into her own resistance and puts her in control. She is telling me how she will sabotage herself; I am not telling her. But more important, having her articulate her resistance in this way often prevents her from manifesting it. For example, one woman's method of sabotage was procrastination. At the second session she admitted that she was not doing her homework but since she had told me that she might procrastinate, she decided to do her homework so that I could not say, "See, you're procrastinating"—this was the beginning of her taking responsibility for herself.

Finally, I assign my book *For Yourself* (1975) to prepare the woman for the group process and the homework exercises. At first I was afraid that the reading would inhibit the process by prematurely giving the women too much information. However, a few of the therapists I had trained began to assign the book when prospective clients initially telephoned. They found, contrary to my expectations, that reading *For Yourself* generally had a facilitating effect. Although some women were concerned about the partner exercises, most of them were better prepared and more willing to undertake the homework than women who had not read the book. The group members reported that reading stories of women like themselves was both reassuring and motivating.

Confirmation

As happens in other forms of therapy, some prospective clients experience so much anticipatory anxiety about the process that they either forget about the first session or cancel at the last minute. This can be devastating to a closed group whose success depends on an optimal size and a balanced makeup. Collecting a reasonable deposit is one way to insure attendance. Fee collection depends on the policy of each therapist and on the ability of the client to pay. Some therapists collect half the fee as a deposit and the second half midway through the group. Others collect by the session or by the week, with the deposit used as payment for the last session or two.

I inform all the women that the group starts on time: nothing dampens enthusiasm more than waiting for stragglers, and soon those who normally arrive on time begin arriving late. Therefore, I always start at the appointed hour. I generally find that after a session or two everyone comes early. Once I arrived five minutes late for a group and found the members already meeting with the door locked. I really felt I was doing my job well when they expressed enough self-confidence to begin the session without me.

CHAPTER 5

The Early Sessions

THE FIRST FEW meetings are the most structured of the series. Didactic material is presented on such topics as the anatomy of the female genitals and the physiology of the sexual response cycle in order to replace myths with solid factual information. The same homework assignments are prescribed for all women in the group (with occasional exceptions); whereas in later sessions homework is tailored to the needs of each individual.

The therapist's role in the early sessions is to support and understand each woman's sexual attitudes and experiences to counter her tendency to feel somehow wrong or inadequate. A woman can listen to and absorb advice, interpretations, suggestions, and instructions only after she feels that she is understood and accepted. If the therapist is too quick to give advice, the woman may conclude that the therapist does not understand her, and she is then likely to reiterate her plight until she believes that her experience has been acknowledged. Intervening before rapport has been established frequently makes the woman feel that she is being criticized and engenders a defensive reaction. Initially the therapist should listen well. She can be more confrontational after rapport has been established.

General Issues

SIMILARITIES AND DIFFERENCES

The therapist, in addition to lending support, aids the group process by pointing out both the differences and the similarities among the participants. The women readily perceive their similarities. However, differences are often overlooked, and it is up to the therapist to protect and even encourage them. If this is not done, a group norm of "sameness" may be established that results in the censure of dissenting opinions or divergent experiences. Such a group norm can prevent progress if the women feel coerced to be like one another in order to be accepted. Consequently, important issues may be suppressed only to haunt the entire group at a later time.

Stressing differences among group members at this early stage begins to give the women a sense that there is no right or wrong way to experience sex; that each is unique and will develop along her own lines, within her own relationship, and at her own pace; and that differences are not only acceptable but also highly desirable. I speak again and again in my groups about uniqueness among women. This concept is crucial to the development of a strong sexual identity and the ability to attain orgasm.

RIGHT TO PLEASURE

Also addressed repeatedly in the initial sessions is the woman's right to pleasure and her responsibility for obtaining it. At the outset, this discussion focuses on each woman's ability to handle the details of her life in such a way as to guarantee her time for the home assignments. The leader can be most effective at this stage by reinforcing successes and overlooking failures. It will soon be clear to all group members that those women who do their homework are making strides and feeling better about themselves whereas those who do nothing are not moving forward.

The mere setting of priorities to encourage the women to put certain personal needs before some responsibilities promotes the notion of the right to pleasure. The beginning of an understanding that this right is innately theirs and need not be earned gives the women a sense of control and optimism. This part of the process is set in a framework of reduced demands as far as orgasm is concerned. It is important to relieve the pressure the women feel to have orgasms and to promote the concept of learning to enjoy their own bodies simply as a source of pleasure.

PARTNER'S REACTIONS

Every relationship is a system. The interaction of two people creates a whole that is greater than the sum of the parts. Consequently, when one person in a system makes certain changes, the whole system changes (Watzlawick, Beavin and Jackson, 1967). Women who participate in preorgasmic groups strengthen their sense of self, their self-worth, and their ability to be assertive. These changes naturally will affect their relationships. However, while change is taking place each woman is receiving considerable support from the group to assist her until a new equilibrium has been established. The excluded partner often receives little, if any, outside support and must weather the changes alone. It is not unusual, therefore, for partners to feel threatened, especially during the early sessions. Some men experience transient episodes of erectile problems or rapid ejaculation during this time. The partner's anxiety generally diminishes as the woman becomes more interested sexually, more willing to initiate sexual activity, and better able to communicate her specific sexual likes and dislikes.

The women in the group can make the process easier or more difficult for their partners. I emphasize this point by asking the participants to imagine how they would feel if their partners were involved in a sex therapy group. The women usually say they would feel anxious, threatened, and uneasy about how their partners would represent them to the other group members and would worry about what the others might think about them. I then explain that they can expect their partners to feel much the same way and that these worries are natural and appropriate reactions to the situation. I tell them that either they can use the group to enhance their relationships and bring them closer to their partners or they can use it as a sledgehammer to disrupt the relationship. It's up to them.

In this way, I return the responsibility for dealing effectively with partners to each woman, where it belongs. I am not interested in running man-hating groups—and this form of therapy could easily degenerate into a man-hating group if the leaders were to permit it. I was once consulted about a group in which none of the women had reached her goal and none had done the assignments. Instead, the members spent most of the group time discussing how their partners sabotaged their efforts to do the homework. The leaders were unwittingly supporting the women's "poor me" attitude rather than putting the responsibility back on them to change their situations so that their needs could be met and the homework carried out.

Pamela put the matter most effectively in the following exchange.

JOSEPHINE: Yeah, I get mad, too.

PAMELA: I feel a little sour, disgusted, disappointed.

B.J.: There is a word to describe what I am feeling. It has to do with relationships. Men are fucked up these days. They assume you have nothing to do and they can drop over any old time and you'd better be ready for them with no consideration at all.

PAMELA: I would like to say something. I think whatever we say should be coming from our own experiences. This could go on to be a whole big discussion about men and how horrible they are and not get around to us. I don't care about the men. I want to do something for myself. Let's forget about them. We could really get hung up on this and they are not paying for this.

[Laughter]

THERAPIST: I think a very good point has been made.

Emphasizing from the very first meeting that the women have responsibility for their own sexual satisfaction helps to avoid relationship problems. I do not suggest that all relationships survive the therapy intact, but most women who are forewarned can anticipate the problems and reassure the partner. When she notices that he is feeling threatened, she can let him know that his response is perfectly natural, at the same time attempting to make the process as easy as possible for him by sharing her thoughts and feelings about the group and her own sexual blocks and breakthroughs.

RESPONSIBILITY

The women are also told that they are responsible for what they get out of the group. They will get as much out as they put in. Many women enter the group saying that they are coming only for their partner's sake. This stance protects them from facing the problem fully and from the possibility of failure. Unfortunately, it can create a self-fulfilling prophecy. A woman who is afraid that she will fail may not try wholeheartedly and thus may unwittingly bring about the very failure she has been dreading.

Confronting such a woman with her defense at the start, while she is using it to protect herself, is likely to threaten and alienate her. Her willingness to come to the meetings and to do an hour of homework a day "for his sake" is sufficient initially. Later, if this stance seems to be inhibiting her progress, it may have to be addressed directly. But this need rarely arises once the notion of sex for the woman's own pleasure has been established.

Session One

When the women arrive for the first group meeting they are generally tense and anxious. Therefore, they may not retain much of what is said, and important details will have to be repeated in later sessions.

On rare occasions, it turns out that two of the women know each other and are quite surprised to find themselves together in the group. It is important to deal with how each acquaintance feels about the situation. Encouraging both women to express their feelings generally clears the air, and I always explain to the entire group, for ethical as well as practical reasons, that what is talked about in the meetings is strictly confidential and is never to be discussed outside the group in any explicit manner.* If either acquaintance nevertheless wishes to join a different group, she is free to do so.

I usually begin the first session by asking how the women feel about being there. This question enables them to verbalize their anxiety and, by doing so, to get beyond it. It also serves to set the process of group identification in motion.

JENNY: What I am feeling right now is that everything that everybody is saying is interesting and fine, but I am not going to

*Members are free to discuss general subjects brought up during group meetings, but they are not to divulge any identifying characteristics of other members or their partners.

relate to this. It actually has nothing to do with me. That's fine, you go talk about your thing, but I'm different. Actually, I am not, but what my feeling is is that I am less of a woman. To admit difficulty in having an orgasm, or not having an orgasm, or having an orgasm by myself, or whatever, then I am the weird one.

After I have a sense of the group and of how the women feel about being there, I want to find out what sex is like for them and what it is like for them not to experience orgasm. I go into this area as explicitly as possible with all the women who are willing to talk about it. Those who are reticent are in no way pressured to speak. I want the women to have an opportunity to hear one another's stories and to get to know one another. This process forms the basis for the development of group cohesiveness and trust. Even women who are reluctant to speak in the initial session can become very involved in the process merely through listening attentively to what others say. Rather than confront, interpret, or make suggestions, in this session the therapist's job is to listen carefully and acknowledge each woman's story.

For example, some preorgasmic women are disappointed and frustrated by their sexual experiences, especially when their partner appears to get so much enjoyment out of sex and they get so little. Anger at their partner for not having all the answers is understandable. After all, women have been taught that men are the experts on sex, when in fact men are often just as confused as women are and may feel themselves to blame for sexual problems that exist in the relationship. It also seems reasonable for a woman to cry when her partner has ejaculated and she still feels frustrated. Crying can provide release when sexual release has not occurred. It is likewise not difficult to comprehend that some women no longer feel anything during sex and try to get it over with as quickly as possible. Experience has shown them that sex always ends in frustration, and they prefer to shut off feelings early because when sexual tension does not build, the resulting sexual frustration is less. Shutting off feelings becomes a self-protective mechanism. Often, women fake orgasm because they find it the easiest way to manage this problem: they protect both themselves and their partners from feeling like failures; faking may induce a considerate lover to stop when the woman can think of no other way to terminate the sex act; and it will obviate those tense discussions about what went wrong and who failed and why, discussions that can be especially depressing when no one has a solution. The following transcript illustrates the typical feelings expressed in the first session.

> THERAPIST: I know the particulars of all of you, but you don't know each other. So, maybe we can share our feelings about what it is like not to have orgasms.
>
> PAMELA: Well, I feel a tremendous frustration and anger and turning inward and hating myself for not being able to be a complete person. I don't want to be with men anymore because there is this feeling that I can't have an orgasm, and I am tired of lying about it all the time. I would just like to be able to experience whatever I want to feel, even for myself without a man there, just for me.
>
> ABBY: When I was 18, 19, and 20 I think I should have gotten an Academy Award for my performance. It was great.
>
> MARIA: To get married and find the right man and live happily ever after—the magic penis. And if you want kids, you have to have an orgasm; there is no way out of it. It's supposed to be the only way to conceive. But I can't masturbate and I get mad at him if he doesn't give me an orgasm. I am waiting for the "Doc" to come along and give me my orgasm for today, or whatever. It is like I freeze up. I just start getting real stiff.
>
> B.J.: For two years, I've been thinking it is a problem, it isn't a problem; it's a problem but the hell with it, I'm not going to do anything about it. It is a psychological thing that I can't have a strong orgasm.
>
> THERAPIST: Some of you have been to groups and all kinds of things. How many of you have worked on this before?
>
> ABBY: I went to a sex therapist and she helped me a lot.
>
> B.J.: I have talked to physicians and so forth. They have nothing to say!
>
> PAMELA: What about gynecologists?
>
> MARIA: They just say, "Don't worry about it." It has always irritated me. I wondered if I should see somebody, because I feel cheated. They'd say, "Don't worry about it." That is the way medical men seem to be. Now, I hardly waste my time asking because they always say, "Oh, just go out and have fun. Find a man and have fun."

Women frequently use the first or the second session to talk about messages they received or did not receive about sex from their mothers and fathers or sisters and brothers. My job at this point is to keep the discussion focused on sexual topics.

JENNY: The way I feel right now is that it is lack of knowledge per se. My parents never taught me about it. I feel like it is something that we just can't talk about.

BEVERLY: The average people of my generation don't talk about it. I remember standing in front of my mother and I was going to sleep in the living room and I was really tired. I was getting undressed and she said, "You're getting undressed here? Grace might come up." This young girl of 20. So I got undressed, I put on my nightgown, and she says to me, "Did you bring a robe?" All I could think of was, "Mother, you should just know about this class."

[Laughter]

I'm 62 and her thinking has never, ever changed. I wanted to say, "Mother, you are damned wrong! Why don't you face that?" Because she won't ever accept it anyway. It's a little late. We've just let her get by with it, myself and my two sisters. I asked my younger sister, "You can answer it or not answer it, however you please, only I'm curious to find out because I'm going to a sexuality class." So I said, "Ellen, did you ever have an orgasm?" And she says, "If I did, I didn't know it." She is the kind of person that I would have thought *did*. We just had never discussed it. I was really surprised.

THERAPIST: What do you make of that? How do you see that relating to your own situation?

BEVERLY: Ellen is a very sexual person and did lots of things with men all her life, much more than I did. What do I make of it? I just think that there has got to be something in the upbringing of us girls. We never saw any sexual displays or any real affection. And my mother even told me before I got married—that was the only time she ever talked to me about sex—that I should always pretend it hurts!

THERAPIST: Pretend it hurts?

BEVERLY: Whether it does or not. Those are the kind of things Mother always put into our heads. I recall once getting undressed when I was about five years old in the backyard and turning the hose on myself and on my sisters and really being *swooped* up and taken into the house and put into a room and that kind of stuff.

THERAPIST: Did any of you others get similar or different messages?

ABBY: I'm wondering just how much of these messages we got. We knew that what they were saying was not how we really felt, but how much of it we really believed—because mothers know best—you know.

JENNY: With me I didn't want to discuss it or argue with her because I knew I differed with her so I just didn't respond. So she would think I was agreeing.

ABBY: What I think we're getting at is that all of us got this big set of messages.

MARIA: All I got was a book.

JOSEPHINE: On menstruation and eggs and sperm.

JENNY: Right. And then Bambi came bouncing through.

THERAPIST: After a movie in the sixth grade I told my mother, "I understand about the eggs and the sperm, but I don't understand how the sperm gets to the egg." And so my mother took this deep breath and explained it to me, and I looked at her and said, "You and Daddy don't do that, do you?" And she wanted to die. That was it—that was the last time we ever talked about sex.

[Laughter]

ABBY: Well, my mother's dead now, but all the time we were growing up they had separate rooms and they never touched each other. Never, but I was curious as to why.

JENNY: I know my mother told me that all men do is they do their thing and then they roll over and go to sleep. That's it. You know, she always had a very negative attitude about sex.

THERAPIST: Did anybody here have a mother with a positive attitude toward sex?

ABBY: Mine had a funny kind of thing about it. My mother said that she liked to make love. That was the only thing she ever said about it. That seemed like enough for her and that was the end of the conversation. And then, when I was married, she said, "How is Abe in bed?" Here's my puritan mother, you know, and it was just very strange. I mean there's a mixed message there, which I've never quite been able to figure out.

HOMEWORK

I save 45 minutes at the end of each session to introduce the homework assignments for the following three or four nights.

Reading

Part of the initial homework assignment is to read *For Yourself* (1975) and the chapter on sexuality in *Our Bodies, Ourselves* (1971) by the Boston Women's Health Book Collective. The readings furnish factual information and provide input for the second session. Some women may have neglected to bring up an important issue because of the fear that the other women would reject or not understand them. Reading about women with similar problems frequently gives members the permission and the courage to broach a difficult issue in the following meeting.

Kegel Exercises

Some of the exercises developed by Kegel (1952) to strengthen the pubococcygeal muscle (which covers the pelvic floor, including the opening to the anus and vagina) are assigned in the first session. The women are told to do Kegel exercises not only throughout the course of the group but also throughout their lives to keep this muscle healthy and well toned. Kegel developed the exercises to help women who tended to expel some urine involuntarily when they coughed, sneezed, or had an orgasm. After approximately six weeks of practicing the exercises, Kegel's patients began reporting heightened sensitivity to sexual sensations in the vaginal area, in addition to a greater ability to withhold urine. Consequently, many of them were finding intercourse more pleasurable.

I usually assign the following Kegel exercises, excerpted from *For Yourself.*

To locate your pubococcygeal muscle, urinate with your legs apart; the muscle you squeeze to stop the flow of urine is the PC muscle. Practice stopping the flow of urine a few times in order to become familiar with the muscle. Then, lie down and put your finger in the opening of your vagina and contract the PC muscle. See if you can feel the contraction around your finger.

After practicing the following exercises for about six weeks, see if you notice any difference in the strength of your PC muscle when you put your finger in your vagina and squeeze.

The first Kegel exercise consists of squeezing the PC muscle for three seconds, then relaxing the muscle for three seconds, and squeezing it again. At first, do ten three-second squeezes at three different times during the day. It may be difficult at first to keep contracting for a full three seconds. If that is the case, contract for one or two seconds and build up the time as the muscle gets stronger. The advantage to these exercises is that you can do them anywhere and at any time and no one can tell you're doing them. Practice when you stop the car for a red light or in the morning when you wake up. Or do them when you answer the telephone at home or at work, or when you are lying down to rest. The muscles surrounding your anus may also move during the exercise, but if you find that you are moving your thigh muscles, your stomach or buttocks, you are probably squeezing the wrong muscle.

The second exercise is like the first except that the objective is to squeeze the muscle, release it, squeeze again and release as quickly as possible. This is nicknamed the "flutter" exercise. Again, squeeze and release ten times at three different times during the day. When you first start doing this exercise, it may feel like a tongue twister; you may not be able to tell if you are contracting or releasing and for a while it may keep getting muddled all together. However, after working at it slowly, you will gradually be able to do the flutter more rapidly.

The third exercise consists of imagining that there is a tampon at the opening to the vagina and that you are sucking it up into your vagina. Gloria was actually able to suck water into her vagina and then spurt it out again when she did this exercise while taking a bath.

The fourth exercise consists of bearing down as during a bowel movement, but with the emphasis more on the vagina than the anal area. This exercise is more apparent to an observer. Both the sucking in and the bearing down should be held for three seconds, as with the first exercise.

All four exercises should be practiced ten times each at three different times during the day. As you progress with these Kegel exercises, slowly increase the number in each series until you are able to do twenty of each series in succession. You can do them as frequently during the day as you can find time, but consider three times daily a minimum [1975:54–55].

Even though the benefit of increased vaginal sensitivity will not be realized for about six weeks, assigning the Kegel exercises in the first session has several advantages. It allays anxiety for women who fear they will urinate when they have an orgasm (although some inevitably will, particularly if they use a vibrator, which has a tendency to irritate the urethra). More important, however, the Kegel exercises are assigned at the beginning because practicing them gives the women the feeling that they are finally able to do something about a problem that always seemed beyond solution. And they are doing something nonthreatening. They do not have to touch their genitals, yet practicing the exercises frequently makes them aware of sexual sensations in the genital area. This result creates optimism while it teaches the women to focus on sexual sensations, an important foundation to be used in later homework assignments. Finally, by learning to exercise the pubococcygeal muscle, the women are gaining a sense of control over this formerly alien part of their bodies.

Relaxation and Private Time

The next two homework assignments are to be carried out during the private hour the women are to set aside every day. The therapist must stress the necessity of setting aside an entire uninterrupted hour of private time. The women may have to put a lock on the bedroom door so that children cannot enter unexpectedly, turn up the heat if the room is too cool, or take the telephone off the hook, and they should do whatever is necessary to make the space comfortable and sensually attractive. (Some women enjoy burning candles or incense or playing soft music.)

It is also important for the women to find a way to relax from the stress of the day before doing the homework. It is difficult to get into a sensual mood when other business has been left unfinished, especially since the women have to create the sensual experience alone. Slowing down, or relaxing, can be accomplished in many ways: some women enjoy a leisurely bath or shower; others find sipping wine or reading a newspaper serves the same purpose. The highly effective Jacobson technique of tensing and then relaxing various muscle groups can be used to relieve tension (Bernstein and Borkovec, 1973). I also frequently teach group members the following simple relaxation exercise.

The first step in this exercise is to assume a comfortable position. Either lie flat, recline in a comfortable chair, or lean against a pillow. Close your eyes, then breathe deeply and regularly. As you are doing so, try to visualize the air as it goes into your mouth, down the trachea, and into the lungs. When the lungs are filled, imagine the reverse process as you exhale. After doing this a number of times, imagine the air being taken into the fingertips of your right hand, up through the right arm and shoulder, into the lungs—then back out again, following the reverse path. As you imagine the warm air going through your arm, notice any areas of tension in the arm and imagine the warm air gently relaxing those areas as it flows through. After you have inhaled and exhaled a number of times and your right arm is relaxed, repeat the process for your left arm, then the neck, torso, pelvic area, and each leg until the whole body is relaxed.

I suggest that the women practice relaxation during the group meetings to clarify the process so they can repeat it at home. After practicing this exercise a few times, the women often find that they need less time to attain the same results.

Body Viewing Exercise

After the woman is in a relaxed and sensual mood, she is to look at her nude body in the largest mirror she has, preferably a full-length one. Women in our society are taught that there is one standard of beauty, and inevitably they do not fit it. Whether they choose a *Vogue* model or a *Playboy* bunny, most women select for themselves an ideal of beauty that differs markedly from their own body type. If a woman is tall and broad-shouldered, she will envy petite women. If she has large breasts, she will wish they were smaller; if they are small, then larger ones are considered more sensuous. Women who feel good about and enjoy their bodies are by far the minority.

The body viewing exercise—incorporated from the Lobitz and LoPiccolo (1972) program—is a good way for a woman to begin to feel more comfortable with her body. A woman who is not comfortable with her body will probably feel awkward when she is nude with her partner. Accordingly, she may try to position herself so that her thighs appear less large, maneuver her lover's hand off her less than taut stomach, or refrain from trying certain positions that would make her breasts appear to sag. Such self-consciousness can easily inhibit one's ability to relax and focus on sexual sensations, whereas if a woman is more accepting of her body she may be more relaxed with a partner.

A woman's feelings about her body frequently reflect her feelings about herself. If we engineer a change that allows her to be more self-accepting physically, emotional self-acceptance can be expected to follow more easily. This is all part of the process of helping the woman to accept her uniqueness on a number of levels.

I ask each woman to look carefully at herself from every direction and to assume many different stances (e.g., lying down, sitting, looking backward between her legs) while nude. She is to examine her body as if seeing it for the first time. I want her to start at the top of her head and slowly work down to the bottom of her feet, stopping every few inches to comment, aloud or silently, about the details she is noticing. Is her right eye rounder than her left? Are there any new wrinkles on her face? Is her right shoulder higher than the left? Slowing the process down and attending to details, even if it is boring to do so, may enable the woman to see her body in a new way. This exercise also paves the way for the masturbation assignments, which will require an even greater ability to focus her awareness.

Women who feel awkward and uncomfortable about their bodies resist doing this homework assignment. Consequently, I use a tactic that encourages completion of the exercise. After I have explained the assignment to the group, I ask each woman first to describe the part of her body she likes the least or is least comfortable with and then the part she likes best or is most comfortable with. I also want to know what it is about each part that makes her feel the way she does about it. If I neglect to say that some women may like all or none of their physical parts, a group norm of "I hate my body" may evolve, persuading women who like their bodies to search for faults in order not to appear in some way better than the others.

A number of things can happen as the women share their feelings about their bodies. Listening to another woman describe her "problem area" may allow a woman to feel better about herself if she likes that part of her own body. For example, she may feel better about her strong legs when she hears another complain about her weak knees. Learning that another woman is also self-conscious about big feet or an appendectomy scar will make her feel less alone with the problem. Hearing another woman's positive reaction to some part of her body may enable the listener to appreciate that area in herself. For example, if one woman says her face is her favorite part, another woman may silently compare her own face to the speaker's and conclude that perhaps it is not as bad as she thought since her nose is straighter, her complexion better, or her chin shapelier. She may walk out of the session feeling much better about herself.

Reality testing is another way of gaining greater self-acceptance. If, for instance, one woman mentions how much she detests a bump on her nose and two other women, unrehearsed blurt out, "Where?" she has to show them. The others have to lean forward to locate this terrible deformity. At this point many women realize that things they dislike about themselves are frequently not even noticed by others.

Fran had had a mastectomy, which she felt made her ugly and sexually unattractive. Another woman in the group spontaneously asked whether she could see the scar since she had never seen a mastectomy scar and was curious. Fran hesitated for a minute, then lifted her sweater and prosthesis and let the other women come closer to look and touch. The group was not revolted. As a matter of fact, one woman commented that seeing the scar lessened her fear of breast cancer. Fran felt wonderful. She had taken a risk and found that it was worth it.

Once a woman tells the group about the part of her body she likes least, she tends to be relieved—the shameful secret is exposed yet the reasons for her shame are not confirmed by the reactions of other group members. This experience can enable her to be more comfortable with the body viewing assignment and, hence, more likely to complete it.

As the women go around the circle saying what physical feature they like least about themselves, I assign an exercise to exaggerate this area when they examine it at home. For example, I may suggest to a woman who does not like her stomach because she feels it is too big that she practice sticking her stomach out as far as possible and then sucking it in as far as she can while looking at herself in the mirror from different angles and positions. Similarly, I may ask a woman who feels she has fat thighs to jump up and down and jiggle the fat as much as possible. I ask a woman who feels she is hirsute to look at her hair through a magnifying glass. Of course, every time I make such a suggestion, I am careful to determine whether the woman is willing to give it a try. If she is not, I acknowledge her right not to do the exercise and reinforce her self-assertion. Ultimately, it is more important that the woman learn to stand up for herself than to carry out a particular assignment.

One object of the exaggeration exercise is to enable the women to face the reality of their situations. Many women avoid looking at the parts of their body that they dislike and mentally magnify their "defects" out of proportion. Having them carefully examine and exaggerate these areas can help give them perspective; for some women, the defects no longer seem as bad as imagined. For others, however, the exaggeration exercise confirms their negative feelings. But at least they can confront the problem honestly and directly. If the feature cannot be changed, they have to learn to live with it; if it can be changed, they can choose whether or not to do so. (Some women go on diets or exercise regimes as the result of this assignment.) Exaggerating the areas also provides a light and playful touch. It breaks the deadly serious tone of the orgasmic problem and helps the women have fun and even laugh at themselves as they approach their sexuality. Furthermore, group members recall these assignments and question one another about them at the next session, which encourages group interaction.

Some women, particularly obese women, have such an aversion to their bodies that it may be necessary to break the body viewing assignment down into smaller steps. Such a woman may look first at only her face and arms or these areas plus her lower legs; then gradually add other sections, trying to look at some new areas each day.

Being part of a group of women who do not look like the ideal helps drive home the fact that there are really very few women who meet the standards this society sets for beauty and that everyone is attractive in her own way. The women can then ponder the absurdity of such a standard. Meanwhile, each woman can better accept her uniqueness.

Body Touching Exercise

The body looking exercise is assigned as the first night's homework. On the second night, after relaxing and getting into a sensual mood, the women are to experiment with touching their bodies all over. I ask them to approach this exercise from two perspectives. The first time they do it they are to concentrate on what their fingertips and hands feel while touching the body, as if touching someone else. How does the skin feel? Is it smooth in some places and rough in others? What do the fat, calluses, hair, bones, blemishes feel like? Frequently women find that the area least comfortable to look at feels best to the touch. Again, starting at the top of the head and slowly moving down the body while verbalizing (aloud or silently) what she notices helps the woman attend to the task.

During the same hour, I ask the women to touch themselves all over once again, but this time to see what it is like to *be* touched in different ways. Which parts of the body are sensitive to which types of touch? A woman may notice that her breasts respond to almost nothing except hard squeezing of the nipples, that her neck enjoys feather-light circular strokes, that her stomach finds similar strokes ticklish, and that her shoulder responds best to firm pressure. Again, beginning at the top of the head and translating feelings into words helps keep the woman focused on the exercise.

If there are four nights between the first and second sessions I ask the women to alternate the exercises, spending two nights on the body looking assignment and two on the body tocuhing assignment. If there are only three nights between the sessions, I may assign body looking the first night and body touching the second, repeating the two assignments on the third night but in half the usual amount of time for each. In general, I want the women to reapeat each exercise at least once to notice whether any differences appear the second time. Sometimes women find the second attempt easier and less anxiety producing. This effect can illustrate that although the assignments may be uncomfortable initially, they become easier the more they are practiced. Generally, however, the women notice that the way they feel about their bodies is largely dependent upon their outlook on a particular day; in other words, although their appearance remains objectively unchanged, their subjective evaluation of themselves will vary with their mood.

Ban On Orgasm

The only other assignment I give in the first session is the paradoxical instruction to women who are not orgasmic at all or who are not orgasmic in partner sex deliberately not to have orgasms during sex with a partner. The rest of the group is instructed to have orgasms only during sexual activities in which they are reliably orgasmic. In other words, orgasm in any new way is forbidden at this point.

When I began running preorgasmic groups, banning intercourse was the first rule of sex therapy. But I feared that if I did so, I would have a number of angry partners on my hands. I knew the process would be threatening enough, and I did not want to encourage partner resistance. Consequently, I decided to tell the women to have sex with a partner as frequently or infrequently as they liked, but that during such activity they were to focus on which types of touch, which positions, and which activities produced greater or lesser sensations. They were to forget about orgasm while interacting with a partner, that would come later, during their homework hours.

To date, no preorgasmic women have started having orgasms as a result of this assignment; however, some situationally orgasmic women have. Women who have had orgasms sometimes experience them again simply by having the pressure to perform removed. For preorgasmic women, however, the goal of this self-monitoring exercise is to relieve the pressure to perform when they are with a partner, which frees them to concentrate on what they are feeling. These feelings in turn provide valuable information for future self-stimulation and partner related exercises. If a woman desires a ban on intercourse in later sessions, she can give herself that assignment for reasons that make it appropriate.

Finally, after making sure that everyone understands the assignments, I ask the women how they feel about the first session in general. I like to save time to ask this question after every session. First, if the women keep me apprised of their feelings I am less likely to overlook important concerns that may develop into negative group norms. Second, it helps the group feel more responsible for the process and what they get out of it. If the women are unhappy about something they have the opportunity to change it. Having the women assume some responsibility for the 10-session process is a first step in teaching them to take responsibility for other areas of their lives.

Session Two

The second session is obviously the first one in which homework can be reported. From this session onward, homework advances and setbacks determine the major content of the meetings. To ignore the homework details by spending excessive group time on other issues conveys the message that the group process is more important than the homework. This can lead to the illusion that progress is being made when in fact progress can occur only as the result of confronting the anxiety by attempting to change the behavior.

Anxiety about doing the homework is to be expected, and resistance is the norm at this juncture. Common excuses include lack of time, unusual obligations, entertaining houseguests, fear of intrusion on the part of children, and forgetting. I have found that the best way to deal with resistance during the early sessions is to ignore it. I express agreement that being a mother does cut into personal time and space and suggest that the women think about how they can overcome whatever obstacles they face to get a little time for themselves since not finding the time would preclude a successful outcome. If they act especially apologetic and guilty in offering their excuses I may wonder aloud how they imagined I would punish them for failing to do the homework. Frequently members will reply, "You wouldn't do anything, I suppose. I know I have to do the assignments to get anywhere." It is far better for the women to make this point and to take responsibility. If I make it, I place myself in the mother or teacher role, treating them like bad little girls.

Resistance can lead to insight if a woman is not made to feel defensive. One woman who had offered numerous excuses for not doing the homework finally volunteered at the end of the fourth session that she was anxious about doing the assignments and, although she wanted to do them, found it difficult to begin. After this admission she began completing the homework.

Remember, there is no way a group leader can make a woman do the homework; she does it only when she has decided that she wants the results it can bring. Consequently, I spend as little time as possible in the early sessions on women who are procrastinating but instead devote myself to reinforcing the women who do the homework by exploring their findings and feelings in detail. Women who gain something from the exercise will encourage the resisters more effectively than I could. In fact, the women who do not complete the first assignment generally reassign it to themselves at the end of the second session, when the new homework is being given. I also assign the Yes-and-No exercise (pp. 129–132) for women who do not feel they have a right to pleasure and are having difficulty taking time out of their busy lives for themselves.

HOMEWORK FEEDBACK

I want to know specifics when getting the homework feedback. Eliciting the details of when, where, and exactly how the women did the homework teaches them the kind of details they need to attend to while doing future homework assignments. I also need a picture of exactly what they are doing to determine what they should emphasize or vary in order to attain orgasm.

I want to know whether the women are having problems doing the Kegel exercises. I may ask them to try Kegeling during the group. If I cannot see them squeezing auxiliary muscles and they are fairly confident that they are doing the exercises correctly, I have no reason for concern. If they are experiencing tenderness or mild cramps I may reduce the number of contractions they complete daily.

I want to know specifically how the body looking and touching exercises went. What did they notice? Were any of their expectations or feelings about their bodies confirmed? Did they learn anything new about their bodies or about any particular areas? Did anything surprise them?

I am less concerned about their liking all parts of their bodies than I am about their acceptance of reality. The purpose is to change from wishing for miracles to accepting reality so that they can make the most of the situation.

The following discussion presents a typical response to the body looking assignment.

JENNY: I found a dimple.

[Laughter]

PAMELA: Where?

JENNY: Right on my tush. I had always felt it was unattractive, 'cause of the fact that my hips are wide. But I think it's been overemphasized by style and my family. It really is not that bad. And I saw this kind of crevice the first day, and I thought it was a crevice, you know—it was fat or something hanging over. I thought it was something disgusting. And, I guess it was last night, I realized it was a dimple.

[Laughter]

Yeah, it was a large one. It was a large dimple. And some of the muscles are starting to sag. I know I don't have the behind of a five year old.

BEVERLY: Or a 25 year old.

[Laughter]

JENNY: All right. Let's not get nasty about the whole thing. But it's true. And when I bent forward all the skin stretched out, and it looked very nice. I mean that the sagginess was gone and I bent forward and it was nice, round, big, you know, very round.

MARIA: That was interesting about the hips because I went home and looked in the mirror, and I'm always trying to make my hips wider and larger 'cause I think it's very womanly and I just kept thinking about it. There are these people who have womanly hips and they don't like it. I was amazed. I'm doing

95

these exercises to try and make my hips come out, you know. Doesn't work, but I like doing the exercises. I even went to sleep seeing my own image in my dreams. I really like looking at my body, and even my calves looked okay to me.

BEVERLY: I know.

MARIA: It felt good. Everything felt great.

BEVERLY: The one part I think I mentioned last week that I didn't like was my stomach. But when I looked at myself and leaned completely over and looked under my legs, I thought, "My breasts are saggy." How could I have the nerve to say that? There's no muscle there. There really isn't. Then I looked at myself more. I could just remind myself that I did life drawing and I used to like to do life drawing if somebody had a big bottom, so you could really get into it. And that's just exactly what I look like. I was big and full.

THERAPIST: Isn't it amazing? We've always gotten messages about how we ought to look, which is, of course, always the way we *don't* look. Because, I mean, if you have large breasts you should have small ones and if you have small ones you should have larger ones. We're all built differently and we're all unhappy.

B.J.: The grass isn't always greener on the other side.

[Laughter]

JENNY: It's like my friend telling me that the object of learning to *dress* is to get as close to Polly Perfect as possible. And this friend of mine is going on about Polly Perfect and how she knows she doesn't look like that. And I found myself thinking that I'm not Polly Perfect. I don't ever want to be. I just realized it—that this is the only body I've ever lived in and it's not perfect, but it's the one I'm familiar with and it's fine. I have other things that I can change. I can't change the fact that I am short and my body's shape went out with Rubens. And, also, probably in the time of Rubens, I would be considered skinny. But, I don't know, I guess I reached a point where I just thought that the things I'm gonna change are the things I have control over. There's some things I just don't *have* any control over and I'll just learn to live with them.

I also want to hear about the body touching assignment. Which areas felt sensitive to which types of touch? How did the women feel

96

doing the exaggeration exercise? How did it affect their feelings about that area? Have they a new sense about how their partners may feel about their bodies?

The following transcript from a second session is indicative of responses to the body touching assignment. It also illustrates how the women begin learning from one another.

B.J.: I did it and, well, the first time was the best. There is something special about the first time. I can't look you in the eye.

THERAPIST: Isn't that all right? You don't tell a stranger every day about how your nipples and your breasts feel when you're being touched.

JENNY: This is not cocktail party conversation.

THERAPIST: Right. Did you like those feelings? Did you like the softness?

B.J.: Yeah, but.

THERAPIST: Can you say "and" instead of "but"? Because when you say "but" to something, it disqualifies it and you don't want to disqualify it. You did real good.

B.J.: It wasn't as good because I was doing it to myself.

THERAPIST: So you would have preferred to have someone else do it?

B.J.: Yeah.

PAMELA: It occurred to me that while I was doing it, there were certain things that I could tell somebody that I liked.

B.J.: Yeah, but it's so hard.

JENNY: Oh, yes! But the next morning I may tell them. One of the things I found I really liked was having this part here touched, my shoulders. And that, I think, I could tell them easier—that I liked my shoulders touched—than where on my clitoris to touch. That might take me until the second episode in bed. But maybe when I first met him and if my dress was cut out or something, I could say, "Gee, it would feel nice if you would touch me on the arm." I think that's a pretty safe thing for me to do. The touching part. One of the things I found, and I had forgotten about it, is I like the feeling of my nails on my behind. Not digging in—not enough to leave a white mark. And it brought back something that happened once. I met this guy at a conference and I spent the night with him; at some point, I don't know how I got it across to him, I got him to pull my hair. It was at a pretty high point of excitement, and it really felt good. So a little later on, he tried hitting me with quite a bit of force, and I didn't like it. It was much too painful, and he said, "Oh, okay, I can tell the limits on how much pain you want." But, I guess I do enjoy a certain amount. It felt good. Last night I found myself standing in front of the mirror and noticed moles. Different skin markings. I also thought of my skin because it's oily and very soft, but parts of it are softer than others. I didn't find any of it that I would consider ugly or rough. I liked the touching part better than the looking part.

PAMELA: I did, too. For me, just allowing, giving myself time. I turned the T.V. off, lit some incense, and just relaxed and allowed myself a half hour or so feeling myself all over. And I rather enjoyed it and I started to talk. I tried, you know, to imagine how I would like to be touched if somebody else was touching. I was thinking that. But also for myself, too. It was just nice as I did my whole body. And I tried at different times of the day; after a shower, before a shower, after I'd been active. And the best times were when I was feeling a bit sweaty and my body was oily. Right after a shower, there was no oil. I didn't like to touch myself after the shower. But before it was okay. And I also found through most of my body, just soft touching with my nails, lightly with my nails, felt good.

THERAPIST: Any place in particular?

PAMELA: My stomach.

THERAPIST: Did you notice how your back felt to be touched?

PAMELA: I didn't do that. I'm very rigid. I lie on my back, in bed, with a cover over me. So there's no way I can reach back there, and I didn't even think to turn over.

THERAPIST: You get one way to do something in your head and you don't think that there are alternative ways.

PAMELA: Right. There are such dumb things that you don't think of.

JENNY: One of my ways of relaxing is a hot bath and I fill it up with bubbles and I take the bubbles and I smear them all over me and I feel great. Well, when I get out of it, I'm tired and very relaxed, but my skin, as you say, all the oil just washed off. It never occurred to me to try it before the bath or to relax in some other way. And I think tonight, I'm gonna try it.

PAMELA: Or oil yourself afterwards.

ANATOMY AND PHYSIOLOGY

I save 45 minutes to an hour at the end of the second session to describe the anatomy of the female genitals and the physiology of sexual response. My goals in the didactic presentation are to supply good, solid information, to demystify the process of orgasm, and to stress individual differences. Chapter 5 of *For Yourself* (1975) and Chapter 1 of *The New Sex Therapy* by Kaplan (1974) contain most of the relevant physiological material.

I also show drawings of female genitals, followed by photographs or slides. I use the drawings in *Liberating Masturbation* (Dodson, 1974). (I point out, however, that some of the clitori in Dodson's drawings are unusually large so the women do not become upset when they compare their own.) The therapist can take her own photographs or slides of women's genitals or use the color photograph in *The Yes Book* (Ayres Rubenstein, and Smith, 1972) or those in *I Am My Lover* (Blank, 1978). Viewing pictures of women's genitals desensitizes the women to looking at their own and makes it clear that every woman's genitals are unique. The therapist should also explain that size and placement of each part has no effect on functioning, just as large eyes do not necessarily mean better vision or widely spaced eyes mean greater visual acuity.

I identify the inner and outer labia, the hood of the clitoris, the clitoral body, the glans of the clitoris, the urethra, the vagina, and the perineum. I note that the clitoris has the greatest density of nerve endings sensitive to touch and that consequently the majority of women find the clitoral area the most sexually responsive. Some women are most sensitive just above the clitoris; others feel the most sensation when the area next to or below the glans is touched. Many women enjoy direct stimulation of the glans whereas others find this contact uncomfortable and even irritating and enjoy a lighter touch or indirect stimulation.

Most of the nerve endings that are responsive to touch are in the first third of the vagina; those in the inner two-thirds respond mainly to pressure. Some women experience most of the sensation during intercourse at the opening of the vagina, and some get pleasure from deep thrusting. Many women feel very little sensation vaginally or seem to respond more to stimulation around the urethra. Numerous women report that they have similar feelings to those that accompany urination when they are aroused during intercourse. Frequently this sensation is caused by the pressure of the penis against the urethra.

The analogous tissue development plate included in Netter (1965) does more to dispel the myth of the vaginal orgasm than do hours of rhetoric. The illustration shows that male and female embryos are identical until the sixth week of development. With the introduction of testosterone the embryo will develop into a male; otherwise it will continue to develop as a female. If the genitals of both sexes originate from the same tissue, it follows that there must be counterparts between them.

No one will ever know how it feels to a person of the opposite sex to be touched on the genitals. Even within each sex there is great variability in the sensitivity of different areas, but the origin of the tissues can give us some sense as to male and female genital counterparts. The same type of tissue that makes up the scrotum makes up the outer labia. The tissue that forms the hood over the clitoris and the clitoral shaft makes up the shaft of the penis. More sensitive is the tissue that forms the midline of the penis and the inner labia and opening to the vagina. Finally, the areas of greatest sensitivity are the glans of the penis and the glans of the clitoris.* Both these areas have about the same number of nerve endings, but the nerve endings are far more densely clustered in the clitoris than in the penis because of its smaller size. The diagram in Netter (1965) makes it clear why so many women do not have orgasms through the thrusting of the penis alone: during intercourse, the male's most sensitive area is being stimulated directly; the female's most sensitive area is being stimulated only indirectly. Hite (1976: 612) found that only 30 percent of the women in her sample were able to reach orgasm through the indirect stimulation of coitus alone. Moreover, many of these women had discovered intercourse positions that provided sufficient clitoral stimulation with a particular partner.

Even if the leaders have the best available information on female sexuality, the women will bring up concerns that have not yet been researched. I always enjoy these questions because they give me an opportunity to show that I do not have all the answers and thereby to give the authority back to the questioner. She can go home and ex-

---

*It is important to remember that the sensitivity of specific areas of the genitals varies from individual to individual. For example, many circumcised males report that the area of greatest sensitivity is located at the intersection of the midline and the circumcision scar.

periment to determine the answer to her question or other group members can join the effort by collecting their own data.

It is important to describe the physiological process of sexual response as flowing rather than as occurring in fixed stages. Sexual arousal can begin with anything—a touch, a thought, a memory, an image, a smell. Sexual arousal includes a variety of physiological reactions: neurological, muscular, vascular, and hormonal. The most dramatic of these changes involves the vasocongestion of the pelvic area and increased muscle tension: "Evidence suggests that the female orgasm reflex is usually elicited by the stimulation of special sensory nerve endings of the clitoris . . . [and] is expressed by motor spasm of the vaginal and circumvaginal muscles [Kaplan, 1974:30]." When vasocongestion and muscle tension reach a peak the process reverses and the accumulated blood flows out of the pelvic region. This reversal of blood flow occurs rapidly with orgasm. If no orgasm takes place, the blood will still flow out of the pelvic area, but the process may take a number of hours. I make certain to note that the arousal process is not linear. The level of excitement normally falls at various points in the arousal process particularly when nonsexual thoughts come to mind or outside noises interfere. This, however, is no cause for concern since excitement will generally rise again once attention is directed toward sexual thoughts and feelings and pleasurable stimulation is reinstated.

In describing the various physiological signs of sexual arousal I say, "Some women notice . . . ," "Some women find . . . but others don't," "It's possible that . . . ," thus emphasizing that every woman's reactions are unique. Differences in sexual response occur in the amount and consistency of lubrication; release of lubrication at orgasm; breast sensitivity; nipple erection; muscular tension; breathing patterns; body movement; sex flush; perspiration; intensity of orgasm; number of orgasms and, if more than one, amount of time between them; and presence or absence of vaginal muscle contractions with orgasm. Consequently, external physiological signs will give a woman less information about the process of arousal than will her subjective feelings. And, of course, her subjective feelings will be affected by fatigue, stress, psychological and relationship factors, and the menstrual cycle.

Fithian, Hartman, and Campbell (1978) measured various physiological processes during arousal and orgasm and found the pattern of these responses to be so specific to each individual that they labeled the phenomenon "orgasmic fingerprinting." According to Kinsey and his associates, "There is nothing more characteristic of sexual response than the fact that it is not the same in any two individuals [1953:594]." Not only will each woman have her own pattern, but this pattern will vary from one time to another.

It is important to reassure the women that first orgasms tend to be mild and are frequently not even recognized as orgasms. Therefore, paying attention to small feelings is vital. I make this point for a couple of reasons. First, it is true: most women's initial orgasms *are* mild. This information helps to reduce the women's fears of experiencing something more intense then they feel they can handle. Second, it counteracts the myth of "you'd know it if you had one." I have heard a number of women describe an orgasm when reporting their masturbation homework without labeling it as such. Many women do not recognize the orgasm because they erroneously expect bells to ring and the earth to move.

HOMEWORK

The homework for the second session is assigned to all the group members unless it seems advisable to slow the process down for a particular woman who is feeling overwhelmed or very frightened. Again I emphasize relaxing and creating a comfortable, sensual, and private setting for the homework hour. I remind the women that they are to continue the Kegel exercises throughout the group program and preferably for the rest of their lives.

Genital Looking

As in the Lobitz and LoPiccolo (1972) program, the women are expected on the first night after the second session to examine their genitals in order to identify and locate all the relevant structures. This exercise is to be done slowly and carefully in good light and with the aid of a hand mirror.

Women who feel disgusted by looking at pictures of genitals or who feel that looking at their own genitals will be very difficult can be desensitized by dividing their hour into a number of mini-sessions. First they are to look for only a few seconds in dim light. Very gradually they are to increase the intensity of light and the length of time they look until they can comfortably observe their genitals for

15 minutes in bright light. Some women may require a few sessions to complete this exercise comfortably.

To help the women attend to the assignment of looking at their genitals, I have them draw a picture of what they see. This task forces them to look carefully. They cannot help but notice all the details when they have to reproduce them on paper. The women also enjoy bringing the pictures to the group and sharing them.

The following transcript is from the third session of a group in which the members were asked to share their feelings about the genital looking and drawing homework assignments.

ABBY: I had a lot of resistance to doing this and I saved it for today to do, knowing I had to do it. I wasn't going to come to class without a picture. And then I started drawing, and I drew one picture, and then I started looking and thought, "This isn't right." And then I started doing it again. I got absolutely intrigued, and I kept looking and looking, seeing more things to draw. And I forgot about being hung up on doing it. And, so, it was like I'd look again and see more folds or more this or that or it would change if I would move, which frustrated me 'cause then I'd have to draw it from a different angle. It was seeing and looking and looking and seeing in a more subtle way. Does that make sense?

THERAPIST: Yes. What was it that you had an aversion to doing in the beginning? Now, I understand what made you feel like you did want to do it, it was your own interest in what you saw. Do you have any sense of what it was initially that you didn't want to do?

ABBY: Yeah. The aversion was mainly about it not being quite nice. When I was sitting there drawing I was thinking it was no different than drawing any other part of my body. I mean, if you had said, "Draw your nose," I would have drawn my nose. My imagination created a far worse situation than actually existed.

PAMELA: I got into drawing, trying to draw me with my legs closed and then spread, with my vagina spread apart and just trying to get various angles on it. I was interested in where the clit was. Finding it took a lot. I wasn't exactly sure where it was. I had seen it before, but I never really studied it before. On top of the inner lips, but back a little bit, under the shaft. And the shaft is connected to the inner lips on the top. You

103

know, you can talk about it all the time, but until you actually see it for yourself you know it's just words. And that's what I discovered. This was really a part of me.

THERAPIST: How did the other drawings go?

MARIA: I did three of them because I had to do it a couple of times. I'll just pass around that one.

ABBY: It looks wonderful.

JENNY: This is the outer lips and the other lips are kind of one pushed over the other.

MARIA: Folded.

PAMELA: Did you find folds?

MARIA: Oh, lots of them. I was trying to draw them. That's what got me into doing a couple of models because I couldn't get them all.

PAMELA: Yeah, mine have extra skin.

JENNY: Yeah, and crevices and.

MARIA: Right.

THERAPIST: What was intriguing about this?

MARIA: It's new. And I would look and it wouldn't stay the same. I would see deeper. I would just see more crevices, more contours, more space. Rather than just looking at it and going ho hum, I was looking again and again.

I ask the women, after they have finished drawing the picture, gently to explore their genitals with their fingers. The exercise is introduced as a clinical examination. Does the hood move freely back and forth over the clitoris? Can they feel the shaft of the clitoris above the glans? Is there somewhat more sensation above, below, to the right, or to the left of the clitoris? Is one inner lip more sensitive than the other when stroked? Do the sensations feel different if they use oil as compared to no lubrication? If they put a finger inside the vagina can they do the Kegel exercises and feel the muscle squeezing around the finger even faintly? With a finger inside the vagina do they notice any difference in sensation if they press the finger toward the perineum, toward the pubic bone, to the right, to the left, or toward the areas in between? How do their natural lubrications smell and taste?

I explicitly state that the intent of the genital looking and touching exercise is not to arouse them and that most women do not feel much, if any, sensation while doing this assignment. They are simply to notice any small differences they feel. By lowering their expectations, I make sure that they cannot fail. They need not be concerned if they feel very little, and if they feel more they have an unexpected success.

During the second day's hour of homework I have the women repeat the genital looking and touching exercise but without drawing another picture. I want them to see whether they notice anything different from the previous day's session.

Breast Examination

In the second group meeting, I demonstrate a breast examination on myself, while wearing a blouse, and ask the women to do the exam on their own bare breasts as part of the second hour's homework. This assignment is not an essential part of the process of learning to have orgasms, but I feel strongly about a woman's responsibility for her own body and health and so I include this exercise in the groups I run. Women are generally reluctant to examine their breasts for fear of finding lumps. By learning to know her own breasts and their normal tissue masses, a woman can be more expert in detecting abnormalities than a physician can in a yearly checkup. In the group we sometimes briefly talk about fears related to breast cancer.

Luxuriating

I assign an hour of deliberate luxuriating for the remaining day or two before the next session. Some women stroke their bodies with textured materials such as silk scarves, rose petals, leather, or burlap. Others lie in the sun, have a massage, or take a long bubble bath to fulfill this assignment.

This exercise encourages the women to begin taking time for themselves simply because they have a right to pleasure. The women who complete this assignment are on the road to accepting the positive aspects of the word "selfish." Women who cannot take the time, do not feel they have the right to it, feel that others need them, or do not remember where the time went, may find the road to enjoying sensual pleasure a bit harder and longer. But even some of these women fulfill the assignment after the following session, when they see that those who did the exercise felt better about themselves afterward. We are embarking on a process of counteracting the notion that it is better to give than to receive in all instances. We are saying that it is as important to take care of oneself as it is to take care of others. For some women this idea is revolutionary. Jenny's experience, as shown in the following transcript, is not unusual.

JENNY: I think I overdid it a little. Saturday, I decided I was going to eat spaghetti with my hands. Never tried it before. I did my grocery shopping and I bought spaghetti with a can of sauce and I made it. Of course, it was too hot at first, so I let it cool down. And I had a lot of fun. I was eating with my hands with a big glass of wine. This was in the middle of the day and the wine made me just sleepy enough that I curled up on the couch, wrapped up in an afghan, and listened to good classical music, which I love, and just really felt good. But, I finally had to get myself up to clean the house.

THERAPIST: How much time did you give yourself?

JENNY: A good hour and a half or two hours between the cooking, the eating, and the lying there enjoying myself. It was really very nice. It would have been great if I'd had a maid to come in and clean.

[Laughter]

ABBY: I find your spaghetti weekend—I want to do it. It sounded really great. I'd like to try it sometime.

JENNY: Yeah, well. And then today, I went and had a facial. So, that's what I mean. I think I overdid it a little.

THERAPIST: Do you really think you overdid it? You feel too good?

JENNY: It feels too good and I'm geared more to do things for other people rather than to do things for me. I'm a social worker. I make a lot of money doing things for other people. I have a Yiddish mama who taught me very early to wait on my husband. About eight or ten years ago, I had a group of people over to my house and I was serving something and I picked up a coffee cup and handed it to the man sitting next to me. He said if I had lived in Japan, I would have made one hell of a geisha girl. I said, "What do you mean?" He said, "This is America. You serve the women first." I was just used to serving men first.

Talking to Mothers

This exercise, which is optional, was designed by Lowry (1975) for women who carry a lot of anger toward their mothers for not having given them the information or attitudes to help establish positive sexual growth, as well as for women who would feel tremendous guilt if they allowed themselves to be more sexual than their mothers. Each situation is different: the sexual tie between mother and daughter is highly varied and often quite convoluted. However, even when the dynamics are not completely understood, this exercise can free a group member from her mother's definition of sexuality.

The appropriate women are to ask their mothers about what they learned from *their* mothers about sex and contraception when they got married. If the mother is no longer alive, the conversation can be imagined. For some women nothing is gained from this assignment; for others the results are momentous. A woman generally finds it easier to forgive and to let go of her resentment once she realizes that her mother, too, received little or no sexual information while she was growing up. Some women understand for the first time why their mothers were so puritanical about sex.

Women who do not believe their mothers would ever participate in such a conversation are aided by this exercise regardless of how the mother responds. If she is willing to talk, this gives the daughter a new impression of her mother. If she refuses, she confirms her daughter's prediction, and in the group we can explore whether or not the woman is going to continue to allow her mother's discomfort to interfere with her own attainment of sexual satisfaction. She may have to give up the attempt to reform her mother, but this decision is easier to reach once the woman feels she has tried everything. Having given up on changing her mother, she is a little more free to surpass her mother's sexual limitations in her own life. As one woman described it, "My mother put me in a box not to feel sexual, but now I realize she doesn't have the key. I do."

BEVERLY: I was so positive that the way we were brought up, Mother had never had sex except when she conceived her children. So one day I took her out for a ride and I said, "Mother, I've always wanted to ask you about your sex life with Pa. Did you and Papa have much sex?" And she said, "Of course." I said, "Did you really? I never thought you did." She said, "Yes, we did." I said, "Mother, do you know what an orgasm is?" And she said yes, and I didn't think she did. I said, "Are you sure you know?" And she said, "I think I do." And I said, "Well, what is it?" And she said, "Well, it's the climax of when you're having sexual intercourse." And I said, "How

did you experience it?'' And the way she described it to me—
she did! And I tell you, I really cannot believe it. But I know
she didn't make it up because she didn't read those books. I
never came across those books in her room. But she said that
there was a dragging sensation ''between my legs and my
thighs and a grip.'' And I said, ''Are you sure?'' She said,
''Oh, yes. Lots of times when Pop used to go away on a business trip, and I always told you he wouldn't be home until 4 or
5 o'clock and you kids would stay out and play. Well, he always got home about noon. We wanted to be alone before you
girls came home.'' The funny thing was that I was sitting there
asking her those questions—and then her response. She was so
calm. I've seen my mother get more excited about my not
phoning her. She was completely calm and assured. My first
thought was, ''I don't believe you.'' But I had to believe her
and I was shocked.

Other Exercises

Women who have completed the previous exercises may reassign
them to themselves for any number of reasons—because they did not
do an exercise as fully as they would have liked and can now see another approach to take, because they felt they benefited the first time
and could benefit further if they repeated it, or because the reports
of the homework experience by others gave them insight into how
the exercise could be altered to meet their own needs better. Some
women may have a particular problem related to sex or to the completion of the homework that lends itself to an individualized behavioral assignment (see pp. 126–134 and pp. 144–159).

Session Three

Session three, like all the other sessions after the initial meeting,
revolves around the women's experiences with the homework assignments. In addition, exploration of negative feelings about assignments and discussion of the avoidance of the homework is useful
now that a certain amount of trust has been established in the group.

GENITAL MODELING

Levine (1976), a therapist who has been running groups for some time, has the women sculpt their genitals out of modeling clay during this session. She feels that working with the clay facilitates the desensitization process. In the following sessions the clay models are used to demonstrate precisely how the gential stimulation is being done.

GOAL SETTING

In this session, I spend some time focusing on the goal each woman hopes to attain by the end of the group. Most of the preorgasmic women will have the goal of reliably experiencing orgasm through self-stimulation. Goal setting for the situationally orgasmic women is a bit more complex. To accomplish this task, I elicit two objectives from each woman—a maximum and a minimum goal. The maximum goal is her long-term sexual goal. The minimum goal is a reasonable goal that would justify to her the time and money spent in therapy. It is important to specify these goals in behavioral terms. If a woman's goal is "to be more turned on" I ask her to explain how she would know when she had attained her objective. Would she behave differently? "Feeling turned on" is too subjective a goal to evaluate accurately. However, if a woman states that she would intitiate sex with her partner if she were more turned on, then we have an observable behavioral goal by which to evaluate her progress. Most women are realistic about what they expect to achieve in 10 sessions. And the explicit setting of goals helps therapist and client to keep focused on the essential issues for each woman.

MASTURBATION

The last 45 minutes to an hour of the third session are set aside for discussing myths about masturbation, showing a film of a woman masturbating to orgasm, and sharing the feelings the movie generates.

Masturbation is probably the most frequently practiced and least discussed sexual act engaged in by human beings. Eighty-two percent of the women polled for the *Hite Report* (Hite, 1976) masturbated. This figure is considerably higher than the 62 per cent found by Kinsey and his colleagues in the early 1940s (1953) and the 63 percent found by Hunt in the early 1970s (1974).

Until fairly recently, masturbation was blamed for numerous mental and physical problems such as warts, hairy palms, acne, failing eyesight, criminality and insanity. Some people feared that masturbation could transform an individual into a homosexual or a social isolate. The assumption was that masturbation would be so compellingly pleasurable that one would become addicted to it and either never leave the house or prefer only same-sex partners. Neither fear, of course, has any factual basis. Masturbation, like other physical and sexual activities, is self-limiting. A person can masturbate for only so long before fatigue sets in.

The cultural taboos surrounding this innocent and pleasurable experience have caused many psychological problems.

> Millions of females in the United States, and a larger number of males, have had their self-assurance, their social efficiency, and sometimes their sexual adjustment in marriage needlessly damaged—not by their masturbation, but by the conflict between their practice and the moral codes. There is no other type of sexual activity which has worried so many women [Kinsey et al., 1953:170].

Until recently, the numerous benefits of masturbation have gone untold. It is a pleasurable activity available to anyone of any age. It requires no money, academic degree, standard of physical beauty, intelligence, or particular personality characteristic. It can be enjoyed when one is too tired to meet the needs of another—quietly, noisily, gently, vigorously. Masturbation enables one to be sexually active without having to be involved in an unsatisfactory relationship. We are now seeing women orgasmic with intercourse who want to learn to masturbate to orgasm because they feel this ability will give them greater independence and self-sufficiency. They do not want to have casual sexual relationships in order to enjoy sexual release.

The tide is changing; not only is masturbation becoming acceptable but it is beginning to be viewed as a healthy aspect of sexuality. After all, masturbation is the way most men and many women learn about orgasm. And it is the simplest, easiest, and most direct approach to learning about orgasm for preorgasmic women since the feedback is unobstructed by another's presence and the woman can clearly ascertain the best location, pressure, and rhythm of the stimulation. The fact that no other person is present during masturbation minimizes potential distractions and eliminates pleasure-inhibiting concerns about looking ugly, taking too long, or satisfying one's partner.

Kinsey's data also seem to indicate that masturbation is a positive way for women to learn to have orgasms reliably. He found that women who were orgasmic with masturbation could attain orgasm this way 95 percent of the time (1953:132) and that having orgasms with masturbation facilitates rather than inhibits the ability to experience orgasm with a partner. As has been noted earlier, women who had experienced orgasm *by any means* prior to marriage were two to three times more likely to experience orgasm in sex with their husbands than were women who had no prior experience of orgasm (p. 385). (Of course, it may be that women uninhibited enough to masturbate or pet to orgasm prior to marriage were predisposed to having less difficulty with orgasm than were women who had not previously felt free to experiment.)

Masters and Johnson found that women generally experienced their most intense orgasms with masturbation. Consequently, since I have found that first orgasms typically are quite mild, those experienced through masturbation are more likely to be identifiable. In addition, the absence of distractions associated with partner sex makes it more likely that the orgasmic sensations experienced in masturbation will be recognized.

Most women in preorgasmic groups have never masturbated and those who have done so have rarely used their hands. A majority of them have been given either overt or covert negative messages about self-stimulation. Receiving permission to masturbate from a knowledgeable authority, a therapist, may be sufficient to persuade some women to try it, but merely debunking the myths about masturbation and touting its benefits may not convince women with inhibitions. For these women desensitization occurs slowly by actually engaging in the behavior and by dealing with negative feelings as they arise.

FILM

The next step in the desensitization process is most easily accomplished by showing a film of a woman masturbating to orgasm. I generally introduce the film by asking for the women's experiences with and feelings about masturbation—sometimes supplying an anecdote from my own life to overcome their inhibitions.

JENNY: The first time I ever did it, I didn't know what it was. That's how little I knew about it.

THERAPIST: How old were you?

JENNY: 19.

THERAPIST: How did you do it?

JENNY: You know, I really don't know. I can remember I was in bed. I was in college, but I don't know what got me started. And I remember lying there. "Oh, my roommate's going to hear me." I knew it was terrible right away. I don't ever remember getting information, but I knew it was sinful.

THERAPIST: I thought it made me sick. I just happened upon it. I just sort of did it and I thought I was the only person in the world who had that feeling. Nobody else had it. It wasn't sexual. I mean, I didn't think of it as having to do with sex. I was 18 years old, and I had taken a nap in the middle of the day. I had masturbated before I took a nap, and I woke up throwing up because I had the flu. I was convinced that masturbation had caused it. I don't know where I got those messages.

ABBY: I got the message that if you masturbated, you weren't going to be sexually potent. It was going to take away your sexual energy. You'd waste it. It would go away. You just wouldn't be able to enjoy sex with a partner. If you masturbated with your boyfriend, then you would never be able to have sex.

MARIA: I think sometimes I felt more sexy when I was in grade school—before I got to junior high. Then I didn't after that because that's when I started thinking that that was wrong to do. And I just didn't do anything. Didn't masturbate, just waited for the right guy to come along and marry me and then it would be all right.

THERAPIST: There's one woman who was in sex therapy and the therapist told her to masturbate. So she went home and she did what she thought masturbation was. And the next session he said, "How did it go?" And she said "nothing much happened." He dropped the whole thing. And it wasn't until she saw this movie that she said, "Oh, that's what masturbation is." He hadn't even asked her enough details to find out what she was actually doing.

The importance of an explicit female masturbation film at this point in therapy cannot be exaggerated. On one occasion, the group leaders were unable to show the film until the eighth session because of mechanical problems. Delaying the presentation not only retarded the group members' progress but also kept the leaders from comprehending the extent of the phobic reaction of one member toward sex and masturbation. Until the film was shown, she had reported wonderful but vague experiences with the masturbation homework. During the film, she found it necessary to leave the room to vomit. Afterward she was able to share with the group how uncomfortable she had been with the assignments and how terrified she was of stimulating herself. Had the leaders been aware of her feelings earlier, they could have reduced the pressure and enabled her to confront these feelings more gradually.

A number of female masturbation films are available.* The film should fulfill several critera. (1) The model should not be a beautiful actress. A nondescript or even overweight woman is generally easier for most group members to identify with. (2) The model should masturbate to orgasm using her hands rather than a vibrator. Some women who are orgasmic with a vibrator join groups to learn how to masturbate manually. (3) The model should spend considerable time masturbating. Thus, women who become aroused slowly will not get discouraged by what might appear to be a quick and effortless process.

In preparing the group for the film it is important to stress that the woman shown masturbates in her own way, which may or may not be pleasurable for other women. She also has an orgasm that may or may not resemble theirs. It is also important to acknowledge that responses to the film vary. This caution enables each woman to accept her response as normal. The film turns some women on, others are repulsed, and some feel neutral.

Women who are excited by watching another woman masturbate generally fear that they have "latent homosexual" tendencies. I approach this issue by saying that it does not make sense that only men should feel excited by women's bodies and that only women should be excited by men's bodies, just as it does not make sense that a married woman should never find any man other than her husband attractive. Many of us have learned to turn off our sexual feelings when we think they are not appropriate. It is important to emphasize

---

*I prefer the film *Reaching Orgasm*, produced by C.O.R.T. at the University of California Medical Center, San Francisco. Other films are available from the Multi-Media Resource Center in San Francisco.

that it is natural to feel sexually stimulated by many things. Whether or not one chooses to *act* on these feelings is up to the individual. A woman may prefer a partner of a certain age, religion, height, hair color, body build, and gender. If she is attracted to someone who does not fit this pattern, she must decide whether or not to act on her feelings. It seems a shame to ward off the good feelings. The message I give is that a woman is free to feel whatever she feels because she has control over whether or not she acts in accordance with her feelings. If the woman does not wish to act on the sexual feelings they can be enjoyed in fantasy and no one need ever know unless the individual chooses to discuss them.

It is essential to set aside at least 15 minutes after showing the film to deal with any discomfort it generates. As always, it is better for the women to talk about their negative feelings in the group than carry the feelings home with them, where they are bound to interfere with the homework.

If no one volunteers any negative reactions to the film during this discussion, I actively encourage the members to express some. Most women do not want to appear shocked by the film. Others are afraid to say it made them feel disgusted or turned them off because they do not want to appear different or unusually inhibited. Many women assume that the leader showed the film to get a positive, not a negative, response. Women in this culture are trained to do, think, and feel what they believe is expected of them, and many lack the self-confidence to express feelings not voiced by others. I usually say, "I'm surprised no one has any negative feelings about the film. This is the first group that hasn't expressed any. Are you sure there are *none*?" Generally, such permission is sufficient to elicit the negative reactions.

THERAPIST: What did you think of the film?
PAMELA: My heart's beating fast.
   [Laughter]
JENNY: I'm thinking of leaving the room
B.J.: I had that feeling, too.
JENNY: Somehow, for me to do the same thing is okay, but to watch her doing it—I mean, if she wants to do it behind a door without me watching, that's fine, but to be watching her do it. The point at which she was exploring everything—it was sort of like, I hate to use the word, it was almost dirty. In the sense of dirt, not in the sense of taboo.

MARIA: I don't really feel she cared about herself.

JENNY: That's it. Just the touching and poking into her body. It wasn't exploring: it was poking. That was what I felt.

MARIA: And you're saying when you touch yourself you feel dirty?

JENNY: Yeah, and there are times when I avoid poking inside. I'll stay outside. She did a lot of exploring and spreading with her legs apart and really looking up inside her. I mean that it just never occurred to me.

PAMELA: What bothered me, one of the scenes—after she finishes touching herself—they switched it, and her hands are all over her face.

[Laughter]

ABBY: Wait a minute, now, hang on. If somebody's down there having oral sex with you, you figure you damn well better taste good.

JENNY: Now, it doesn't bother me to have oral sex and then to kiss him. That's fine. It's part of the whole bag. But the idea to stick my finger and give a lick. Yechhh!

B.J.: This film was supposed to give you permission to do it. That's what I felt.

PAMELA: I liked watching her touch herself and I kind of wished she was touching me. Because she was just lying there and she's really getting into it. She seems very free with her hands, just moving back and forth, and she used both hands, and just getting the feel of it, and touching her breasts. I feel inhibited.

THERAPIST: So you don't touch yourself that way?

PAMELA: I don't think I do. I think I may use one finger because I have one finger down there. So, like using all fingers might be something to try, too.

ABBY: What was most valuable to me was the thing about the leg muscles tensing up because as soon as I start feeling that, that's when I get scared.

THERAPIST: And what did you come away thinking it was like?

ABBY: Well, it's fine. The leg muscles tense up.

The expression of the negative feelings produced by the film has a freeing effect on the women. In the first group I ran, I showed *Shirley*,* and the members' responses were so negative I feared the

*Produced by Multi-Media Resource Center, San Francisco.

film represented a permanent setback. The women thought the model was too hairy, too angular, and too unfeminine in her strong grimaces and orgasmic spasms. As they shared their negative reactions, I silently vowed never to show the movie again. Much to my surprise, the women returned two sessions later and responded that they felt like the woman in the film when doing their homework. Having verbalized their negative reactions they had transformed her into a positive role model. It may be that the woman in the movie freed them to be more sexually expressive: if she is a model of sexuality, they compare favorably. In any case, *Shirley* facilitated rather than inhibited the process.

The film is also instructional. Many women who have never masturbated do not understand how to do so. Women who try masturbation on their own after they have experienced intercourse often assume that they should be stimulating themselves in the vaginal area even though they know the clitoral area is considered the most sensitive. They may not quite understand how one does the touching. Showing the film is an attempt explicitly to provide the information they need without producing the anxiety that might be generated by having a live model or a group leader demonstrate masturbation.*

Another function of the film is to demystify orgasm. Many women expect to scream, thrash about wildly or lose consciousness when they have an orgasm. Even though they may understand intellectually that orgasm is a normal and safe bodily response and realize that many women around them are orgasmic and still alive, observing the process helps to alleviate their anxiety and make them feel more secure.

HOMEWORK

In the third session, the women are directed to masturbate for an hour a day using oil, saliva, or vaginal secretions as lubricants. I generally ask them to buy some oil, alone or with a partner. They may use anything from peanut oil to expensive massage oil† but should be warned against products that contain alcohol or any other sub-

---

*Betty Dodson, however, uses a live demonstration in her Bodysex workshops for sexual enrichment and this approach seems to work well for many of her clients.

†Women have recommended coconut oil, mineral oil with vanilla or almond extract added, and various commercial products such as Albolene, Johnson's Baby Oil, and Physician's Emollient.

stance that can irritate the mucous membranes. Some women may be or may become allergic to a particular oil. Complaints of soreness or genital irritation after masturbation are more likely to be related to an adverse reaction to the oil than to the assignment itself. Changing the lubricant while continuing the daily homework generally solves the problem.

It is essential when giving the first masturbation assignment to instruct the group members *not* to have an orgasm. They are to concentrate on whatever small feelings they have. Some women feel nothing the first few times they masturbate. If by chance a group member should experience intense feelings or should become uncomfortable while doing the assignment, she is to stop stimulating herself immediately resuming only when the strong sensation or the discomfort subsides.

This caution is important for several reasons. For women who are very fearful, the permission to stop stimulation when they become uncomfortable provides a sense of safety in uncharted territory. It also teaches them that they have control over the stimulation they receive. In situations where the partner is providing manual or oral stimulation the woman who wants to experience orgasm but is afraid of the intensity of the sensations she is beginning to feel will unintentionally tense her muscles and in other ways block off the physical sensations rather than learn to relax and go with them. If, however, she can allow the feelings to build at a manageable pace, with full knowledge that she has the power to stop them whenever she wants to, she will be more free to relax and grow accustomed to increasing sexual intensity. With time, she can develop sufficient comfort with sexual excitement to allow herself to continue the stimulation to the point of orgasm.

The instruction prohibiting orgasm also provides a dictum to be resisted by those women who would resist anything they were told to do anyway. Such women have no sense of positive power but only the negative power of withholding. The paradoxical injunction to do exactly what they are already doing allows them to express their negativism against the leader by having an orgasm—a no-lose situation!

In my second group, a woman who had received the instruction not to have an orgasm reported an orgasm in the fourth session. Unfortunately, I responded enthusiastically, and she did not have another orgasm until the eighth session. It took me four sessions to disentangle myself from a power struggle I could have avoided simply by *not* responding with praise and enthusiasm. To make up for my initial error in strategy I had to withdraw totally from the struggle. I accomplished this by meeting each of her unsuccessful homework attempts with perplexity: "The first orgasm must have been a fluke—perhaps it's the only one you'll ever have. But maybe since you figured out how to have an orgasm that time, you can do so again." (See Chapter 6 for more details on handling resistance.)

Session Four

The fourth group meeting is the last session in which any formal didactic information is given and the first session in which the bulk of the homework is individualized. From this point on, each homework assignment will build on the individual woman's success or lack thereof in the previous assignment.

The educational material covered in the fourth session deals with the erotic component of sexual arousal. Merely touching the right areas long enough is generally insufficient to produce orgasm without accompanying mental arousal. Mental arousal is particularly important with regard to self-stimulation because the women are not accustomed to providing the cues themselves; they are used to having a partner provide the cues for arousal.

DISTRACTIBILITY

Women have a tendency to be easily distracted during sex. They find themselves attending to outside noises, thinking about uncompleted chores, and wondering whether they are performing well sexually and whether their partner is receiving sufficient pleasure.

Some women who are distracted to an unusual degree by outside sounds find that white noise helps cut out the interference. White noise is any constant drone such as that provided by a fan, hair dryer, air conditioner, running water, or vibrator. White noise machines are sold commercially as are records of Seashore or forest sounds. One sex therapist I knew was convinced that vibrators are addictive and in support of this view told of a woman who was so habituated to the vibrator that she needed to have it turned on during lovemaking with her husband even though she did not actually use it. It seems far more likely that her addiction was to the humming noise emitted by the vibrator, which helped her tune out intrusive sounds and focus better on the stimulation she was receiving from her husband.

The techniques of erotic arousal discussed in the fourth session are intended to keep the woman's mind focused and in tune with the physical stimulation being applied. These erotic enhancements, which are fairly easy to manipulate, fall under the categories of visual, kinesthetic, and auditory stimulation.

VISUAL STIMULATION

Fantasy

Fantasy is a tool available to everyone, but some women fantasize more readily than others. Daydreams with sexual content span a tremendous range from fleeting visual images or series of images all the way to full-blown movies with plot and dialogue.

Fantasies keep the mind focused on erotic stimuli and away from distractions and pressuring thoughts of orgasm. Telling a woman not to think of orgasm is like telling her not to think about pink elephants. It simply does not work. The best way to eliminate the thought is by replacing it with another. And fantasy provides an involving substitute.

The greatest problem with fantasy is the feeling that particular subjects are unacceptable. But since sexual titillation is often associated with the illicit, it is only reasonable that sexual acts that would not be enjoyed or even tolerated in real life often are pleasurable when explored in the imagination. Yet many women fear that if they fantasize about a particular activity, they must really want to do it. Thus, fantasies concerning rape, sex with women, group sex, incest, or sex with children may be threatening and indicative of abnormality in the minds of some women. I worked with a group of feminist therapists who argued that it is sexist to derive pleasure from rape fantasies or fantasies that portray male domination. It was difficult for them to separate the sexual pleasure the fantasy provided from its political interpretation. I also knew a lesbian therapist who nearly panicked when she found herself having heterosexual fantasies, fearing that she might be a "latent heterosexual." Whatever their content, fantasies should be treated as always harmless and sometimes helpful mental meanderings.

119

From a study of women's fantasies during intercourse, Hariton and Singer concluded that "clinicians must be careful to avoid interpreting a given patient's reports of fantasies as indicative of sexual dysfunction, gross pathology, or profound masochism to the fantasizers [1974:321]."

It is beneficial when talking about women's fantasies to take a permission giving approach rather than an analytic one. Accepting fantasies is a far more sensible stance than attempting to change them. Fantasies easily change of their own accord when the negative charge of unacceptability is removed. Indeed, once a formerly unacceptable fantasy becomes acceptable, other fantasies become more prevalent and the originally unacceptable fantasy tends to occur with less frequency.

If a woman feels a certain fantasy is unacceptable, it is unlikely to lose its negative charge merely because the therapist indicates that it is perfectly normal. If the woman is really disturbed about a given fantasy, I will ask her to exaggerate it as part of her homework, elaborating and embellishing the story and carrying it out further and further. This exercise brings the fantasy under the woman's control. As she gains confidence that she will not act out the fantasy, it loses some of its frightening aspects.

A number of trials with the same fantasy generally will make it seem less interesting. One woman reported that her father kept appearing in her sexual fantasies. This so distressed her that she would immediately stop the fantasy, and her arousal level would drop dramatically. She thought I was crazy when I told her to keep her father in her fantasies and to exaggerate his participation in the sexual activity, but she agreed to try. She allowed herself to imagine having sex with her father in many different positions and under varying circumstances. After two or three trials with this fantasy she found herself losing interest in it and was able to respond to other fantasies. Another woman in one one of my groups was disturbed by sexual fantasies that included her four-year-old daughter. She kept exaggerating the fantasy until she imagined actually having a sexual interaction with the child. Although at first she could not verbalize her fear, once she exaggerated her fantasy and realized that she was not going to lose control over her impulses and actually seduce her daughter, she felt very relieved; thereafter, the fantasy occurred less frequently and with less anxiety attached to it.

If the therapist agrees to the client's request for help in changing her fantasies, the therapist is giving the woman the message that there is something wrong with the fantasies. Regardless of what the therapist says, trying to help a client change her fantasizing may make the woman feel even worse about herself when she cannot suppress her imagination. Meanwhile, all the attention on the fantasy acts as a bellows put to an already existing flame—it makes the concern burn more strongly.

Erotica

Women who do not readily fantasize should be encouraged to obtain written, graphic, or photographic erotica to use while masturbating. Sometimes I suggest that a woman read a compilation of female masturbation fantasies such as Friday's *My Secret Garden* (1973) or *Forbidden Flowers* (1975) to get an idea of what women's sexual fantasies are like. She may use these stories as a jumping off place from which to create her own fantasies. Such classic erotica as *The Pearl* (1968), an anthology by an anonymous author, *Fanny Hill* by John Cleland (1963), and *Delta of Venus* by Anaïs Nin (1977) also may prove helpful. And, of course, adult bookstores usually carry a large selection of both written and graphic erotica. The erotic materials are assigned to increase the women's arousal while doing the homework, to keep them focused on erotic thoughts other than orgasm, and at the same time to provide subject matter for future fantasies.

Some women prefer written erotica; others, visual erotica. Both types differ in style, subject matter, and explicitness, so the women may have to explore a number of examples before they find sources they like.

Since women have been socialized not to find erotica stimulating, many initially report not being aroused by it. Research by Heiman (1975) indicated that 42 percent of her subjects who showed the largest physiological change in vaginal blood volume while listening to erotic tapes reported not feeling any physical response. However, there are few women who, once they have received permission from the therapists and other group members to enjoy erotica, continue not to find some such stimuli exciting.

The only drawback with erotica is that it can prove a distraction. The woman may become interested in the story and find the logistics of turning pages while stimulating herself frustrating, or the nonsexual details may interfere with her mood. Thus, many women prefer to read a few pages of a particularly erotic section, then put the book aside and fantasize a bit or focus on physical sensations while masturbating, and pick the book up again only when arousal level decreases.

KINESTHETIC STIMULATION

Learning to focus on pleasurable feelings in an almost meditative way is an approach that works for many women. The idea is to concentrate totally on the tactile and sensual feelings so as to learn to be less and less distracted by extraneous thoughts or outside noises. One woman said that she was so tuned into her genitals that when she had her first orgasm, she felt as though her clitoris was at her chin. Most women who begin to masturbate at a very young age learn to do so by focusing on the feelings generated by the physical stimulation and frequently keep this as their major source of arousal.

AUDITORY STIMULATION

Some women find that auditory stimuli enhance their sexual arousal. Those who do may play music they find particularly arousing (strongly rhythmic selections such as Ravel's *Bolero* are popular). Some women make tapes of sexual experiences with a partner or of a partner or themselves reading pornography, telling erotic stories, or saying words that turn them on. These tapes can then be played during masturbation.

HOMEWORK

The homework for the fourth session is to have the women continue to masturbate while experimenting with each of the different erotic enhancements to see which are the most comfortable and effective for them.

Important Issues in the Early Sessions

During the first few sessions certain critical issues tend to arise. Anger, lesbian sexuality, strong feelings of disgust, sexual trauma, and inability to accept pleasure must be dealt with as early as possible.

ANGER

Though the expression of anger is not very acceptable in this society, anger is a powerful emotion felt by most preorgasmic women in relation to sex, and it is perhaps the central emotion to tap in attempting to mobilize group members toward experiencing orgasm. They may be angry at their mothers for never having explained sex properly or for not providing a healthy sexual role model; they may be angry at a boyfriend who called them frigid, who put them down sexually, or who was not aroused by them; they may be angry at a current partner for getting enjoyment out of sex while they do not; or they may be angry at themselves for not being more sexually responsive.

Because these women do not feel that their anger is acceptable it remains bottled up inside, resulting in depression, guilt, or sadness. Delving beneath the surface within the group situation, where the woman feels supported by her peers, almost always helps to release some of the anger. Any therapeutic techniques that facilitate the expression of anger, such as role-playing or pillow pounding, are useful. I have found time and time again that groups in which one or two women get in touch with their anger early in the process move much more quickly than groups that avoid dealing with these feelings. Consequently, I actively elicit the anger, even to the extent of provoking the women into directing it toward me.

One woman related a recent experience with her partner that left her feeling furious. She had finally allowed herself to overcome her inhibitions and make noises during sex. Her partner responded by asking her to be quiet as she was distracting him. Her worst fear had come true. She immediately shut up and shut off. She arrived at the next group meeting seething. We gave her a pillow and told her to imagine the pillow was her lover. She beat it with her fists while shouting aloud everything she wanted to say to him. She felt better and resolved to express her anger more directly the next time. Meanwhile, another woman wanted a turn with the pillow to deal with some of her angry feelings toward a partner. She, however, merely hit the pillow and whined for a while, stopped and whined a bit more, and never really released her anger. I grabbed the pillow away mid-beating and said, "Well, I guess she's finished." A stunned silence filled the room. I then asked how people were feeling; one member said she wanted to take the pillow away from me and give it back to the other woman. I asked why she did not. She said, "You're supposed to be the therapist—you know best," to which I replied, "Would you jump off a bridge if I told you to?" Everyone realized that she was responsible for herself everywhere, even in a therapy session. This was a turning point for the group. At the end of the session, when I gave out the assignment to be totally selfless and accommodating (see pp. 132–134) one woman organized the others to resist doing this exercise. Thus, the group members for the first time realized their own power. My provoking them helped them to understand both the power they had and how they tended to give it up.*

Expressing anger can be the first step a woman takes toward assuming responsibility for changing her sexual life. After she has expressed her rage toward her parents or partner, I ask whether she likes the situation as it is. Of course she does not. Then I want to know what she plans to do or whether she derives satisfaction from helplessness and suffering. The usual response, "I'm tired of waiting," ultimately gives way to "I guess I'll just have to change things myself." In this way, the anger, once acknowledged, is free to mobilize the woman to take a more active role in deciding the quality of her sexual life. Hence, it may motivate her to complete the homework assignments more conscientiously.

The nice thing about a group is that not every woman has to deal with her anger individually. If one or two women who are most in touch with these feelings are encouraged to vent them, all the group members will benefit vicariously.

LESBIAN SEXUALITY

Some lesbians prefer to join an all-lesbian group. Others, however, are willing or even prefer to participate in a group with heterosexual women. When there is a gay or bisexual woman in the group, the issue of women loving women needs to be addressed. It is necessary first to find out how the group members feel about homosexuality. Usually, at least one woman is very uncomfortable with this kind of discussion.

---

*Not every therapist would feel comfortable with such a provocative stance; however, the importance lies not in the style but in the ability to utilize the women's anger as a mobilizing force.

If the group includes a gay or bisexual woman it is important to ask her if she wants to know how the others in the group feel about her sexual orientation. She can then ask for feedback from those women she is concerned about. After she has elicited responses from the other members I point out, once again, that what turns people on and how they actually express their sexual feelings can be very different things and that the latter is more a matter of choice.

In the group each woman's individuality merits the utmost respect. The intent is not to encourage the women to conform to a particular lifestyle but to help each individual to discover her own personal and sexual needs and develop them in the most satisfactory way. Whatever her sexual orientation, every woman to be orgasmic will have to learn about her own responses first and then find out how to communicate what she has learned about herself to her partner, male or female.

SEXUAL TRAUMA

Not all women who have been raped or molested as children or who have had sexual relations with a family member experience sexual problems in later life, but some do. No therapy can erase the trauma, yet it can help make the experience a less painful one. If a woman believes that a traumatic sexual event has some bearing on her inability to reach orgasm, it is important to explore this possibility. The exploration is pursued with the intent of disconnecting the negative experience from the woman's current sexuality so that it no longer has a hold on it.

A woman who has experienced sexual trauma will generally bring up the subject in one of the early group sessions. If I think the experience is somehow related to the woman's lack of orgasm I want to obtain the details as soon as I feel the woman has developed sufficient trust in the group to be comfortable providing them. At that point, I may ask the woman to close her eyes and experience the event again while she describes it aloud. This retelling is generally very emotional. Then I want to find out how she feels about having shared her experience with the group. One woman who had recounted such an episode told the group after she finished that she felt as if she had just shown everyone her wooden leg. She needed to know how they felt about her, given this terrible and shameful deformity. The group members are nearly always sympathetic, reassuring, and caring. After the woman receives sufficient feedback to feel sup-

125

ported I make it clear that there is no way we can make the memory disappear. However, she can either allow the negative experience to influence her sexuality for the rest of her life of she can attempt to get beyond it. To date, I have not found that sexual trauma prevents women from becoming orgasmic.

DISGUST AND AVERSION

One of the most effective ways to work with disgust about and aversion to one or another type of sexual activity is to give the woman permission to have such feelings and even to encourage her to exaggerate them. I always acknowledge and accept the feelings as normal, given our society or the attitudes of her parents, and reassure the woman that the intensity of her feelings will decrease over time. Meanwhile, I encourage her to follow through with the homework assignments while fully experiencing the aversion.

A woman who recently completed a group called me to tell me how helpful the program had been for her. She especially wanted me to know, because she felt it would help me to help other women, that my telling her to let herself experience her feelings of disgust when she masturbated helped her more than anything else. She could now masturbate comfortably and even though the negative feelings appeared from time to time, she could accept them and still allow herself the pleasure of the experience.

Some women find that certain negative thoughts tend to appear while masturbating or making love with a partner. These thoughts or images not only distract the woman from the pleasure she is experiencing but frequently change her mood from arousal to revulsion. In these cases also, the woman is asked deliberately to exaggerate the negative thought or image. For example, one woman was repulsed when her husband sucked on her nipples. The image of farm animals suckling flashed before her. She did not understand why this thought should disgust her and could recall no negative experiences involving animals or animals suckling. She was given the assignment of exaggerating the image whenever her husband kissed her breasts. After imagining one farm animal suckling, she was to imagine others, then to imagine the animals fornicating while suckling or performing whatever act came to mind. Thought-stopping was the next part of the procedure: when the image of suckling animals flashed, she was told to redirect her attention consciously to the pleasure she was experiencing in another part of her body, her genitals, for example. With some practice at exaggerating and refocusing, she found that negative thoughts only minimally intruded on her sexual pleasure and that when they did, she had sufficient control to refocus on something pleasurable, thereby restoring her sexual arousal.

THE RIGHT TO PLEASURE

The greatest single problem in the initial sessions of the group is helping the women feel justified in spending time on the homework exercises. These are women who are well socialized in the female role. Giving is more important that receiving. Others like you better if you fulfill their needs first, and to be liked by everyone is one of the most common measures of self-worth for the American woman. The result is that women either do not even recognize their needs or, if they do, refuse to acknowledge and fulfill them. At the same time, they feel growing resentment, which cannot be expressed at all or can be expressed only indirectly so as not to threaten their sense of security.

Many women feel they are worth less than others. And without a sense of self-worth, how can a woman feel justified in asking for more time for lovemaking, more body massage before genital stimulation, specific types of gential touching, or other prerequisites for orgasm?

BEVERLY: When I get way up there, I feel stimulated the rest of the day.

THERAPIST: And that's why you should do your homework the next day or later on that day again. You didn't get a vibrator.

BEVERLY: I'll have to. I want to feel this release aside from feeling that I'm close to it.

THERAPIST: Who's going to give you the answer?

BEVERLY: Nobody.

THERAPIST: Because I have a feeling—and I could be wrong—I have a feeling that you think the answer is somewhere outside. Either you will have to have a partner, it's going to be in a book, a therapist will give you the answer to it, if you just breathe deeply, if you read the right book, and what you are not quite doing enough of is spending this time with yourself. When you do it, when you spend the time with yourself, you really do move somewhere. And then you wait a whole other week before you really do it again.

ABBY: I was observing the same thing. What I wanted to say is that you've got the answer. Nobody else has the answer. I have a feeling that there are a lot of ways you expect other people to give you the answer, the leadership.

BEVERLY: Maybe in this particular thing, yes, but ordinarily, no.

THERAPIST: I have a question. Do you really think you have a right to this?

BEVERLY: It's not having a right. I don't deserve things. I put myself last.

THERAPIST: Right. You put yourself last.

BEVERLY: I know that. With people I've gone to as therapists, they've said part of what you're saying. They just haven't seen, or been exposed to, someone who puts herself at the last, first taking care of her husband and mother and the children, and always the big rescuer. Which I realize I have been all my life, never speaking up for myself.

THERAPIST: You're still not thinking of yourself. We have to realize that you're hard-core so when you're making changes, part of you is looking at how difficult it is and how many more changes there are still left to make.

BEVERLY: The release would make me feel good, wouldn't it?

THERAPIST: You don't do *anything* that makes you feel good. That's the basis of this whole thing. Putting yourself at the bottom in a lot of things. What's not an easy thing for you to do is to make yourself feel good. You don't have much practice at it—in a lot of areas.

BEVERLY: The goal—isn't it to make me feel better?

THERAPIST: Yeah, but how are you doing that in other parts of your life? I'm wondering how you can let yourself feel good sexually if you don't let yourself feel good in a lot of other ways. Also, you have a kind of goal orientation. Like, if I have my orgasm I will do better. The orgasm is pure pleasure. That's all the orgasm is, letting yourself build up and enjoying the pleasure and taking the time to do that. And in order to do that, you have to start feeling that somehow you have a right to take this time, relaxing with yourself, feeling good with yourself, saying no to other people because they are taking up all of your time when you need some for yourself. It's not like,

"Okay, I have two hours to get to that goal." How are you feeling now?

BEVERLY: No, I think, my first thought was that nobody really will like me. It's hard for me to ask for something from them. [Starts to cry]

THERAPIST: Try asking. Stay with your feelings.

BEVERLY: I'd like a hug. Abby?
[They hug]

THERAPIST: Is there anybody else you want a hug from?

BEVERLY: Each of you.
[She gets a hug from each woman]

THERAPIST: How are you feeling right now?

BEVERLY: I feel good.

THERAPIST: What you just did here was take care of yourself. I just want you to think about that because that's what you did by asking for hugging and some caring and that's one way to get it. The other way is to relax and spend some time with yourself.

In teaching women to be orgasmic, these groups give them a new sense of their right to be respected and to have pleasure and a feeling of internal strength and security that enables them to disagree with others and still feel worthy of being loved. Possibly these dramatic changes occur with such rapidity because the group process rides on the coattails of a natural developmental process. The majority of women attending the groups range from their late twenties to their mid-forties. According to Sheehy, "The passage to the thirties stimulates a subtle psychological shift on all fronts. 'Me' is just starting to take on as much value as 'others' [1974:140]." The groups support this internal shift by giving the women permission to place themselves and their needs first.

Yes-and-No Exercise

The assignment that is most helpful in effecting this change is the Yes-and-No exercise. It is the single most useful exercise I have found for psychotherapy clients with low self-esteem.

The noes were developed to overcome the difficulty many women had in finding time to do the homework. The exercise requires the women to say no to three things they do not want to do but would ordinarily agree to do. They can say no to themselves about something they feel they should do as well as no to someone else when a request is made of them.

In this assignment, I am giving the women permission to do what they really want to do anyway. Many women have reported at the next session that the only reason they were able to say no was because it was an assignment. If the experiment did not turn out well, they could always put the blame on me—after all, they were just following directions. But the results almost invariably surprise the women. They are delighted with the free time they gain by not being encumbered with unacceptable and unnecessary responsibilities. They also end up feeling really good about being able to say no and having their stance respected. Their worst fears are not realized. The people they turn down do not shun them; their husbands do not leave them. Most of the time, their response is accepted immediately with no argument at all. This result encourages them to try the exercise again—and slowly produces a new sense of self-worth and power. To help insure that the experience will turn out favorably, I encourage the women to say no to small things and to people who are good friends: refusing to admit a babysitter who always arrives an hour early and has to be entertained; saying no to a relative who wants to be taken shopping on the woman's only free afternoon; not doing the dishes when the woman would rather go to sleep and clean up in the morning. I discourage applying the exercise to major issues for the first few trials. Nonetheless, one woman told a co-worker that she would no longer do extra typing because it was not part of her job, a task she had been resenting for months. Another returned a used automobile to the dealer after discovering that her request for a new transmission had somehow been "overlooked." Soon the women begin to realize that they have rights and they start to stand up for themselves.

The Yes exercise is the opposite side of the same coin. The women are to ask for or let themselves have three things they would like but ordinarily would not seek or accept. Again, I am providing permission for them to do what they really want to do. The yes task is difficult for those women who have an intense fear of rejection. Soon they begin to realize that if they never ask for anything, they never get rejected, but they never get what they want either. One therapist I trained is fond of saying that if she is not *turned down* three times a day, she has not asked for enough. The more she asks for, the more she is likely to receive. This exercise helps to sever the connection be-

130

tween being refused something and being rejected personally, an important distinction.

Again, in assigning the Yes task I stress the importance of small requests at the beginning: asking their husbands to make dinner or get them a glass of water; treating themselves to something they want but have denied themselves. The result of saying yes is similar to that of saying no. The women are amazed when their partners are willing to help them out, if their partners refuse, they are amazed that they are not devastated. And refusal gives them stronger permission to refuse requests in turn when they feel so inclined. The women soon see the extent to which they have been depriving themselves, and this realization mobilizes them to take charge and get more for themselves.

By the third or fourth session I assign the No exercise to aid women who are having difficulty setting aside time to do the homework. Although the assignment is prompted by one or two women who are finding that ouside demands are interfering with their homework time, I usually ask all the group members to complete it. Sometimes I assign both parts of the exercise together; sometimes I assign the No task at one meeting and the Yes task at the following session, depending upon how much other homework has been assigned. It is not uncommon for group members or for myself to reassign the Yes-and-No exercise when it has been of benefit.

JENNY: It's the business of saying yes. And I'm really having a hard time. Friday night something happened that really showed me how difficult it was for me. I came home late and I was going to the theater that evening. So I called the couple I was going with and I said, "I just got in. I have to change and eat something. Why don't you drive around and pick me up. It will give me a couple of minutes." So I was racing around the house madly and the phone rang, and she said, "Barry is not leaving the house for five minutes," by way of telling me that I had more time and I could slow down. But I heard, "Well, since you have more time, why don't you walk around the corner." And this is all of a three-second hop. I said, "I still would rather you pick me up." And she says, "Oh, no. I'll still pick you up. I just wanted you to know that you had a couple more minutes. You could slow down so as to not get indigestion." And I said, "Oh, thanks." So, I did ask for something, which I normally don't do—and then the bit of threat that it was being taken away from me. And I haven't asked for anything since. So asking for things I need is still very difficult.

MARIA: I did something. We were going to sleep at night, and I felt really turned on, and I wanted to have sex with him. Usually I just think he's so tired and I turn over and go to sleep sadly. This night, I was so turned on, I wasn't going to let him sleep. So I went straight for him, for that beautiful penis, and he said, "Please massage me first. You make me feel like a sex object." It was so funny. I started laughing and I started massaging him.

JOSEPHINE: I did something at work. I asked if I could work a Wednesday night and not a Saturday night. I've been working weekends for two years. And he said, "No, we can't do it." So I came back later and asked again. He said, "Well, no. I can't take the night away from the other waitresses." But he said I could have Saturday off anyway. I thought about it and even though I really can't afford it, called him up and said, "Okay, I'm taking Saturday night off."

The Yes-and-No exercise not only affects the women's self-esteem and sense of power but also paves the way for necessary sexual changes. If a woman feels she has no right to say no to sex and must participate whenever her partner so desires, she will view sex with resentment. She may fulfill his needs, but she will not enjoy herself. Only when she can say no to sex without feeling guilt is she free really to enjoy sex and even to initiate it. This dynamic is particularly apparent in women who claim they have little or no interest in sex.

Learning to ask for things outside the bedroom and not feel devastated when a request is refused or when results prove disappointing paves the way for being able to ask for things inside the bedroom. A woman must make specific requests of a partner regarding the kinds of touching she likes if she is to find sexual interactions fulfilling.

Totally Accommodating and Selfless Exercise

Most women are so well socialized into the role of caretaker that they frequently anticipate the needs of others. Often they end up anticipating needs which don't actually exist. This habit leaves the woman feeling short-changed and resentful. She believes that her favors are never returned to the degree to which they are given. She then blames those around her for being insufficiently responsive when the problem generally lies in her own overresponsiveness to others and lack of self-caretaking.

To make the women more aware of this automatic process so that they can gain conscious control over it I ask them to set aside one to four hours one evening or afternoon in which to be totally accommodating and selfless: they are to be the perfect caricature of a wife who not only fulfills her partner's every wish but even satisfies those he has not yet thought of. The woman is not to tell the partner about the exercise ahead of time to insure that he does not abuse the opportunity, though I encourage the women to tell their partners about the assignment after they have completed it. Remarkably, most partners notice no difference in the women's behavior, a result that emphasizes, the excessive degree to which the women usually are accommodating and selfless.

Frequently, group members resist doing the exercise, claiming that they are trying to eliminate this particular form of behavior. In such cases I make it clear that they are doing many things unconsciously and that the exercise will make them more aware of their behavior so that they can begin to control it. For example, one woman carried out the exercise for an hour. After she decided to stop, she experimented by telling her husband she was thirsty. He merely replied "Uh-huh." She was furious at the next group session, saying that if he had said *he* was thirsty she immediately would have gotten him some water or tea. After some group discussion the woman realized that her response was inappropriate and that her husband had acted quite reasonably: she never actually asked him for a drink; she only mentioned that she was thirsty. She began to understand that she was over accommodating and that her husband's lack of appreciation might stem in part from the fact that he may not have wanted some of the things she had been providing. Consequently, the woman stopped being so accommodating. She felt less resentful, and her husband was happier because she was not angry with him all the time.

This exercise had an unexpected result for another woman. She was often upset with her husband because she felt that although they both worked he failed to do his fair share of household chores. One night when he arrived home from work she told him to sit and relax while she fixed him a drink and dinner. In a few minutes he was in the kitchen insisting upon helping her. The next time she tried this tactic, the same thing happened. Finally she realized that she would usually criticize her husband for not helping before he had an opportunity to offer his assistance. As she complained less, he helped more.

Other women discover different things about themselves, but few have not benefited considerably, in awareness if not in behavioral change, from the exercise in being totally selfless and accommodating.

CHAPTER 6

The Middle Sessions

SESSIONS FIVE THROUGH SEVEN constitute the major working portion of the group. The stage has been carefully set and a sense of group trust and cohesiveness should be well established. The therapists have had the opportunity to learn more about each woman and how she responds to the homework assignments, as well as to various therapeutic approaches and stances. The task now is to individualize the homework assignments and the therapeutic strategy to meet the special needs of each group member.

Individualizing the Therapeutic Approach

Each woman is unique and therefore requires a therapeutic approach that takes account of her particular personality. Of course, some women fulfill their goal regardless of how the therapist interacts with them, but others may fail to respond to treatment if the interactional stance of the therapist is not appropriate. Previous chapters have suggested some of the techniques in the therapist's arsenal.

Support, paradox, abdication, confrontation, and joining the resistance are the principal interactional styles. During the sessions, the therapist spends time with each woman according to her need in terms of dealing with obstacles to becoming orgasmic as well as according to her readiness to work. It has always seemed to me a waste of time to struggle with someone who is not quite ready to change when there are other group members who are ready. Those women who make no progress in the early meetings usually become sufficiently disappointed or angry to take charge of the session in order to obtain the time and information they need later on.

PROVIDING SUPPORT

A supportive, accepting, permission giving approach is generally a useful one for the therapist to follow in the first three sessions. With a woman who is very tentative and frightened, such a stance provides a sense of security and safety and should be maintained beyond the third session as long as the woman seems to be doing her homework and confronting her fears at a reasonable pace, given her personality and history. Cory, for example, entered the group feeling quite depressed about sex, her marriage, and life in general. After the second session, in which she was very emotional, crying and expressing her feelings of hopelessness, she began to do the homework. By the fifth session, she was feeling better and looking better, even to the extent that her cheeks were pinker and her complexion less sallow. The group she was in appeared to be stuck in the sixth session—no one had had an orgasm—so I gave the women the assignment of imagining how they would feel thirty-five years later still never having had an orgasm. This exercise was an attempt to break the group norm of no one succeeding (see pp. 169–170). At this point, Cory turned sallow again and said how disappointed she was. She felt that earlier I had given her hope and that this had enabled her to make progress. Now that I was pessimistic she felt like giving up. The assignment, while appropriate for the other group members, was clearly inappropriate for Cory. Thereafter, I resumed my supportive stance with Cory and she became orgasmic before the eighth session.*

---

*I learned from this error never to give any assignment to a whole group without considering its appropriateness for each individual.

DEALING WITH RESISTANCE

All forms of sex therapy work by attacking the client's defenses directly. This frequently increases his or her anxiety and thereby actually engenders resistance. Some people's ego boundaries are so poorly defined that they need to defend themselves vigorously against being overwhelmed by another person. In sex therapy, which produces a high level of anxiety, they express this need by resisting both the therapy and the therapist.

Women in preorgasmic groups who present difficulties because of their passive resistance can be easily identified in the first or second session. They generally present themselves as being helpless. They may report incidents of reacting to a partner in a passive-aggressive manner. They frequently question the therapist's authority and imply that they do not like to follow orders or have always been "rebellious." Sometimes they indicate that they do not expect the program to work for them though they are willing to go through the motions. It becomes perfectly clear that despite their helpless, inadequate manner, these women are firmly resistant to the help they solicit. The resistance is a response to their feeling a lack of control over their lives. They carefully guard their boundaries for fear of merging or losing themselves, and they prove their strength by showing that others cannot change them. Although this process is self-defeating, it generally represents a lifelong pattern. In therapy, these are the women who win by defeating the therapist. Sometimes, however, they experience orgasm after the group is over, thereby proving that the leader and treatment program were of no assistance and that they had to do it by themselves. If I perceive that a woman is manifesting this form of resistance, I discontinue the supportive stance and abdicate, join the resistance, or use a paradoxical approach.

Abdication

The resistant woman can "win" by withholding her orgasm, thus proving her autonomy. She is the client most likely to fail in groups led by inexperienced therapists. It is crucial for the therapist to recognize this common resistance, withdraw from the perceived power struggle, and, in doing so, relinquish her investment in the client's achievement of orgasm.

137

Sometimes the therapist can clarify the power struggle by describing and interpreting it dynamically, but in a brief therapy program such as the preorgasmic group process it is far easier for the woman to achieve orgasm if the group leader takes a helpless rather than an authoritative position. Not surprisingly, when a woman gives herself credit for attaining orgasm despite the therapist, she is beginning to redefine herself as a winner—as someone who has the power to go after and obtain what she wants. This aspect of the leadership role, which enables a woman to break away from the authority figure in a healthy way, may be one of the primary factors in her starting to take control of her life.

The therapist's willingness to be "defeated" early in the group by not having all the answers, by making mistakes, by being ignorant in a way that requires the woman to help her find answers rather than fight her, and by being excessively understanding, exaggerating the difficulty of the woman's situation in such a way that she is required to assume positive control in order to correct the therapist—all help bypass the resistance. The resistant woman still wins by defeating the therapist, but attains her original goal as well. Examples of this will follow.

Joining the Resistance

Sometimes I visualize this dynamic as a seesaw. If a woman tells me how terrible her situation is and I counter by saying it really is not so terrible, or if she acts confused and I give her the answer, we remain locked in equilibrium. I provide her with an opponent to prove wrong. We each defend our positions and a stalemate results.

Figure 6-1

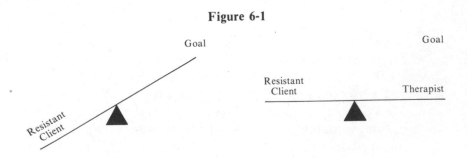

However, if I join her, acknowledging that things are terrible—so terrible I am surprised she can attend the group sessions, let alone do the homework—if I suggest that she is trying to move too fast and should slow down (when in fact she has not tried at all), and if I say I have no answers to her problems, I move over to her side of the see-saw. To fight me, she must move to the other side. Hence, by remaining in opposition, she finds herself on the side that is most likely to enable her to achieve her goal.

Figure 6-2

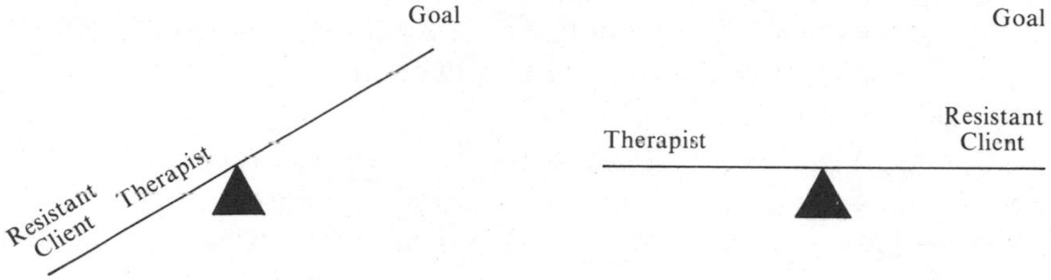

Goal   Goal

Therapist   Resistant
Client

Resistant Client   Therapist

Paradox

The paradoxical approach, as described by Watzlawick and various co-workers (1967, 1974), consists of directing the client in various ways to continue or to exaggerate self-defeating or anxiety-producing behavior.

> If one person wants to influence another person's behavior, there are basically only two ways of doing so. The first consists of trying to make the other behave differently. This approach fails with symptoms because the patient has no deliberate control over this behavior. The other approach . . . consists in making him behave as he is already behaving. . . . If a therapist instructs a patient to perform his symptom, he is demanding spontaneous behavior and by this paradoxical injunction imposes on his patient a behavioral change. The symptomatic behavior is no longer spontaneous; by subjecting himself to the therapsit's injunction the patient has stepped outside the frame of his symptomatic game [Watzlawick, Beavin, and Jackson, 1967:237].

Prescribing the symptom results in giving the woman a new kind of control over her behavior because she can no longer indulge in it unconsciously while claiming to be helpless. What occurs by this intervention is a change in the system: "Symptom prescription—or in the wider, non-clinical sense, second-order change through paradox—is undoubtedly the most powerful and most elegant form of problem resolution known to us [Watzlawick, Weakland, and Fisch, 1974:114]."

The use of paradox is illustrated in the following transcript.

PAMELA: It just happens. I block the feelings.
MARIA: Spontaneously?
PAMELA: Yeah, I can't plan it.
THERAPIST: Well, then notice it. Actively block the feelings.
PAMELA: I would think that if it happens that I feel turned on I should build up that feeling.
THERAPIST: That doesn't work for you. Because even if you build up, you'll still block eventually. Seems to me more reasonable at this point to find out how you block, to get that more under your control by blocking actively, noticing that process better.
PAMELA: I think it's a very unconscious thing, very subconscious.
THERAPIST: Maybe as you're doing the blocking, actually cut off the feelings and see if it gives you an idea.

Examples of ways to handle resistance are contained throughout this book, but I shall present a couple of cases here to illustrate the aforementioned approaches.

Dale was never able to complete her homework: friends, family, illness, and other concerns kept interfering. When the group members or therapists tried to help her solve her problems (fighting her resistance), she always had an explanation for why their solutions would not work. Her responses usually took the form of "Yes, but . . . I can't afford a baby sitter;" "Yes, but . . . he would get angry if he had to take care of the children." The therapists realized what they were up against and, rather than try to help Dale further, they clearly acknowledged how stressful and complicated her life was (which was true) and suggested that it might be reasonable for her, in view of her life circumstances, to expect to have to attend two or more groups in order to reach her goal (joining her pessimism). Consequently, it seemed to make sense for her to lower her expectations and set a homework goal that she could fulfill. The leaders decided that setting aside a total of 10 minutes a day for herself would be a sufficiently difficult task. Finding enough time to masturbate to orgasm was clearly out of the question for the moment. (In other words, the therapists prescribed the symptom of not doing the homework.) Dale felt this solution was going a bit overboard and thought she could find a half hour. The therapists replied that it would be fine if she could find that much time but cautioned her not to pressure herself. She should aim for 10 minutes and any time beyond that would be fantastic but understandably very difficult to accomplish. Dale responded by being relieved but somewhat miffed. In the following session, she reported having found a little time to practice masturbation, was reinforced for doing so by the therapist, and again was advised to spend a much shorter time with the homework than the prescribed hour—perhaps 15 minutes daily. This time, she found an even longer period in which to practice and was rewarded by having an orgasm.

Mary always did the opposite of whatever the therapists suggested. She became orgasmic with masturbation in the sixth session, once the therapists discontinued assigning her specific homework tasks (abdication). Later in the group, when some of the women were given the assignment of practicing masturbation with candles and other phallic-shaped objects inside the vagina to pave the way for orgasm during intercourse, Mary suddenly developed vaginismus, a tightening of the muscles surrounding the vaginal opening that prevents penetration. Consequently, she could not insert an object to masturbate with. The therapists instructed her to take a vacation from homework which was exactly what she had been doing (paradox). Accordingly, Mary made considerable progress before the next session and experienced no difficulty inserting a candle. The therapists never asked how she managed to do the homework for fear she would begin to resist them again.

Once the strategy of abdication or paradox is employed successfully, it is important not to assume a more interested or supportive approach. There is nothing more inviting than a woman who has made a breakthrough after sessions of being stuck. However, if at this time the therapist attempts to "help" the client, especially by telling her what to do, resistance will arise again. It is essential to maintain the approach which has produced the positive results.

Some therapists do not like to use paradox because they deem it manipulative or dishonest. On the contrary, telling a woman to do something she already is doing gives her the opportunity to monitor her behavior closely and hence to gain control over it. My expecting little because the woman has accomplished so little is a reality. My giving up in defeat is reasonable. She can beat me hands down. She has control over her body; I have none. So, the therapist can either fight the client's resistance or use the power of the resistance to help attain the goal.

Some clients will refuse to carry out a paradoxical assignment. At this point many therapists are at a loss; they do not know how to present the paradox in a way that would make it acceptable. The following transcript illustrates a situation in which a client initially rejects such an assignment.

ABBY: What I'm experiencing, and you picked it up, is the feeling that it's not gonna work, but I'll keep trying. I've had to be in the city every day and I just haven't felt like masturbating, but I know I could have found the time if I wanted to, if it had been top priority. So what I think I'm doing is repeating an old pattern of not following through.

BEVERLY: I have been doing the same thing and behind that is the fear that I'm not going to be successful. I'm really trying to shake that fear.

THERAPIST: Abby, I'd like to give you a different kind of assignment because I think there is a good reason for you to be exactly where you are now. There may be something important to learn from the doubts you have before we throw them away. What I'd like you to do rather than go home and try to do the homework and fight the tendency not to do it is to go home and get in touch with what it is going to be like for you to never have an orgasm.

ABBY: I've done that.

THERAPIST: How much time did you spend on that?

ABBY: How much time? I could get into it right now. What it would feel like to me would be that a part of me would stay dead. About not realizing my own potential as a person.

THERAPIST: But what would it feel like? Would you close your eyes for just a second? Imagine yourself getting older, going through the years. Visualize yourself getting older. Imagine what is going on in your life. Imagine yourself not having orgasms. Getting older and still not having orgasms. What is it like?

[Silence]

142

ABBY: I see two things. I feel one part of me is very used to being like that. It is a comfortable way to be. It doesn't feel bad because I don't have the other side of it to know how good it could be.

THERAPIST: So it is comforting. Maybe that is how your life is going to be for you.

ABBY: Ooooh. I don't want to live through that part of me.

THERAPIST: I think it is important to get in touch with the fact that that is the way your life is going to be. Has that not been true for you up until now? Is there a part of you that puts a lid on things you feel uncomfortable about or is it just in sex?

ABBY: Sure, but that is not comfortable either.

THERAPIST: I would still like you to go home and, even if you are going to still do the masturbation, really get in touch with that comfortable part of you and acknowledge it. This is very important because this is a very important part of you.

ABBY: I could say I was willing to do that, but that would mean cutting off a part of me that doesn't need to be cut off. What I may be saying is that I don't find it very helpful to be told that that is maybe the way I'm going to live my life.

THERAPIST: And my feeling is that that is a real possibility and it is really important for you to look at it because there is a very strong force here. I think that if you just say, "No, it's not there," and avoid it, it keeps creeping in.

ABBY: In other words, I have to face the enemy?

THERAPIST: What I'm saying is that for where you are right now, you need to face that side of you and just to pretend that it is not there and you are just going to be the other way is not working very well.

ABBY: Yes, but it is too easy to slip into that way because it is what I've done all these years. I've worked too hard at it and thought about it too long to do that. I've been hopeful all my life that it was going to happen.

THERAPIST: And you can keep being hopeful until the end. There is a state called being hopeful and you can just continue to be hopeful. And it will be very upsetting for you to think about what I'm telling you to think about. You've ignored it and pretended it wasn't there. It's very strong and being hopeful won't make it go away.

ABBY: It seems I've made the choice, but I keep going back and forth. Maybe I don't stay with one or the other long enough.

THERAPIST: Well, that would be my homework assignment for you.

ABBY: To go home and fantasize what it would be like to never have an orgasm?

THERAPIST: To experience that side, to really feel what that side is like. Obviously, you can do for your homework whatever you want to do, but that is what I would assign you to do.

CONFRONTING FEARS

If a woman is not resistant but is overly fearful, I generally become more confrontational after the initial sessions. I encourage her to note the feelings that pass over her as she completes the assignments. In the sessions I may spend considerable time working with her in an attempt to isolate and identify the fears and personality dynamics that might be tied to the orgasm so that we can focus on them in appropriate future assignments.

Carla consistently did very little of her homework. She appeared very shy and naive about sex. She had had two lovers in her 45 years, to one of whom she was married for 15 years. She was now considering marrying the other man. Because of her discomfort in discussing sex, I took a supportive role with her until the fifth session. Since I was quite sure that her withholding was not an expression of resistance but of fearfulness, I then took a more directive role, again explaining the importance of the homework and giving her a vibrator to try. (She had been too anxious to buy one herself.) Within a couple of sessions she was orgasmic with the vibrator. In the last session she told me she felt I should have been more directive earlier and that I should force all the women to get vibrators and stress the importance of doing the homework more heavily.

Areas and issues that may require confrontation commonly include, but are not limited to, failure to express anger and sadness, lack of assertiveness, aversion to sex, as well as other psychological issues discussed throughout this chapter.

Individualizing the Homework

The middle sessions are characterized by individualized homework assignments. For the homework to be effective, there must be a specific reason for making each and every assignment. If a woman is failing to progress, it is sometimes better to make no assignment at all or one that has no goal other than to allow the woman to observe or monitor the process that is causing her difficulty.

Beyond the first four sessions, there is no preordained order to the homework assignments, and no one assignment is mandatory. A creative sex therapist could, with the help of the client, devise a potentially unlimited number of assignments to fit any particular problem. The concept of designing small steps toward reaching a goal rather than developing a list of specific exercises is important here.

Small steps and *safety* are the keys to tailoring the homework. Small steps means breaking down a goal into a number of subgoals. Safety refers to the physical and psychological components that enable the woman to feel secure and in control in the learning process. Small steps can take the form of variations in duration, activity or setting, and intensity. For example, I may instruct a preorgasmic woman to masturbate for only five minutes daily at first, expanding the time until she is comfortable masturbating for an hour or longer (increase in time). She may begin with gentle manual masturbation and increase the speed and intensity of her touch or incorporate a vibrator (increase in intensity). Once she is orgasmic alone the next step might be for her to masturbate with a partner present but not participating in the actual stimulation initially (change in setting).

The individual woman needs to be consulted in order for the group leader to determine which small steps are appropriate with which safety measures. The therapist should ask questions to help ascertain the woman's fears or other problems in relation to a particular goal so that she can participate in designing the appropriate homework. The right approach to the solution of any problem is the one the woman feels is best suited to her own needs. The therapist helps isolate the problem, but the woman herself solves it—with some monitoring from the therapist.

Suppose a woman has become reliably orgasmic with masturbation and now wants to experience orgasm with her partner. The successful experience thus far has been her pleasuring herself in a certain manner while alone. The jump from this step to trying to have orgasms during intercourse would be too large for most women and might easily lead to failure. Therefore, taking what works (masturbation) and putting it in a new setting (adding a partner) is a reasonable first step. How the woman feels about this assignment will determine exactly how the homework should be designed; she and the therapist will pay special attention to what safety measures need to be employed.

Let us say that a woman is very fearful of looking ugly and thus disgusting her partner when she has an orgasm. For this woman, masturbating to orgasm in front of a partner would be too large a first step. The therapist and the client together can break this task down into a number of substeps. For instance, if the woman indicated that she would feel more relaxed if her partner were not watching her when she had an orgasm, I might suggest that she begin by masturbating with him outside the room but aware that she is masturbating. Perhaps she would prefer to have him in the room but with his back to her while she masturbates. Given that the woman's major concern is her appearance *at orgasm*, I might add the instruction that she masturbate but *not* have an orgasm the first time, as a way to maximize her sense of safety and comfort. Once she has succeeded in masturbating with her partner in the same room, she may then feel ready to masturbate to orgasm with him looking at her.

LEARNING FROM FAILURE

If a subgoal is not attained through a particular homework assignment, this does not necessarily mean that the assignment is inappropriate. Important learning can result from an unsuccessful attempt at change if one can determine not only what does not work but also why it does not. The incident is frequently only one example of a typical pattern of handling certain areas inappropriately, and the so-called failure can help to point up the negative pattern quite clearly.

Grace could set aside only five or 10 minutes a day for her homework because of family obligations. She was thus unable to learn much about her sexual responsiveness. However, while telling the group about her difficulties in finding time for the homework, she realized that she had no time for herself because she put everyone else's needs before her own. This realization caused Grace to reevaluate her role in her family. Soon thereafter she decided that her needs were no less important than those of the other family members and began to set aside time for the homework.

DEALING WITH BLOCKS

Some women may be unable to carry out their assignments without first going through the desensitization process of practicing the homework in fantasy or role-playing it in the group. Again, take the example of a woman who is orgasmic on her own and desires to reach orgasm with a partner. When we talk about masturbating in front of her partner she becomes very anxious and says she could not possibly do it. Questioned further, she says she would have less difficulty doing such an exercise if her partner were to suggest it. Thus, it becomes more clear that the problem centers around her discomfort in *initiating* the exercise with her partner, not in actually doing it. The appropriate first assignment might be to have her practice initiating the exercise with a group member who is pretending to be her partner or to imagine the sequence of events in fantasy.

The homework assignments deal with the physical and mental components of sexual arousal. Other intrapsychic or interactional issues, however, are sometimes linked to orgasm and have to be resolved or considered separately from the sexual problem before orgasm can be attained (see pp. 159–166). Homework assignments can be designed to help resolve such issues as well so that the path can be cleared to work on orgasm.* In some cases the nonsexual problems are so severe or persistent that the woman must attend a second (or third) group or seek therapy for the other issues before tackling her sexuality.

Homework assignments are designed to overcome particular blocks to experiencing orgasm. Common points in the arousal process at which blocks occur are lack of arousal, intermediate arousal, and high arousal with no release.

LACK OF AROUSAL

Many women report feeling bored, embarrassed, or foolish when beginning to masturbate. For some, this reaction is merely a stage in the process, and with the aid of fantasy or pornography (see Chapter 5) they soon learn to arouse themselves. Many others, however, lack perseverance and after a number of unsuccessful attempts feel both frustrated and helpless.

Vibrators

The use of a vibrator often enables such women to get over the hurdle of boredom and frustration. Using a vibrator, which supplies

---

*Structured homework assignments have been so successful that I use this approach with all my psychotherapy clients. Once the concept of tailoring homework to fit a particular problem or situation is understood, it is quite simple to generalize the process to other issues.

effective stimulation, is frequently also the easiest way for a woman to experience her first orgasm.

Vibrators are often discussed during the first few sessions either because a woman has heard about them and wonders about their effectiveness or because she is already orgasmic with a vibrator but not with other types of stimulation. Many women worry that vibrators are addictive or can decrease one's responsiveness to a partner. For many women the vibrator offers a quick and effortless route to orgasm, and some prefer to use a vibrator when they masturbate and even during partner sex. In this sense, a vibrator is no more addictive than enjoyable sex: it feels good and the procedure is consequently repeated.

Women who learn to have orgasms using a vibrator become accustomed to attaining orgasm very quickly, but the type of stimulation afforded by a mechanical device is significantly different from that afforded by a human being. Consequently, learning to reach orgasm through manual self- or partner stimulation may be as time-consuming initially as becoming orgasmic for the first time. However, because of their previous effortless experiences, women who have used vibrators successfully tend to be more impatient and more easily discouraged and frustrated with manual stimulation than women who have never had an orgasm. It is important, therefore, to assign preorgasmic women the use of a vibrator early in the group—no later than the fifth or sixth session—so as to leave ample time before the group terminates to provide the continued support necessary to learn to achieve the orgasmic response with nonmechanical stimulation.

Some few women are orgasmic with a vibrator but are unable to respond orgasmically to any other type of sexual stimulation. I believe it is important to inform group members that this outcome has occurred. They then have the option to choose orgasm with a vibrator over no orgasm at all. And until there is evidence that vibrators cause physical harm, there does not seem to be any cause for concern about their use. Women who are pregnant or who have medical problems should, however, consult a physician before using a vibrator.

My concern about assigning the vibrator initially is that some women may use it as a way to avoid touching their genitals, especially when discomfort in touching their own genitals is related to discomfort in having a partner touch them. Accordingly, I explicitly address the issues involved and suggest that the women use the vibrator over their hands or that they alternate using the vibrator and a hand, whichever is more comfortable.

BEVERLY: Where do you go to get all these vibrators?

PAMELA: I got mine in New York.

JENNY: Drugstores. I ask for a body massager.

JOSEPHINE: The one I got has a rubber tip. I got it through a place in Los Angeles. They had a table where they displayed a number of different kinds.

PAMELA: You can send for them.

THERAPIST: How many of you have orgasms with the vibrator?

JENNY: I have. I went for a lecture by Betty Dodson, at a women's workshop. She had a stainless steel one that was wonderful. I started thinking that if I got involved with a vibrator, it is such a gross sensation, just massive, it might not be good. I was told by someone to stay away from the vibrator if at all possible.

BEVERLY: Because you might become dependent upon it?

JENNY: It's not that I would become dependent. It is just that it is not what generally happens with an outside stimulus. It is a more subtle thing if you use your hand.

ABBY: Have you experienced sensations from your hand?

JENNY: I can do both. I feel different with the vibrator.

THERAPIST: All orgasms are different, from morning until evening and from day to day.

PAMELA: How long does it take you with the vibrator?

JENNY: I can't give you the time, but sometimes it takes as long with the vibrator as it does with my hand. The vibrator is no guarantee that it is going to be quick. Sometimes it is.

PAMELA: I felt like a vibrator was a little more painful or too intense. But then I thought, "Maybe if I could just start having orgasms with the vibrator." It is that initial awakening or whatever.

MARIA: For me, the vibrator is easier than with my hands because it seems as if it's something else or someone else. It's not me doing it, so that takes away some of the guilt that I have. Because it's the vibrator that's doing it to me.

THERAPIST: And if it were you doing it?

MARIA: Then I would be doing it, and I can't take that.

THERAPIST: Because?

MARIA: Probably the same way as I feel about looking at my vagina. I think there's something about touching it that's, it's just that, I don't know. It's just—I can't touch it.

Many women are reluctant to purchase a vibrator even though they are sold in the small appliances section of most department stores. Frequently, overcoming the embarrassment and buying a vibrator, alone or with a lover or friend, is an important step. However, sometimes I lend a vibrator to a woman who is indigent or very fearful. Of course, vibrators can be ordered through the mail,* but the process generally takes longer than the time available to the group.

Most physiologically sound women will become aroused by vibrator stimulation. However, a particular woman may have to try a few different types of vibrators before she finds one that meets her needs. Some women seem to require intense vibrator stimulation; others prefer milder stimulation. The Prelude vibrator, designed specifically for sexual use, is one of the few electric models that has two different intensities and a special attachment for clitoral stimulation.

Some women do not enjoy vibrator stimulation. However, if a woman who is not averse to their use has tried a few models without success or if she typically requires more than a half hour of direct genital stimulation with a vibrator to reach orgasm, her problem is likely to be an inability to concentrate. The additional assignment of fantasy or pornography will generally resolve her difficulty. If fantasy or pornography also proves unsuccessful, psychological issues related to orgasm may be at work. A woman who resists by withholding and who is likely to try to prove the therapist wrong should not be given the assignment to use a vibrator. If the issue of vibrators arises, it is generally best to present this method as likely to fail in her particular case.

Clare was the epitome of a woman who resists by withholding. She complained in the middle sessions that she found masturbation so boring that she preferred to be in the library studying. She was separated from her husband so masturbating with him was out of the question, and since she did not feel comfortable enough yet with her new lover to tell him about the group or her problem with or-

*Many vibrator models can be ordered through Eve's Garden, 119 West Fifty-seventh Street, New York, New York 10019. The Prelude vibrator can be ordered directly from Sensory research, 2424 Morris Avenue, Union, New Jersey 07083.

gasm, it appeared that Clare had all routes to attaining orgasm blocked. A vibrator was the only hope, but I knew that if I suggested it, she would find a way to dismiss that possibility also. So I told her, "Clare, I'm really stuck. I know that you find the masturbation assignments boring and doing it alone doesn't turn you on. I can understand that you don't want to try it with your husband since you're separated. You could try the vibrator, but that probably wouldn't work. And I can understand why you might not be comfortable enough yet with Paul to try it with him. I don't know what you should do." Clare decided that the vibrator made the most sense. At the next session she arrived looking quite different. Her hair had been cut and styled and she was dressed in a skirt instead of her usual jeans. She did not say a word and I refrained from asking about her homework. After the session had officially ended, one of the group members asked Clare what had happened with the vibrator. She matter-of-factly replied that she not only was having orgasms regularly with the vibrator but had almost had an orgasm when her husband stimulated her manually.

There is no reason for a woman who is orgasmic only with a vibrator to feel she has a problem unless she wishes to respond to other types of stimulation as well. When teaching women to transfer having an orgasm from the vibrator to the hand, take care not to indicate that there is anything wrong with the use of a vibrator or with orgasms experienced in that way. All sexual successes are important. If either the leader or the woman herself treats the vibrator as a last resort, to be used only if she fails the "real way," the woman might end the treatment program reliably orgasmic with a vibrator but still feeling like a failure. However, if orgasm resulting from vibrator stimulation is perceived as a positive outcome, the same woman could from a position of strength work on enlarging her options if she wanted to do so.

Myrna learned after the second group session that her husband of six months was having an affair and desired a separation. She was very upset but wanted to continue the group anyway. After the fifth session Myrna became orgasmic using a vibrator. She wished to become orgasmic manually as well but felt her current crisis was interfering with her ability to relax and concentrate on more subtle stimulation. Consequently, she decided to defer that learning until she felt less distracted.

Women who enter the group orgasmic only with a vibrator generally wish to become orgasmic with other sources of stimulation.

Initially I prohibited the use of a vibrator for the duration of the program to encourage such women to do the manual assignments more diligently. This approach backfired. Some women perceived the prohibition as deprivation and either continued to use a vibrator surreptitiously and felt guilty or followed the instruction and failed to progress because they resented being deprived.

Since then I have found several methods to teach women who are orgasmic with vibrators to reach orgasm in other ways. I have the women experiment with integrating manual and vibrator homework to see which combinations work best for them. One solution is to separate vibrator and manual masturbation assignments. The woman can use a vibrator one day and her hand the next or begin with her hand and use a vibrator after a specified period of time. (This approach needs careful supervision because some women get almost to the point of orgasm and then use the vibrator and wonder why they cannot have orgasms through manual stimulation.) Some women find that starting with the vibrator helps to turn them on; they then discontinue its use and build arousal with the hand. Others find the vibrator numbs them so that they are insensitive to later manual touching.

Another approach is to reduce the intensity of vibrator stimulation by having the woman place a towel or her hand between the vibrator and her genitals or use the vibrator in a more gentle, teasing fashion while intermittently providing manual stimulation. This procedure slows down the arousal process and enables the woman to become accustomed to taking longer to reach orgasm with less discouragement. (Although reaching orgasm is taking longer, the woman anticipates success because of her prior positive experiences with a vibrator.)

Most women can transfer the orgasm from mechanical to manual stimulation if they put in enough time and effort. However, during the course of the group, some women realize that they are unwilling to expend the energy to learn to have orgasms in other ways and as a result accept the vibrator more completely. By the sixth or seventh session I encourage these women to use the vibrator with a partner if they are not already doing so. My goal is not to wean them from the vibrator but to give them permission to use whatever techniques prove to be satisfying. A woman who is satisfied using a vibrator alone and with a partner is limited only by electrical sources and batteries. If her partner does not mind or enjoys the vibrator, this outcome may be perfectly acceptable.

Some women use vibrators as a weapon against their partners, saying, as it were, "The vibrator can do it, but you can't." Often, such a woman is reluctant to become orgasmic using her hands for fear that she will have to be orgasmic when her partner stimulates her manually. Because of her dissatisfaction with the relationship, she is invested in withholding sexually. I reassure her that she probably will not lose her ability to withhold orgasm during partner sex: she has become too proficient at it. I bring up this point to show the woman that she is making choices and that she is not "inadequate." Of course, conjoint sex or marital counseling would be in order if both the woman and her partner were willing to participate.

Withholding

The topic of resistant women, those who feel their only power is to withhold, has been discussed throughout the book (specifically on pp. 137–144). I bring it up again here because withholding is probably the most common dynamic involved when women say they feel little or no sexual arousal. These women either do very little of the homework or, being "good girls," do absolutely all the assignments, but in neither case do they "own" the process.

Joyce, age 28 and married five years with two children, did the homework regularly but felt nothing. When we tried to pin her down on details she gave evasive answers. After three frustrating sessions of little progress, we told her that we had no other information to give her; she was just different from everyone else we had worked with. Consequently, she would have to design a program to fit her individual needs and then perhaps we could learn from her. Joyce was angry and totally taken aback by this suggestion. However, after a few more sessions of receiving no assistance or instruction, she began to report progress. She had discovered some massaging techniques that were working for her. We continued to claim ignorance as well as amazement at her ability to design her own program creatively, and after another session she experienced her first orgasm.

Anxiety

Fearful of being overwhelmed by the anticipated intensity of orgasm, some women initially feel very little sexually when they masturbate. Usually this anxiety response first presents itself when the woman feels intense sexual feelings during masturbation (often by using a vibrator or running water over her genitals), at which time her fear of losing control causes her to cut off her experience of these feelings. Such women must be instructed to slow down and begin again very gradually. A temporary vacation from the homework may produce a sense of safety. When the woman starts doing the assignments again, she should try to feel only mild sensations and slowly build on these. After such a scare, experience has shown that it is realistic to suggest that more than one group may be necessary for her to reach orgasm. In general, very gradual desensitization works best with highly anxious women; pressure to move quickly to orgasm may retard progress.

Gerri knew that masturbation might help her experience orgasm but was unable to accomplish this goal herself so she joined a group in the hope that therapy would assist her. Initially, she felt very little sensation from masturbating manually. Then another woman in the group discovered that stimulation by water flowing from the bathtub faucet resulted in orgasm, so Gerri decided to try this technique. The first time she tried it she experienced very intense sensations and panicked. She felt that she was going to explode. After a couple of days she forced herself to try again but felt nothing. The next few times she tried she continued to feel only very mild sensations. We discussed her fears in the group and assured her that she was obviously capable of having the feelings; in fact, her tremendous sensitivity was creating some of her problem, and we suggested that she slow the process down. She took a vacation from the homework for a few nights and then began again, using her hand. By the end of the group she was able to tolerate mild sensations. It was not until the middle of a second group that she was able to experience orgasm.

Including the Partner

Occasionally a woman is totally unable to arouse herself when doing the homework alone but experiences considerable body and genital sensations while making love with a partner. Such a woman may benefit from doing the homework with a partner present, and the therapist should help work out ways of integrating the assignments into the relationship. The difficulty is that the woman may curtail her own pleasuring by concentrating on her partner instead should she become uncomfortable with the intensity of her sexual feelings.

Phyllis was unable to turn herself on by masturbating alone. She did not fantasize easily, and pornography was unacceptable to her.

However, she always felt aroused when she had sex with her husband and felt perfectly uninhibited in bed with him. When I asked whether she might prefer to do the homework with him present she was overwhelmed with relief. Asked how she would do the assignment, she said masturbating with him kissing her lips and breasts felt comfortable. The assignment to masturbate with her partner in this way seemed reasonable to me as well. If after a few sessions it had worked out poorly because of relationship problems or unexpected discomfort on the part of Phyllis or her partner, we would have had to devise another approach. Returning to solitary masturbation might have worked once she realized that she harbored a fantasy that her husband would do it for her. But in this instance, she felt good about the homework sessions with her husband and after a number of trials Phyllis experienced her first orgasm.

INTERMEDIATE AROUSAL

Once sexual sensations have begun to build, certain techniques can be used to enhance them.

Muscle Tension

Since the physiological components of sexual arousal are vaso-congestion and myotonia (muscular tension), the buildup of muscular tension is important in attaining orgasm. Some women require more muscular tension and find that crossing their legs, squeezing their thighs together, or practicing the Kegel excercises while masturbating helps to increase their level of arousal.

Other women build up too much muscular tension. They become overly aroused and must reduce the tension before they can experience orgasm. A brief rest or a short walk around the house may help. One woman claimed that getting up and brushing her teeth solved the problem. Sometimes pelvic bounces prove effective. This exercise requires the woman to lie on her back with her legs drawn up and feet placed on the surface next to the buttocks. In this position it is easy to raise the buttocks a short distance and then drop them on the surface again in a fairly rapid bouncing motion. A series of such bounces may reduce the tension sufficiently to allow orgasmic release when clitoral stimulation is resumed.

Relaxation exercises also can reduce pelvic tension. The woman should breathe deeply while visualizing that the air she is breathing is going in and out of the vagina. With each breath she can imagine the warm air relaxing the tension in the pelvic region.

Breathing

Breathing patterns are important in the sexual arousal process. Some women are breath holders: they stop breathing as tension mounts and orgasm draws near. Others are panters and take many shallow rapid breaths as arousal increases. Others find that slow, deep breaths increase sexual sensations. Having women pay attention to their breathing and experiment to see which breathing techniques seem most effective in building sexual arousal is advisable (see Rosenberg, 1973).

Miscellaneous Techniques

Some women find that moaning, grunting or talking enhances the arousal process. Others are distracted by sounds and prefer to remain silent. Moving the body, particularly the pelvic area, can foster the arousal process for some women; others need to lie perfectly still as orgasm approaches. Each woman is unique, and should be encouraged to experiment with each of these techniques, one at a time, to determine which heighten her sexual pleasure.

HIGH AROUSAL WITHOUT RELEASE

After learning to arouse themselves sexually, some women reach a high level of excitement but do not experience the release of orgasm. Frequently they report feeling frustrated, nervous, and uncomfortable after such episodes. Several techniques can help women to get beyond this plateau stage.*

Desensitization

A process of desensitization may be useful for women who become fearful as sexual feelings mount. The preferred technique is sometimes called "teasing" because the woman builds up to a high level of tension and then allows the tension to subside a bit by changing or stopping the stimulation; she then builds to a slightly higher level of arousal, stops, and repeats the process once more. During

---

*Sometimes the added intensity of stimulation provided by a vibrator is sufficient to trigger the orgasmic response.

the next homework session she can begin by increasing the stimulation, beginning at the highest level of arousal she attained in the previous session. This method enables the woman gradually to become more and more comfortable with intense sexual sensations while still feeling that she is in control.

Role-playing

Acting out the most intense orgasm they can imagine is a productive assignment for women who reach high levels of arousal but cannot go over the top to orgasm. I generally instruct such women during the group session to imagine the most extreme orgasm they could have. We then discuss the most frightening aspects of the imagined orgasm and design safety measures to protect the women when they carry out the assignment at home. For example, if a woman is afraid she might scream so loudly that she would wake her neighbors, she could turn the radio up or put a towel or sock in her mouth to muffle the noise. If she is afraid that she would writhe around so much she might fall off the bed and injure herself, she could masturbate on the floor. If she is afraid she would urinate, she could masturbate in the bathtub or put a plastic sheet or towels underneath her on the bed. If she is afraid she would lose consciousness, she might call a friend or another group member before beginning the homework, instructing the person to come to her house if she did not call back within an hour.

Some women find that role-playing an intense orgasm causes the fabricated orgasm to turn into a real one. Others never fulfill the assignment and yet experience orgasm by the next session; just talking about their fears is sufficient. For others, the role-playing seems to make no difference whatsoever; they continue to be stuck at the plateau level of arousal.

MARIA: It gets me so mad, walking around with the level of tension that I feel at that point, and I just walk away from it like—bing. It's like building up to such a crescendo—you know my fear of looking epileptic; I think I'm going to be epileptic.

[Laughter]

THERAPIST: Is that what your fear is, that you'll be epileptic?

MARIA: Right. At the point of orgasm.

THERAPIST: I'd like to have you try something, okay? With the homework, as you are feeling a little bit turned on, I'd like you

157

to role-play an epileptic orgasm. I want you to get used to whatever that fantasy is. I want you to act out all those things that you think will happen. Okay? And *still* don't have an orgasm.

MARIA: I know I'm going to feel silly doing that.

THERAPIST: Okay. Feel silly. Be aware of all the feelings that you have. But do it anyway.

MARIA: I just noticed how desperate I get like when I'm with Bob: "Don't look ridiculous, don't look desperate, or he'll be scared and run away."

THERAPIST: Do all of that with masturbation. Okay?

MARIA: Oh, God.

THERAPIST: That's a tough one for you. If it's too soon, then wait another session before you do it. But I think that that is going to be important for you to at least get a sense of letting go of that. You won't let go of that until you really can experience it and see what it's like.

Assuming Responsibility

In some cases the woman needs to realize that no one can make it easy for her to reach orgasm; she has to take a risk. This may require a leap of faith that no harm will come to her, or it may mean that she will just have to fight the fear and continue the stimulation, even beyond an hour, with the knowledge that no woman has ever died from attaining orgasm. It is sometimes helpful to tell the woman that it is important that she not lose control. In fact, she should understand that the object is to gain control—to have enough control to relax and go with her feelings.

Reducing Pressure

Sometimes the paradoxical injunction of telling the woman to take a vacation for a few days results in her attaining orgasm. Some resistant women may oppose the therapist's suggestions by having an orgasm when told to take a rest. Other women feel more freedom to respond once the pressure to perform has been removed.

The issue of performance pressure in preorgasmic groups is complex. Masters and Johnson (1970) successfully operate under the assumption that the pressure to perform is one of the most common causes of sexual dysfunction, and one primary aspect of their therapy is to remove this pressure. In the preorgasmic groups, pressure to perform can be created by group competition if the leaders are not careful. Since orgasm is the natural result of the buildup of pleasure, one successful way of reducing performance pressure is to change from a goal orientation of focusing on orgasm to a process orientation of experiencing more and more pleasure: emphasize pleasure and deemphasize orgasm.

Misidentification

Some women who claim they are only reaching high levels of arousal are in fact having orgasms. They resist labeling them as such because the orgasm they experience is different from what they expected.

By the eighth session, Kelly, who had come into the group clinically depressed, was feeling better and even looking physically healthier. She was enjoying her homework and claiming that each homework session was better than the last. She expected that orgasm was not too far away but was not concerned because all the exercises were so pleasurable. Since I could not tell where she was stuck or why she was not yet having orgasms I doggedly inquired into the most minute details of her homework sessions. She described her feelings as going up the shaft of an umbrella and then spreading out over the top of it as if the umbrella had opened up, after which she felt relaxed and warm all over.

Her account sounded like a classical description of orgasm, but when I told her so she vehemently disagreed; it did not fit her husband's description of what he experienced when he had an orgasm. Suddenly it became crystal clear: her expectations were creating the problem. Even after I explained that men's and women's orgasms are different Kelly resisted labeling her experience as orgasm. In the ninth session she came in and reported having had three more of "those things you call my orgasms." By the tenth session she, too, was calling them orgasms and seemed very satisfied with her progress.

Psychological Interferences and Relationship Problems

Though I believe that the fear of loss of control is the central dynamic among women who are preorgasmic, I do not adhere to the Freudian notion that anorgasmia is necessarily a symptom of underlying psychological distress. In some women, however, the attainment of orgasm is "hooked," or tied, to another psychological issue or conflict. But even in these cases, it is rarely essential to resolve the deeper psychological problem in order for the woman to attain orgasm. Determining the connection between the issue and the orgasm and then disconnecting the two frequently enables the woman to experience orgasm, although additional therapy may be required for resolution of the deeper problem. Often, the therapist cannot tell that a woman has a problem tied to orgasm until the sixth or seventh session, when diverse approaches have been unsuccessful. The following pages contain examples of some deeper issues that are frequently connected to attaining orgasm.

Expectations of Life Changes

Many women come into the groups expecting that when they become orgasmic their lives will change dramatically. Their belief is that orgasm will bring relief from all their daily problems and struggles and that once they are orgasmic they will become adequate in all the ways in which they feel they are currently lacking.

At first glance, this attachment between orgasm and life change appears to be positive: since the women are looking forward to having their lives change, one would expect that their optimism would encourage the experiencing of orgasm. However, this simplified view overlooks the complexities of a life change. On the one hand, the women welcome the change; on the other, they fear it. If their lives were different, how would they be different? The problems they are currently experiencing may be annoying, but they are at least familiar and predictable. The unknown, even if it is expected to be better, is very anxiety producing. Consequently, as long as orgasm is linked to the unknown, fear of the unknown will interfere with attainment of orgasm.

> MARIA: I did cop out in not coming the last two sessions because I felt the group wasn't what I expected. I did expect more: with sexual orgasms and all I thought that personalities would change. I thought that's why I wasn't having orgasms. Because I expected a whole personality transformation and it never happened and I saw people who hadn't had orgasms were having orgasms and there was no personality change. I thought you become different and beautiful and everything's just so

beautiful and there are no problems in the world. And that didn't happen and that let me down. I expected too much.

ABBY: See, I can say this because I know I was doing it, saying, "If only I could have an orgasm, my whole life would fall into place." And you'll scare any orgasm into the other direction. There's so much expectation laid on those little things.

It is essential to disconnect the prospect of life change from the attainment of orgasm.

THERAPIST: What would be different if you had an orgasm?

BEVERLY: I guess I'd feel more satisfaction as a woman. Completed. It won't make the other things that are happening in my life change at all, but it would make me more even, more tolerating.

ABBY: It isn't that much different. All the stuff is still there. At the time, you feel good. You think, "Hot dog," then the dog bites the postmaster, your mother calls up on the phone, and it's all there.

THERAPIST: Satisfaction as a woman? What does that mean?

BEVERLY: Well, whatever you're supposed to experience as a woman in life. I think that all the years when I didn't have, I was wondering if I was a frigid person. But I was told that I wasn't. I knew I wasn't frigid because my emotions were warm.

THERAPIST: I see. So, this would be a total validation of Beverly. If you were orgasmic that means in some sense that you're okay. And other things wouldn't bother you as much because you could tolerate them . . . being orgasmic. . . . You got a heavy load on this orgasm. How about other people, with your orgasms? Do they solve all your, or at least make you handle all your problems better? Don't you find that your other problems don't bother you because you have orgasms?

Although many women's lives do change once they become orgasmic, in that newfound control over their sexuality enables them to gain greater control over other aspects of their lives, I do not address this possibility. Rather, I explore how the woman expects her life to change: how will it be better and how may it be worse? Eliciting the negative is difficult since the women generally prefer to believe that only positive changes will result. Finally, having elicited all the specifics, I reframe the issues in order to debunk this myth. For example, I may say, ''It certainly would be nice if having orgasms would improve your ability to get another job, but whether or not you have orgasms it sounds like you'll need some further education or therapy to straighten out your job problems. Now, you can seek further education or therapy being orgasmic or seek it not being orgasmic—it's your choice.''

Most women resist this interpretation, but it is important to stand firm. In the long run, it is better for group members to face possible disappointment initially than to have their expectations encouraged and not only have their nonsexual agendas unrealized, but have them interfere with their sexual progress as well.

Fear of Responsibility

Lorie believed that if she became orgasmic she would lose her adolescent freedom and be forced to become responsible, which to her meant getting married, a nine–to–five job, straight clothes, and boring colleagues. I sympathized with the dreariness of this prospect and reframed her concept of ''responsible adult'' by saying that I hoped I would not have to give up my orgasms to remain carefree and spontaneous. The other group members agreed: they did not want to grow up either if it meant fitting Lorie's concept of a responsible adult. Hence, we gave Lorie permission to continue to be totally irresponsible and orgasmic at the same time. She could wait years to grow up and become responsible, but she did not have to wait that long to enjoy orgasms.

Fear of Vulnerability

We did not recognize Brenda's situation at first. She kept talking about how much better she felt about herself since beginning the group—that the assignments were helping her progress from being very controlled and unemotional to being more open and vulnerable in general and particularly with her partner. She was delighted because this change was a goal for her. I did not recognize the problem until she told a story about walking in a rather seedy section of town and being greeted by an unshaven and disheveled man. If she were really open and vulnerable, she felt, she would have responded to him in a friendly manner, but she could not. She felt paralyzed. As she told this story I realized that being open and vulnerable was something Brenda both wanted and feared. So we talked about control and limits and how she could be a little more open without having to talk to everyone who walked down the street, but Brenda insisted that being totally open was her goal and through the help of the sexual exercises she was on the right path; it just might take longer than the three sessions we had remaining in the group. I knew then that disconnecting orgasm from openness and vulnerability was essential so I replied, "I know that being totally open and vulnerable is a goal for you, and it is a valuable goal, but *maybe*, just maybe, by the time you are 65 you'll achieve total openness and vulnerability. Do you want to wait that long to be orgasmic?" Brenda began to cry. I was bursting her bubble of hope: she was so sure she was on the right track. I then gave her the homework assignment of exaggerating her feelings and her sadness to enable her better to comprehend the reality of the situation. She did not like what I had to say, but two sessions later she had had her first orgasm with her partner and by the 10-week follow-up was orgasmic about half the time with him. She was still not "totally open and vulnerable" but was feeling very positive about her progress.

Partner Related Difficulties

Problems in a woman's relationship with a partner are commonly hooked to orgasm. As I noted earlier, some women fear that if they become orgasmic on their own they will have to be orgasmic with a partner. If they are involved with someone they do not trust sufficiently to reach orgasm with, or if they are angry with their partner and view orgasm as a gift they do not want to give, they may resist becoming orgasmic. It is not uncommon for a woman to fear that if she becomes orgasmic her partner, even though he says he wants the change, will in fact be so threatened by the change that he will leave her. Such a woman fears that being orgasmic will make her more dependent upon a partner and that she would therefore be more devastated if the partner were to leave. Or, she might fear the opposite: if she becomes orgasmic she may discover that the relationship is no longer satisfactory for her.

In these situations it is important to separate the orgasm from the relationship issue. The therapist can reassure the woman that she will not lose her ability to hold back her orgasm with a partner if she desires to do so. I explain that it is impossible to avoid making changes in a relationship if it is to last; that if the woman looks back over the relationship she will find that changes have indeed been made without separation occurring; that she would probably be devastated if her partner left her whether or not she had orgasms with him but if she were orgasmic at least she would have a chance of experiencing orgasms with another partner; and that her fears of leaving her partner may have some basis in general dissatisfaction with the relationship—issues that may need to be addressed if the couple is to remain together. Some women do feel more dissatisfied with their relationships once they become orgasmic, but this result may reflect a change in self-concept rather than any relationship change. Frequently, when women become orgasmic they feel less inadequate and consequently believe that they deserve more. A relationship that was satisfactory to someone who viewed herself as a sexual cripple and felt lucky to have any partner at all may not be acceptable to a woman who feels whole sexually.

Sally was recently separated from her husband but was uncertain whether she wanted a divorce. She had a lover with whom she enjoyed sex, although she never experienced orgasm with him. She did not feel at all turned on by her husband but thought of him as her best friend. The fact that they had a young son complicated the matter. After careful probing in the seventh session it came to light that Sally had the attainment of orgasm hooked to her decision regarding divorce. She believed that becoming orgasmic would bring back her sexual attraction to her husband; if it did not she would have to divorce him. Since she was not prepared to make this decision she was holding back sexually. Once I realized that orgasm was connected to divorce, I unhooked the issues by telling Sally that orgasm would definitely not have any effect on her feelings of sexual attraction toward her husband. She still would not be attracted to him and whether or not she became orgasmic she would have to make the decision about divorce quite independently. Sally seemed greatly relieved. Using a vibrator, she had an orgasm before the next session, came close to orgasm with manual stimulation by her husband, found him to be no more sexually attractive, but continued to put off the decision about divorce. (Three months later, they got back together and, to date, are still together. Sally did regain her sexual attraction to her husband—but then she experienced the opposite of everything I predicted.)

Unhooking the Hooks

Detaching orgasm from the issue, conflict, or wish to which it is hooked can be done in a number of ways. Pointing out the issue that is attached to orgasm and then carefully and logically disconnecting the two without discounting either the orgasm or the other issue can be very useful.

I also find it effective to reframe and to exaggerate the attachment until it reaches the level of absurdity. This approach was followed in Brenda's case when I pointed out that if becoming orgasmic meant being totally open and vulnerable she might have to wait until she was 65 to have an orgasm. In Lorie's case I exaggerated the notion of being responsible to make it so uninviting that no one in her right mind would aspire to this goal. Reframing or exaggerating the attachment frequently brings disappointment and tears. I pursue this reaction because it seems reasonable to grieve over the loss of an important fantasy, especially when accepting reality may be the woman's only hope for real change.

Deeper Issues

Although from time to time deeper issues interfere with the attainment of orgasm, they are far less pervasive than we have been led to believe. However, certain negative psychological patterns sometimes must be worked through in order for orgasm to occur.

For example, some women have to get in touch with their sadness and anger before they can experience sexual feelings. Women who withhold all their emotions are likely to hold in sexual feelings as well. It is not uncommon for such a woman to experience her first orgasm after breaking down and crying or having an angry fight with her partner. Techniques to help the woman get in touch with these feelings are the same as those used with any general therapy client in a similar situation.

Pamela, although not orgasmic, was upon closer examination really not a sex therapy case. She described her genitals as being numb and frequently used a vibrator directly on her clitoris for an hour or longer until she felt pain. Pamela was also very depressed but felt no anger or sadness. I did not realize the extent of her problem until mid-group, at which time I decided that working on orgasm was inappropriate without first working on the expression of feelings. I explained to Pamela that her being cut off from her sexual feelings was only one aspect of a more general pattern, that I did not know how successful we would be within the context of the group, and that individual therapy might be required, after which she could work on orgasm in a second group. Pamela agreed. Afterward, I had her lie on the floor, fully clothed, on her back and invited the group members to massage her. This experience brought intense feelings to the fore: Pamela screamed and cried and bit into her fist. Subsequently, she began to take greater risks in relationships and became more aware of her feelings. By the tenth session, she had had an enjoyable sexual relationship in which she had experienced pleasurable feelings. By the three-month follow-up, I was amazed to learn that Pamela had continued with her masturbation assignments and for the previous two weeks had been orgasmic regularly with masturbation.

Group Norms

Each group takes on a life and personality of its own, and each group develops a unique set of norms, the underlying assumptions upon which the group process operates. Frequently, these norms are highly coercive and can either enhance or inhibit the group process. Positive norms—group cohesiveness, openness, and support, for example—facilitate the process of the group. Negative group norms obviously interfere with the success of group members. Yet negative norms are easily reversed, and often one or more women become orgasmic in the session after the one in which a negative group norm has been exposed.

Group norms are usually covert but everyone feels their presence and silently abides by them. These norms are difficult to determine because they are what the women are *not* talking about rather than what they are talking about. It requires skill in understanding group process to recognize and expose group norms. Usually, if no women have experienced orgasm by the sixth or seventh session, the therapist can look to a negative group norm as the cause. In some cases, the group leader can uncover the norm by noting what is *not* being expressed in the group as compared with topics and feelings usually discussed in preorgasmic groups. Likewise, she can use her own reactions in the group as a barometer to evaluate the process. Frequently, group members may be able to explain the lack of progress and clarify the issues that are at the root of the problem. However, such knowledge is often outside their immediate awareness, and having the leader point out that there seems to be a problem can help them attend to and verbalize heretofore unspoken and even unformulated feelings.

One of my groups was unusual in that group cohesiveness had not formed by the third session and I felt ill at ease and somewhat anxious running it. In the middle of the third session I asked the women how they felt about the group so far. Did they feel something was missing? One member asked whether they could bring cheese and crackers to eat at the next session; another wanted to sit on the floor. When I asked why they had not made those suggestions before, they answered that they had not realized they could—they were not sure of the rules. It appeared that a group norm of not transgressing unspoken rules had developed partly in response to my co-therapist, who had never run a group of this type before. Her uncertainty about the process seemed to be mirrored by the group members: everyone was being overly cautious and not investing herself in the process as the members would have had they felt more secure. At the next session, two women brought cheese and crackers, another brought wine, and we sat on the floor. Everyone relaxed and group cohesiveness seemed to form instantly.

Leaving ten minutes at the end of each session for the women to express how they felt about the session, what they got out of it, and what was lacking or needs to be included in future sessions frequently prevents the development of negative group norms. Again, the concepts can be most clearly described through illustrative case histories. The following are some examples of how negative group norms have been isolated and reversed.

In the first research group I ran for my dissertation, I unintentionally created resistance by being too personally invested in the members' experiencing orgasm. At the time it seemed that my graduate degree depended on the success rate of the group. By the sixth session, progress was limited: two of the five members had had orgasms after the third session when instructed to masturbate but *not* to have an orgasm. One of these women failed to repeat the experience. Meanwhile, the group was enjoying heated discussions about their relationships with mothers, fathers, sisters, brothers and how these relationships related to their lack of orgasm. I kept trying to elicit homework details and wondered why no one seemed to be doing the assignments. After the sixth session, I consulted with my thesis supervisor, who commented that I seemed to be more invested in the homework and the orgasm than the group members were. Consequently, when no new orgasms were reported in the seventh session, I told the group what my supervisor had said, adding that I had done what I could and it was now up to them. The women knew what steps to take if they wanted to have orgasms, and I was going to shut up and let them run the group because I felt I was getting in the way of the process. They carried the group on by themselves and I listened. In the eighth session two women reported their first orgasm. In the ninth session the last woman became orgasmic, and the woman who had had only one orgasm had begun having more.

My second dissertation research group kept to the subject of orgasms and completed the homework religiously. But when two women failed to attend the sixth session, and no one had yet reported an orgasm, I knew that another negative group norm was operating. I had no idea what it was so I asked the group members what they thought the problem might be. They quietly began expressing discouragement and frustration, feelings that they had been afraid to bring up because of their expectation that the process was supposed to work. I then realized that in my relief at their dutiful homework participation, so different from the previous group's laxity, I had colluded with the members' wish not to talk about all of their negative feelings. A group norm of "it's only okay to talk about successes" had developed. Accordingly, we spent the sixth session talking about depression, disappointment, and hopelessness. The homework assigned in that session was for the women to get in touch with the fact that they might never have orgasms. One woman angrily stomped out of the room saying that she had already waited 35 years to have an orgasm and was not going to think about waiting 35 years more. The next day she had an orgasm and the domino effect was in motion. The rest of the sessions proved clear sailing.

(My third dissertation research group went like clockwork: only positive group norms developed and one or two orgasms were reported at each of the sessions from the fifth through the ninth.)

Some group leaders consulted with me on a group that had experienced so much partner sabotage that the women could not complete their homework assignments and spent most of the group time talking about partner interference. It became clear to me that the leaders were unwittingly reinforcing the partner sabotage. The women had formed a man-hating group, with the leaders agreeing that their partners were responsible for the women's lack of success. The partner problem had become a form of resistance for the whole group. It was easier for the women to talk about how awful their partners were than to talk about how anxious they felt about doing the homework. Had the issue been raised and had each woman been given back the responsibility to find ways to complete her homework despite her partner, the group norm might have been reversed. The leaders might even have made group discussion of partner difficulties off limits since that topic was interfering with discussion of the masturbation homework.

In another situation, two therapists I supervised were so good that they helped the women not only with orgasm but with many of their other problems as well. However, an unusual process developed in the group. The women would come to the sessions reporting orgasms but complaining about their number, intensity, or some other characteristic. This kind of dissatisfaction had never been manifested in other groups. As we began to observe the process more closely, it became apparent that after making the initial sexual complaint, the women would direct the discussion to other areas of their lives and receive therapy for nonsexual difficulties. Even if sex were going well, they would find a sexual complaint in order to get the therapists' attention. The leaders had inadvertently connected orgasm to other life problems, and a group norm of reporting sexual dissatisfaction in order to get assistance on other issues had developed. Once they recognized this pattern, the therapists could say, "You're doing fine sexually, but do you have any other areas you'd like to work on during this session?" thereby disconnecting sex from other problems. The women received the therapy they wanted, and their sexual complaints ceased.

In one group that I ran no orgasms had been reported by the seventh session. This group was very close and supportive, which led me to suspect that negative competition had developed. Women in this society frequently find it difficult to compete and succeed for fear of making those who are less successful feel bad. Obviously, if no one can win, no one can become orgasmic. So I asked, "Who do you think is going to be the first to have an orgasm?" Everyone immediately pointed to Barbara, the most gregarious member of the group. Barbara said, "Oh, no, not me!" and pointed to the others. I then commented that it looked as though we were going to be there for a long time if no one wanted to be first. The waiting game ended when one woman reported an orgasm at the next session.

Another situation involving negative competition arose when two women announced in the second session of their group that they had had orgasms. We were surprised to discover that despite their early success neither of them found time to complete the homework assignments for the second and third sessions. During the fourth session I noted how interesting it was that both these women had stopped doing their homework since they had become orgasmic. I suggested that for women success is often not a virtue and wondered whether perhaps they might be feeling uncomfortable about being so far ahead of the others. The session ended and no discussion followed, but both women came to the fifth session having had a few more orgasms.

Negative competition can inhibit progress in a group whereas positive competition can enhance the process. On one occasion I was training six therapists who were paired up as leaders of three groups. We all met together weekly in a group supervisory consultation. Two of the groups were moving along nicely; the third was doing spectacularly well, with all the group members orgasmic by the fifth session. I had never seen a group progress so rapidly, and we tried to figure out what the leaders were doing to obtain such rapid results. They could think of nothing except that after every consultation they told their group how much better they were doing than the other two groups. They had inadvertently set up a process of positive competition similar to that researched in the famous Robbers Caves experiment, which showed that campers performed best and were most motivated to win contests when structured in such a way that they never personally competed against their opponents but instead received daily notice from the counselors indicating lower scores for the opposing campers (Sherif et al., 1961). This group had no losers: the losers were in the other groups and no one had to feel guilty about being more successful than anonymous opponents.

These are just a few examples of some group norms and the process employed in dealing with them. It is important to stress again that group norms are difficult to identify because they represent that which is unspoken. However, it is possible for the therapist, with the aid of the group members, to recognize the presence of a negative group norm, isolate it and reverse it thereby freeing the women to become orgasmic.

Attaining Orgasm

It is not uncommon for women who have had their first orgasm to come to the group looking different from the way they looked prior to the experience. Frequently, they have had their hair cut or styled; they may wear makeup to the group for the first time; or they may dress more carefully or in a different fashion. In most cases the woman looks more attractive, as if she is demonstrating that she feels better about herself and deserves to take greater pains with her appearance. It is always a genuine delight to see this transformation.

The first orgasm generally occurs between the fourth and the sixth session. Orgasms occurring earlier are unusual, especially since the homework to masturbate has not yet been assigned. If no woman has had an orgasm by the sixth session a negative group norm probably is in effect and there is reason to be concerned about the group process.

EARLY ORGASMS

Women who become orgasmic by the second or third session are generally those who require little more than a structured, supportive, and permission giving environment. The process of deciding to seek help and applying for group membership is sufficient to enable some women to masturbate to orgasm even before the first session.

Women who experience orgasm very early in the process are often embarrassed and reluctant to share their success with the group. One woman had an orgasm before the second session but did not tell the group until the third and even then was reluctant to do so. The concern of many women who are successful early is that the other group members consequently will dislike them. And, in fact, the other members frequently are jealous.

The real problem with early orgasms from the therapist's point of view is that the other group members may not have developed sufficient identification with the newly orgasmic woman to set off the chain reaction that is a crucial part of the process. The newly orgasmic woman was just like the others before she had her orgasm and she is no different now; her whole life has not changed, but she is having and enjoying orgasms. The other women begin to believe that perhaps orgasm is possible for them, too. For example, when June had her first orgasm she immediately telephoned another woman in her group with whom she had become friendly. The second woman had her first orgasm the same night. But the domino effect requires that group members identify with one another. When a woman becomes orgasmic too early in the process she is seen as being different from the others; they do not easily identify with her. Often, the impact of this first orgasm is insufficient to establish the necessary momentum. In this situation I attempt to promote identification by

171

having the orgasmic woman describe in as great detail as possible any negative feelings, fears, and difficulties she may have had in regard to her first orgasmic experience.

ELICITING DETAILS

The first woman in the group to have an orgasm rarely reports it with certaintly. Typically, first orgasms are mild in intensity and may differ from the woman's expectation. Furthermore, women are hesitant about building up hope that what they experienced was really an orgasm for fear they might be wrong. Finally, as previously mentioned, it is often difficult for a woman in a group situation to "win" by reaching orgasm first.

Because of the woman's difficulty in identifying her first orgasm, it is important to delve into the details of the masturbation experience. I usually get the most reliable clues if I ask the woman when she stopped masturbating and why. If she discontinued masturbating because it was the end of the hour, it is unlikely that orgasm occurred. However, if she stopped because she felt a buildup and then something different, or had a sensation of warmth and relaxation, or just did not feel like going on anymore, especially if her clitoris felt very tender or sensitive afterwards, I can be fairly certain she experienced an orgasm. Most women also note contractions of the pubococcygeal muscle at orgasm. However, contrary to Kline-Graber and Graber, who contend that "these contractions are the hallmark of orgasms . . . without them, *there has been no orgasm* [1975:4]," I find that many orgasmic women either do not experience contractions or are not aware of them. The following excerpt illustrates the details sought to ascertain if a women is orgasmic.

JOSEPHINE: I didn't have any real luck. One day I was masturbating so much that, I was using lotion, that my fingers kept getting all wrinkled. I thought, "Well, I guess I've tried long enough." I kept on trying.
THERAPIST: Well, what happened?
JOSEPHINE: It's just the same as usual.
THERAPIST: Well, what's usual?
JOSEPHINE: I get to a certain point and it seems like something's going on and then I kept masturbating past that, but nothing

more happened. I don't know if I was more or less aroused afterwards.

THERAPIST: Okay, you get to a point where something is happening. What do you mean by something is happening?

JOSEPHINE: It feels like I'm almost at the point where I'm going to have an orgasm.

THERAPIST: What does that point feel like?

JOSEPHINE: I don't know. I'm really turned on and excited. How can I explain it to someone?

THERAPIST: Well, try to explain it. What kinds of feelings are they? Would you give them a word like a tingling, buzzing? Where do you feel them? What's happening in your body? What's your breathing doing?

JOSEPHINE: I feel mostly right on my clitoris and my vagina. I didn't get any tingle from it. Not sure about my breathing. I try to take short breaths and deep breaths.

THERAPIST: Okay, so it doesn't matter much how you breathe. Does it feel like it's intense down there?

JOSPEHINE: Yeah, a little.

THERAPIST: Then what? Does it start feeling different after that or does it go dead or numb?

JOSEPHINE: No, I don't feel dead. I still have a lot of sensations there, but I guess I feel like I want to stop for while and rest. I just want to stop masturbating and rest. But this time I kept on trying after.

In no case can I determine conclusively that another woman has experienced an orgasm. Erring in either direction creates problems. If I mistakenly confirm a report, the woman may become confused and frustrated should she be unable to identify additional orgasms. I may then find myself near the last session with a woman who is bewildered and upset. If I fail to confirm an orgasm, the woman may be orgasmic while continuing to feel sexually inadequate. Consequently, if I think a woman has had an orgasm, I usually say that it "sounds like" an orgasm to me, but since we are not absolutely certain she should repeat the homework, paying special attention to the details. If an orgasm did occur, it is almost always repeated. If it did not, some "optimistic doubt" will often reduce the woman's anxiety about the experience of orgasm itself. If a woman thinks she has had an orgasm and her worst fears were not realized, generally she will be more relaxed and optimistic about future experiences. Many women claim, after they have had a clearly defined orgasm, that previously they had been experiencing "mini-orgasms."

When the first clearly identified orgasm is reported to the group, I generally prefer to let the group members question the woman.* Sometimes the group responds as if they are a bit shell-shocked and I have to initiate the discussion by commenting, "It's interesting that no one is particularly interested in [so-and-so's] orgasm." After the group has elicited the details from the woman, I may have to place her experience in perspective. If her orgasm was intense, I note that most first orgasms are fairly mild. If she reported any idiosyncratic body experiences (urinating, vibrating legs, hot feet, gasping for air), I point them out so that the other women do not expect to respond in an identical manner.

Once the orgasm has been thoroughly explored I always ask the other group members how they feel hearing that someone else has had an orgasm. The response is twofold. On the one hand, the women are hopeful: "If it could happen to her, maybe it could happen to me." On the other, they feel jealous or resentful: "Why couldn't it have been me?" Generally, only the positive feelings are expressed initially. If no one mentions negative feelings, I elicit them so that the women do not go home feeling secretly they are terrible or wicked for wishing ill toward someone who has experienced success. (The danger here, of course, if that guilt about ill wishes can create a sense of being personally undeserving of an orgasm.)

After the first orgasm has been experienced, the woman is instructed to continue the masturbation homework in order to learn more about this newfound process. Orgasm oriented partner homework is not assigned until the woman is reliably orgasmic with masturbation.†

WOMEN SLOW TO REACH ORGASM

A number of approaches can be taken with a woman who has not experienced her first orgasm by the ninth session. The therapist ought first to understand why the woman is encountering difficulty

---

*Every first orgasm reported in the group is explored at length.

†By "reliably orgasmic" I mean that a woman reaches orgasm most of the time she masturbates and has a good understanding of her process of sexual arousal and release.

in order to determine what future approach would be most effective. The therapist should remember that some withholding, resistant women become orgasmic in the month or two *after* the group has ended.

I may offer an eleventh session to a woman who has recently made significant headway and for whom orgasm does not appear to be too far off. She is free to refuse an additional session, but if she says yes, she can determine how much time she requires in the interim and then invite the other group members and the leaders to join her. (The women who wish to attend will have to pay for the extra meeting. The ten session program is very short and most women have sexual agendas, particularly regarding partner exercises, that they are working on. Thus, there may be considerable interest in a postgroup session, which does not take the place of the regular follow-up.)

Another approach is to try to take the pressure off the woman. First, the therapist should discuss with her how it feels to be last—after all, someone has to be last. Second, she should instruct the woman to report at the following session that she has not had an orgasm whether or not she has. This tactic aims to protect the woman from group pressure to perform; women who then experience orgasm always enthusiastically disregard this instruction, as the following transcript, from a final session, demonstrates: Beverly was given the instruction in the ninth session to report no orgasm to the group at the next meeting.

BEVERLY: I had an orgasm. At 3 P.M., reading *Fanny Hill*. I'm embarrassed a little. Everybody was very supportive last week. I was saying, "My God, I'm doing this like a text book. Doing this, doing the breathing." I listened to what everybody had said, "Do your homework and don't expect it." So I didn't. I started reading and doing—I'm still feeling quite as stimulated as I have on other occasions—but it's not going to happen and I thought, "But don't let it happen. Well, it's not going to happen anyway." I was having this conversation with myself. But, I will say that there's no doubt. I really didn't think it would be that sharp a sensation.

THERAPIST: What was it like? Were you using your hands or a vibrator?

BEVERLY: I was using a new vibrator but the position for me was different. It was the way Abby had described it: your legs up against the side of the bed, against the wall.

ABBY: You put them up against the side of the bed or wall and you get resistance. When you're making love with somebody, try that.

BEVERLY: That's what I was doing and I was turning the pages. And kept more or less, more stimulated, and I thought, "No, no, no, turn it off, turn it off." And all of a sudden I felt a flooding and I thought to myself, "I hope this is different." This *is* different and I just put the book down.

PAMELA: Where did you feel it?

BEVERLY: I felt it very definitely in the genital area. Very strongly. There was like an electric current all the way through up to my face. I felt it very strongly. I would say it was the way I anticipated it but didn't think it would be as uncontrollable. I thought that I would have control over it.

THERAPIST: Did that scare you?

BEVERLY: A little, but not enough to make me stop. I couldn't have stopped it really. You really couldn't stop it. It seemed to go on for a long time.

ABBY: What happened with you and urinating? Did you do that?

BEVERLY: Yes, I told you before that I always did that. And what I did because I just didn't want to get up, I just turned over on the towel after I climaxed. I just let a few drops out. And then I thought, "Well, there was no doubt in my mind." So, then I thought, "Should I try it again? Don't press your luck." But I did.

THERAPIST: Now, what was the difference? What allowed it to happen this time and it hadn't in the past?

BEVERLY: I don't know. I have felt as close to it before. I have felt the pressure. I think the position made the difference.

PAMELA: That's a real success story.

THERAPIST: That's wonderful. Just under the wire: 3:17 P.M. today.

BEVERLY: No, 3:10 P.M. to about 3:20 P.M.

LATE ORGASMS

I might be skeptical about a woman who is last or next to last to report experiencing a first orgasm, especially if her account is cloudy or if the woman is unsure. Group pressure is so strong that it is possible for a woman who feels no hope about attaining her goal to report success simply to gain acceptance and approval. Throughout the course of the therapy I make it clear that a woman is not a failure if the group process does not work for her within ten sessions. A second group or even an alternative form of therapy may be required for a particular woman.

CHAPTER 7

Partner Sex

ONCE A PREORGASMIC WOMAN has attained orgasm with masturbation, she can be considered situationally orgasmic, meaning that she is now orgasmic in certain situations (with masturbation) but not in others (with a partner). For most such women, transfer of the orgasm to the partner relationship is fairly easy. Initially, these women had little idea of what produces an orgasm. After they learn and accept that what makes them feel good sexually is normal and right, they can, with little shame or embarrassment, apply this knowledge to their sexual relationships. Women who were situationally orgasmic at the beginning of the group can progress to partner related work once they have become sexually comfortable and secure through bridging and partner preparation assignments. As always, each woman moves at her own pace.

Bridging Techniques

Before couple related exercises are begun, the women can practice bridging techniques designed to teach them the skills and build

178

the confidence needed for work with partners. The main purpose of the bridging techniques is to make masturbation similar to what happens during sex with a partner. These exercises are aimed at enlarging the repertoire of positions and stroking techniques that produce orgasm. Bridging techniques are also useful for women who have no current sexual partner but wish to prepare to be orgasmic with a partner at a later date, as well as for newly orgasmic women who do have a partner but do not feel ready or willing to begin partner work and yet wish to expand their self-sexuality.

POSITION VARIATIONS

A woman who learns to have orgasms masturbating in only one position may have difficulty responding orgasmically by herself or with a partner in other positons. Adding new positions to those with which she is already comfortable (from back to stomach to side, standing, sitting, or kneeling) makes her more flexible sexually. Although learning to switch from one position to another is difficult at first, once acquired this ability is rarely lost.

In trying out new positons, the woman should keep all the other aspects of masturbation constant (her stroking technique, her fantasizing, her setting). The woman can choose either to start masturbating in the new position or to begin in the usual position and switch to the new one once she becomes aroused. The level of arousal can be expected to diminish with the change in position. If the woman cannot regain arousal in the new position, she should switch back and forth between the familiar position and the new one as frequently as necessary until she is able to maintain a high level of arousal in the new position. A number of practice sessions may be required before the woman experiences orgasm in the new position. In the interim, she can reach orgasm in the familiar way if and when she desires to do so.

STROKING VARIATIONS

New stroking techniques can broaden responsiveness. A woman can change the area, speed, and intensity of self-stimulation according to her needs at a particular moment. Her partner, however, does not have instantaneous feedback, so that the stimulation provided by a partner cannot be as precise as self-stimulation. She may therefore become anxious with a partner and find herself turned off or feel frustrated because she believes she can arouse herself better. Trying lighter or less direct strokes or using the hand not usually used can teach her that the stimulation does not always have to be exact in order to be pleasurable and that even if arousal decreases, it can be regained once effective stimulation is reinstated.

Women who wish to become aware of and responsive to more subtle stimulation should try light genital stroking for approximately 20 minutes a day. Those who need hard and direct clitoral stimulation to experience orgasm and even those who are responsive to a more delicate touch may not reach orgasm in this way. The object of the exercise is to identify and enjoy more subtle sexual feelings.

Finally, most women tend to move the hand against the body when they masturbate. A useful exercise is to have the woman move her body against her hand in order to simulate the kind of clitoral stimulation that occurs with thrusting during intercourse.

VAGINAL INSERTS

To simulate coitus, vaginal inserts can be added to the exercise of moving the body against the hand. Some women who have learned to have orgasms by clitoral stimulation may find the vaginal sensations a distraction at first. By having something in the vagina while they masturbate, they can grow accustomed to the new sensations without also having to be concerned about interacting with another person.

Anything that is safe to put in the vagina can be used in this exercise—dildos, vegetables (zucchini, cucumbers, carrots), candles, empty plastic bottles, or phallic-shaped vibrators. Obviously, nothing made of glass, which can break, or wood, which can splinter, should be used. All vegetables should be carefully washed or peeled to eliminate pesticides, which can irritate the vaginal tissue. Women have also found that insertion of vegetables is more comfortable if the vegetables are at room temperature. Scented candles can produce allergic reactions. If small plastic bottles are used, they should be inserted bottom first to avoid creating a vacuum in the vagina, making removal of the bottle difficult or dangerous. Also, any bottle used should be empty.

Inserting something phallic in the vagina not only enhances the pleasure of masturbation for many women but also takes what already works, clitoral stimulation, and adds one new element to make self-sexuality more like sex with a male partner. This exercise paves the way for the later assignment of intercourse with clitoral stimulation.

Considerations about Couple Work

It is important not to assign couple sexual homework until the woman feels confident about her own sexuality and wants to begin exercises with a partner. If she feels insecure about her masturbatory responses, very awkward about approaching her partner, or overly-aware of her partner's feelings toward her, it might be wise to continue working on these feelings, using role-playing and fantasy along with some nonsexual communication and nonsexual touching exercises (pp. 185–193). Although partner homework is discussed in the group, each woman will begin partner assignments only when she is ready to do so. In a mixed group of preorgasmic and situationally orgasmic women, some will begin couple exercises as early as the fifth session; others my not do any partner homework until the group ends.

Many women feel unsure about their newfound orgasms or do not want to share this experience immediately with a partner. To some it feels like giving away a brand-new toy that they have not fully enjoyed playing with yet. They need completely to "own" the orgasm before they feel secure enough to share it. Unless there are serious relationship problems, however, most women want to include their partners within a few months of becoming reliably orgasmic. The therapist should let the woman determine her timetable rather than pressure her to move ahead simply because the group is drawing to a close. Some women may require a second group, but most are able to use the tools they have acquired in the ten sessions to progress on their own after the group has ended.

Giving couple assignments while working with only one partner can present difficulties. The therapist must be knowledgeable about family systems to understand the complexities of relationships and to take a broad range of factors into account as assignments are formulated. The pregroup interview with both partners, as previously mentioned, can provide insight into the couple's relationship. If the therapist knows little about the couple, a conservative stance is wise when introducing specific changes in the relationship.

Although the women's group therapists cannot work directly with the relationship system, as in conjoint therapy, it is still possible significantly to alter this system by changing one of the members. As the woman changes, the relationship necessarily changes, as well. The structure of the therapy places major responsibility for change on the woman's shoulders. She is the one who must relay the relevant information and carry out the requisite homework assignments. Since in most instances, her partner grew up with the same cultural restrictions, anxieties, and negative messages about sex, she may have a delicate task to accomplish. The woman must first overcome her own gender linked cultural expectations and assert herself sexually in order to carry out the exercises. Her partner must overcome his need to be the authority on sex and be willing to learn from his female partner. She must then supply the pertinent sexual information and be strong and secure enough to weather any anxiety they both may encounter. This is a tall order, especially since the role scripting of the woman encourages her to maintain the status quo in order to protect her partner from discomfort and discourages her from initiating and directing sexual interactions.

Not all men are threatened by a lover's growing competence in sexual expression. Actually, most partners are relieved to gain information on female sexuality. By this time in the process many of the men have developed trust in the preorgasmic program simply through watching the women become more sexually responsive, more communicative about sex, and more willing to initiate sexual activities. However, Barbach and Flaherty (1978) studied situationally orgasmic women and found that although the women's group treatment was highly successful for women with casual partners and women in serious relationships of less than 18 months' duration, it was not so successful for women in serious relationships of over three years' duration: 11 of the 14 women (79 per cent) in casual or shorter term relationships had become orgasmic with a partner more than 50 per cent of the time at the 12–24-month follow-up whereas this level was reached by only 6 of the 12 women (50 percent) in longer term relationships. This study may underscore the usefulness of involving the partner directly in treatment in order to overcome negative sexual patterns. However, since the unsuccessful women had also not attempted to carry out the difficult partner assignments, it may also indicate that certain relationship factors must be resolved before some women are willing to work wholeheartedly on partner related sex.

LESBIAN COUPLES

Some of the difficulties that arise as a result of sex-role scripting are often not present in lesbian relationships, but anxiety about sex and other relationship problems are independent of sexual preference: homosexual couples tend to be more similar to, than different from, heterosexual ones in these respects.

Learning to be comfortable with sexual activity has relatively little to do with sexual orientation. A dildo can substitute for a penis in lesbian lovemaking if one or both partners enjoys the feeling of something inside the vagina; similarly, heterosexual couples can have a satisfying sexual experience without ever having the penis enter the vagina. *Loving Women*, a book on lesbian sexuality by Nomadic Sisters, defines a penis as "a substitute for a dildo [1976:3]." The exact reverse is used to define a dildo. It all depends on one's perspective.

Learning to have orgasms with masturbation involves a similar process for all women regardless of sexual orientation. When it comes time to share the experience with a partner, again the process is more similar than different. The partner must be made aware of the woman's unique sexual likes, dislikes, and areas of sensitivity. Each person must learn to communicate her needs to a partner. That the partner is another woman does not mean that she will be any more aware of her lover's uniqueness than a man might be.

Sexual satisfaction requires the same consideration regardless of the sex of the partners. Each sexual experience involving two people is a special meeting of both partners' personalities, past experiences, and comfort with their own sexuality; relationship and situational factors also affect their encounter.

Both homosexual and heterosexual relationships have communication and interactional problems. In both cases the therapist must take into account the partner's possibly negative sexual attitudes, as well as the unique values and relationship dynamics of the couple. In the following descriptions of partner exercises, I sometimes use masculine pronouns to facilitate the flow of the text. However, with the exception of the intercourse exercise, all exercises are equally appropriate for heterosexual and lesbian couples.

PARTNER PREPARATION

To provide permission and information to the partner, particularly before the group begins, is an essential aspect of the group process. And following up the women's group with either between two and four couples' group or conjoint sessions will help to clarify and possibly to resolve many troublesome sexual issues.

It is often useful to distinguish between women who are trying to change an old sexual relationship and those who are trying to begin a new one: the difficulties encountered are different for each. Women in long-term relationships generally enjoy security and trust developed over years spent together. This sense of security can make them more comfortable initiating discussions concerning sex and new sexual activities. However, changing old patterns may require continued attention after the initial overtures are made. New relationships, in contrast, pose the reverse problem: though they do not have to overcome negative patterns and experiences, the women must possess considerable strength and self-confidence to broach the subject of sexuality when no solid foundation of trust yet exists.

In general, I let the group members determine the pace of partner involvement in the sexual exercises. If a couple appears to have serious relationship problems, I usually prefer to prepare them for conjoint therapy rather than have them engage in sexual activities that may increase the stress in the relationship. Whether or not conjoint therapy will be required, the first step is to have the couple begin discussing sexuality. When sexual communication or initiation of sexual activities is a problem, sexual progress typically is slow. Obviously, the woman must be able to communicate what she has learned about her body to her partner in order to teach her partner the kind of sexual stimulation she requires to reach orgasm.

The first task for a woman with communication problems is to learn to talk with her partner about sex or to initiatiate sexual activities nonverbally—whichever process is more comfortable for her. If she wants to reherase verbal initiation of the exercise, she can role-play the interaction with a leader or another group member. To make the role-play meaningful, I may ask her to describe the most unpleasant response she can imagine her partner having; the role-play partner then presents that response. If the woman wants to be able to initiate sex nonverbally, I again ask about her worst fear as to how the interaction could go wrong; then I have her fantasize this outcome and describe how she might deal with it. The role-play or fantasy rehearsal can be repeated for each of the couple assignments as often as necessary until the woman is ready to try the exercise in actuality. (Role-playing is also useful as preparation for women who do not currently have a sexual partner.)

When attempting to explain an exercise verbally to a partner, it is useful for the woman to state first how she feels at that moment. Comments such as "I'm anxious now as I think about explaining our sex homework" or "I'm afraid you won't like this assignment, but it is important to me that you listen" help avoid the possibility that the partner will misinterpret the woman's anxiety as anger, contempt, or rejection and enhance the likelihood that he will listen attentively and respond supportively.

Couple Assignments

Couple homework assignments can be divided into four general areas: nonsexual communication exercises, nonsexual touching exercises, sexual communication exercises, and sexual touching exercises.* These are not necessarily designed as a progression. Some couples benefit from beginning with nonsexual exercises, others may start with those that are explicitly sexual. The assignments described in this section have been useful for many couples and can be tailored to meet the particular difficulties a woman and her partner are having—always using the principles of small steps and safety.

NONSEXUAL COMMUNICATION EXERCISES

Exercises to enhance communication between partners can be assigned at any point at which such an assignment seems relevant to a given group member. Nonsexual communication exercises pave the way for sexual communication. Bach and Goldberg's *Creative Ag-*

---

*These exercises have been gathered from various sources and have been passed around by word of mouth for so long, with so many changes in the process, that I must apologize if the sources I credit are not the original ones.

gression (1974), Bach and Deutsch's *Pairing* (1970), and Bach and Wyden's *The Intimate Enemy* (1968) are useful resources in this area.

Listening

Many couples with sexual difficulties slowly grow apart. As each person becomes more involved with his or her individual problems, less and less time is spent sharing feelings and activities. Closeness in a relationship is built on the sharing of feelings. Sometimes solutions to existing problems are sought in this sharing process, but for the most part a sympathetic ear is all that is required. In fact, many relationship problems arise because one partner seeks solace but instead receives solutions. Teaching couples to listen to one another without problem solving can provide considerable benefit.

I frequently suggest that the couple talk for approximately five minutes every evening about how their days went. While one person talks the other should listen with interest but without offering advice, solutions, or corrections. The only responses allowed in addition to supportive comments are questions asking for further information or clarification.

In one instance, this assignment produced unexpected and far-reaching results. Irene's partner was unwilling to participate in any of the homework exercises and disapproved of Irene's membership in the group. She therefore had to be creative in order to benefit from the couple exercises without angering her partner further. Irene wanted to try the listening exercise, so she engineered it to fit her unique circumstances. When she and her partner were having the kind of discussion that ordinarily would degenerate into a fight, she used the opportunity merely to listen attentively. Irene's partner commented on how good their talk had been. When Irene did not respond in her usual defensive way, her partner felt she understood him and the discussion ended pleasantly.

Active Listening

Active listening is a communication feedback exercise designed to handle disagreement. However, this technique should be practiced first with neutral issues. Exercises using active listening can be found in Gordon's *P.E.T.: Parent Effectiveness Training* (1970). The object of active listening is to slow down the escalation process that occurs during an argument and to keep both people listening to each other rather than formulating defenses (or offenses).

Using active listening requires that after one partner has said perhaps three or four sentences, the listener feeds back the content of the speaker's message in his or her own words. The judge of the correctness of the feedback is the speaker. It is possible for the listener to repeat the exact words the speaker used but with sufficiently different intonation for the speaker to feel that he or she has not been understood. Should the speaker feel misunderstood, he or she is to repeat the message and the listener is again to feed back what has been heard. This process continues until the speaker has completed the message and feels understood. Roles are then reversed and the new speaker presents his or her side of the story with the new listener feeding back what he or she hears. This checking out process significantly slows down the discussion, thus helping the participants to keep it focused. Active listening aims to insure that the two people are in fact disagreeing about the same thing and not responding to what may be erroneous conceptions of each other's position.

Appreciations and Annoyances

This communication exercise is an adaptation of an exercise described by Bach and Goldberg (1974). It takes only three minutes a day and helps keep the air clear of resentments, thereby setting the stage for renewed sexual interest. It also helps teach people to talk with each other about their likes and dislikes. The exercise, used initially in nonsexual areas, can later be applied to sex.

In the evening, one partner begins by stating three things the other did during the previous 24 hours that annoyed him or her. The annoyances should be small ones like leaving socks on the floor or not paying a bill. It is essential that the annoyances have occurred within the previous 24 hours so that the partners do not dig up past grievances. The three annoyances are followed by three appreciations–small things the other person did during the previous 24 hours that were appreciated. An appreciation might be a telephone call at work, a kiss in the morning, or remembering a small chore. The appreciations follow the annoyances to convey the message that "although this, this, and this bothered me, I still love you."*

---

*It is against the rules to be annoyed by an annoyance. That is, it is unacceptable to say, after the first person has stated his or her three annoyances and three appreciations, "I'm annoyed that you were annoyed by. . . ."

After both people have stated their three annoyances and three appreciations, they are to spend an hour thinking about what was said before talking further. Postponing discussion increases the likelihood that they will understand each other's position rather than merely defend their own. It is important that each person comprehend that the other was annoyed even if the action causing the annoyance was unintentional or unavoidable.

Some people have great difficulty finding three items of both sorts, especially if the couple has spent only a few hours together in the preceding 24. In these cases, I encourage the couple to look for very small annoyances and appreciations. If even that is too difficult they can exchange only one or two annoyances and appreciations as long as they are of equal number. To cite only annoyances and no appreciation is unconstructive, and to mention only appreciations and no annoyances may be passive-aggressive. Later, this exercise can be modified to communicate sexual likes and dislikes.

Laura would occasionally park her car in front of the driveway. When her husband came home from work, he would have to move her car before he could park his own in the garage. On these days he would walk into the house angry but would never say anything. The exercise enabled him for the first time to mention this annoying situation. Once he told Laura about it, she stopped parking her car in front of the driveway. With this constant annoyance gone, they began to feel more positive toward one another. These good feelings reinforced continued practice of the exercises, which in turn fostered better communication in general.

NONSEXUAL TOUCHING EXERCISES

When couples are having sexual difficulties, they frequently eliminate all forms of touching from their interactions for fear that a nonsexual but affectionate hug might be misinterpreted as a sexual advance, which, if acted upon, could lead to anxiety or to an unsatisfying sexual encounter. Avoidance of physical contact exacerbates their sense of estrangement. Touching is a very important form of communication for all animals. Having a couple resume nonsexual touching can diminish the feeling of distance between the two and promote intimacy. Touching that prohibits sexual interaction reduces anxiety and allows sexual feelings to surface. Finally, the communication fostered by nonsexual touching exercises helps desensitize the couple to communicating about sexual touching.

Sensate Focus

Sensate focus exercises, derived from the work of Masters and Johnson (1970), are massage exercises that follow certain ground rules. For couples who have avoided sexual activity for a considerable period of time or who are very anxious about reestablishing a sexual relationship, it is often best to begin with massage of the extremities (hands, face, feet). For couples who feel physically comfortable with each other, a back or full-body massage can be assigned initially. When a full-body massage is assigned, I do not place breasts and genitals off limits because I find that more attention is called to these areas by avoiding them. Instead, I tell the couple to treat the breasts and genitals like any other part of the body, not giving them more or less attention than other parts, and not to attempt to arouse the person being massaged. Whenever possible, the touching exercises are to be carried out with both partners in the nude in an area that is comfortable and private. The partners are instructed to take turns giving and receiving massages. However, the massages need not be exchanged on the same night since some people cannot fully enjoy being massaged knowing all the while that they will soon have to rouse themselves to reciprocate.

The sensate focus exercises are assigned from two vantage points: for the interest of the massager and for the enjoyment of the recipient.

Sensate Focus for the Interest of the Massager

The first massage is designed to give permission to the massager to experiment with various kinds of touching, to discover what he or she can about the partner's body, and to learn the recipient's preferences in being touched.

The assignment is explicitly given for the "interest" and not the "enjoyment" of the giver. This instruction discourages the massager from indirectly expressing resentment or feelings of inadequacy by saying that he or she did not enjoy giving the massage. It is difficult to hold people accountable for lack of enjoyment; however, making an experience "interesting" is under the individual's control. If the massager does not find this assignment interesting a discussion can ensue about what he or she could have done to make the experience a more interesting one.

Setting the exercise up in this way frequently exposes a partner's tendency to be more concerned about pleasing the other person than himself or herself. Since the primary problems of women who do not experience orgasm with a partner are the woman's overconcern with her partner's pleasure and the woman's embarrassment if her partner is overly concerned with her enjoyment, this exercise often proves that a physical interaction can be highly pleasurable for both people if they each concentrate on selfish enjoyment. When the giver thoroughly enjoys what he or she is doing the receiver can guiltlessly and unself-consciously enjoy the pleasure received. Consequently, this is one exercise in which far more can be learned by a so-called initial failure than by an immediate success.

I assign the massage for half an hour to an hour unless either partner is uncomfortable with massage or very reluctant. In those cases, I have the couple determine the amount of time they would feel comfortable with and then I subtract five or 10 minutes to help reduce any pressure they may feel.

Since the massage is for the interest of the giver, it is important to build in some protection for the receiver so that the experience is not negative for him or her. Therefore, I stipulate that if the touching is pleasurable or at least neutral, the receiver is to say nothing except to answer any questions posed by the giver. However, if the touching is unpleasant, the receiver is to let the giver know in a positive way; that is, the receiver is to tell the giver how he or she can change the touch to make it pleasurable or neutral. For example: "The muscles are sore in my shoulder. Please massage more gently there"; "That tickles. Would you touch me more firmly?" Too many people, for fear of hurting a partner's feelings, are reluctant to indicate that being touched in certain ways is disagreeable. But this kind of thoughtful deceit creates problems in the long run. If one partner cannot trust the other enough to let him or her know when something is uncomfortable, then the giver must second-guess the partner, which not only takes considerable effort but also detracts from the sexual experience. Trusting one another to say when the touching is not pleasurable is fostered by instructing the giver to elicit at least two negative responses from the receiver even if to do so requires actively producing a negative reaction. This aspect of the exercise can also ease concern about pleasing the partner.

After the massage, the couple is to spend 10 or 15 minutes discussing what the experience was like for each of them. This postmassage conversation frequently is more important than the massage itself since it enables deeper feelings to be explored and shared.

I rarely put a ban on intercourse for women with concerns about orgasm, but in order to separate the touching from sex I have the couple agree that no genitally oriented sexual activity will occur until at least an hour after the exercise has ended. This helps prevent the anticipatory anxiety that the massage might turn into a sexual event, an expectation that can keep sexual feelings from surfacing.

Sensate Focus for the Enjoyment of the Recipient

The purpose of massage for the recipient's enjoyment is different from that of the previous exercise but the instructions still include a ban on sex for an hour afterward, a 10- to 15-minute discussion about the massage once it is over, and alternation of roles as giver and receiver on the same or consecutive days.

This exercise is designed to encourage assertiveness in asking for specific kinds of pleasuring. The receiver is responsible for indicating the areas and types of touching preferred throughout the massage. Many women feel that if they request a certain type of stimulation from a partner "it had better work." If they are not certain that the stimulation will produce an orgasm, they are reluctant to ask for it. This exercise takes the pressure off requesting specific types of touching.

Many men think they should know the kind of touch a woman prefers and hence are not comfortable asking about what feels good. Men in particular, but many women as well, hesitate to experiment with sensual or sexual activities because of feelings of inadequacy and fear of failure. This exercise supplies the massager with specific information on the kinds of touch the partner finds pleasurable. Because explicit information is being transmitted, the giver is protected from the possibility of failing.

To create a situation that both encourages the recipient to ask for specific types of touch without feeling she or he has to perform and provides the giver with maximum feedback, I tell the receiver to supply a constant flow of instructions and reactions. For example: "Please massage my stomach. A little firmer touch, please. Just a bit higher. There—that feels terrific. That feels so good I'm going to be quiet for a few minutes just to enjoy the sensations. That was lovely.

191

Could you try stroking higher up for a bit now?'' If I give specific examples of what I mean by feedback, the women have a clearer understanding of the exercise, and with better understanding comes greater confidence in carrying out the assignment.

Home Sexological Exam

The sexological exam (''playing doctor'') was designed by Hartman and Fithian (1972) to desensitize couples to touching each other's genitals, as well as to provide a forum for exchanging explicit information about genital sensitivity. This exercise is similar to the women's genital exam assigned in the second group session but is carried out with a partner.

In giving the instructions I always mention that the couple will probably feel very awkward and uncomfortable when they are about to begin the exercise. They may find themselves giggling and wondering whether such a seemingly absurd experience could teach them anything. They are directed to continue with the exam even though it may seem very contrived.

The couple decide who will explore the other's genitals first. Then, with the aid of a mirror and diagrams of male and female genitals, they are to point out and label all the anatomical structures. They are then to explore the various areas of the genitals using strokes of different length and pressure. After every stroke, the person being examined rates the sensitivity of the touch on a scale from -3 to $+3$, with -3 being very unpleasant, 0 neutral, and $+3$ very pleasurable. A minimum of ten minutes is assigned for each person's exam to insure that the couple's anxiety does not lead them to gloss over the exercise too rapidly.

The therapist can reduce the partner's anxiety about doing the assignment by giving suggestions on how to proceed. I suggest that the scrotum, shaft of the penis, glans of the penis, outer labia, inner labia, clitoral hood, and glans of the clitoris, for example, be explored to see whether strokes using the index finger in a downward direction are more pleasurable than those in an upward direction or whether a firmer touch is more pleasurable than a lighter touch. If a finger is inserted in the women's vagina and they imagine the vaginal opening as the face of a clock, does she feel more sensations when pressure is placed at 12 o'clock, 1 o'clock, 3 o'clock, 5 o'clock, and so on?

I make it clear that a man's genitals can be explored whether or not he has an erection. In either case, the woman is encouraged to squeeze the penis slowly and firmly until her partner indicates that the pressure is becoming uncomfortable: she thereby gains some security in touching him without fear of hurting him. Stroking the man's inner thigh and observing the premasteric reflex, which causes the hair follicles on the testicles to undulate is almost always found interesting. If the man gets an erection it is useful to repeat the stroking motions to see whether there are any differences in preference between the flaccid and the erect state.

Repeating the entire exercise using oil can yield additional information. For example, a woman may realize that the difference between a pleasurable and an unpleasurable touch depends on the presence or absence of sufficient lubrication.

SEXUAL COMMUNICATION EXERCISES

The following exercises are designed explicitly to improve sexual communication. They can be assigned before, during, or after the sexual touching exercises.

Asking for One New Thing Sexually

This exercise is similar in purpose to the sensate focus for the enjoyment of the recipient. Lack of assertiveness is almost always involved when women do not experience orgasm with a partner. Requesting specific kinds of sexual stimulation has not been a part of female role scripting, and women generally feel insecure and embarrassed when they even contemplate making sexual requests. To give a woman practice with this new behavior she is told to ask for or initiate one new thing each time she has sex. The initiation can be either a verbal request or a nonverbal action. For example, the woman can ask to be stimulated orally; actually get on top during intercourse; move her partner's hand to a new position while being manually stimulated; place her own hand on her stomach, slowly move it toward her genital area, and, when that behavior becomes comfortable, stimulate her clitoris herself; or request that her partner continue a particular kind of stimulation for a longer period of time. Initially, the attempt is almost always very awkward, and the woman may be too anxious to enjoy the interaction she has initiated. But after a few trials she generally becomes more comfortable in asserting herself, and her partner is able to stimulate her more effectively with every new piece of information received.

Sexual Readiness Scale

The sexual readiness scale, developed by Engel (1977), is helpful for couples with seemingly dissimilar sex drives. In such cases partner 1 thinks, "My partner never wants sex. If I don't have sex now, goodness knows when I'll have another opportunity." In partner 2's view, "All my partner ever wants is sex. If I give in now it will just be one more time." Each person is so concerned with what the other wants that neither thinks about whether or not he or she is in the mood for sex.

The sexual readiness scale is also useful for couples who are awkward about initiating sex. If one partner strokes the other tentatively for a few seconds and gets no response, he or she will give up. Then, a minute or two later, the second person will begin stroking the first but also will give up quickly if there is no response. Awkwardness prevails until one partner eventually makes his or her desires known or both will give up and go to sleep.

Finally, the sexual readiness scale is useful for women who claim that they never feel turned on, that is, who are out of touch with fluctuations in their sexual feelings.

The sexual readiness scale is a way of rating sexual interest. The scale ranges from 0 (the person is not interested in sex under any circumstances) through 5 (the person is not motivated in either direction and is willing to go along with the partner's desires) to 10 (the person is very much interested in sex). The other numbers represent gradations in between. Later on, the scale can be used to indicate interest in various kinds of sexual activities; for instance, "I'm a 2 for intercourse but an 8 for cuddling."

I usually assign this exercise to be practiced first in nonsexual situations. For example, I have the woman mentally check in with herself to determine her level of sexual readiness three times a day or, if she is in a relationship, instruct her to share sexual readiness information with her partner face to face or by telephone thrice daily during times when they cannot have sex. After a week of sharing this information, couples with dissimilar sex drives gain a more realistic appraisal of their actual differences. The partners generally realize that one is not always a 10 but is frequently a 1 or a 3 and the other is not always a 0 but is sometimes a 4 or even a 6.

After the couple has practiced using the scale outside the bedroom, they are assigned to communicate their sexual readiness level to each other at bedtime, in the morning when they awake and at various other times during the day when sex might possibly occur. This device not only enables both people to consider their own level of sexual interest before reacting to the partner's stance but also helps alleviate the awkward beginning moments of a sexual interaction. If both are at 7 it is safe for them to proceed sexually. If one is at 2 and the other at 3 it is clear that sex is not on the agenda. If they are at 8 and 2, respectively, negotiations can begin.

If the partners' interest in sexual activity differs, one person can obtain sexual release while leaving the other free to participate only to the degree to which he or she desires. Once sexual pleasuring without intercourse becomes acceptable, neither partner needs to feel exploited or deprived when their interest in sex differs. (This subject is discussed later in the chapter under sexual touching exercises.)

Rhonda experienced difficulty using the sexual readiness scale. She generally desired sex far more often than did her partner and had been told about the scale by sex therapists she had seen some months before joining a group. Initially the scale had been effective for her and her partner. However, she had recently reinstated the exercise on her own and felt it was causing problems. When we discussed the details of her use of the scale it became clear that she would ask her partner for his number whenever she was interested in sex. Consequently, the scale was not being used as a way to check in with her partner but was experienced by him as one more sexual demand. So we changed the procedure and had them communicate their numbers on the scale at predetermined hours three times a day rather than whenever Rhonda was in a sexual mood. This modification helped relieve her partner's feeling of being pressured because he could see that Rhonda did not always want sex either. As a result, the frequency of their sexual interaction increased.

SEXUAL TOUCHING EXERCISES

The explicitly sexual touching exercises combine all the earlier exercises of touching and communication in a sexual experience specif-

195

ically designed to enhance learning and promote orgasm. All sexual touching exercises should end with a 15-minute discussion of the encounter by the partners.

Masturbating with a Partner

The seventh step in Lobitz and LoPiccolo's (1972) masturbation program is for the woman to masturbate in front of her partner. Masturbation taken out of the secretive context can create a high level of sharing and intimacy between partners. And masturbating with a partner present is frequently the easiest way for a woman to have her first orgasm with partner sex because it takes what already works—masturbation under the woman's control—and adds one new element—the presence of a partner. However, the partner is not responsible for or in control of the stimulation; the partner merely participates in whatever manner is mutually acceptable.

Having the woman stimulate herself in view of her partner is one way of teaching the partner the exact areas and types of stroking that give the woman the most pleasure. The partner can observe the woman's techniques without being immediately responsible for replicating them, thereby forestalling the anxiety and frustration that could develop if he were immediately expected to apply the stimulation.

This exercise also helps desensitize the couple to masturbation in general so that it can be used as a respectable form of sexual release, particularly when other sexual activities are precluded by physical illness or dissimilar levels of sexual interest. To expect two people from two different backgrounds, with differing daily experiences, heredity, levels of stress, fatigue, preoccupation and frustration to be sexually interested at exactly the same time all the time is totally unrealistic. However, many couples interpret any reduction of sexual interest as lack of caring. This misconception can lead to feelings of inadequacy, especially if the absence of orgasm or erection results from concomitant feelings of anxiety or resentment. Natural differences in sexual interest, which can produce a feeling of distance between two people, are exaggerated when one partner chooses to masturbate in private to gain sexual release and the other accidentally discovers this practice. However, when such differences are seen as natural and reasonable, and carry no messages about being loved and accepted, the couple can use masturbation creatively together, thereby enabling the partner with less sexual interest to participate as much or as little as he or she desires while still sharing the experience. In this way neither feels deprived or resentful.

Although some women are able to initiate self-stimulation with a partner without first preparing the partner, in most cases it is essential to make a preassignment to discuss both individuals' feelings about masturbation and exactly how the exercise will be carried out. The woman's partner has not had the opportunity she has had to become desensitized to masturbation, and his attitude toward it may be negative.

Denise left books and articles about masturbation around the house for her husband to read. When he did not comment on them, she very tentatively broached the subject of masturbation. Her husband replied, "Adults do not masturbate. You do not masturbate. I do not masturbate, and I don't want to hear anymore about it." Denise did not feel sufficiently confident to challenge his beliefs, so she did not initiate this exercise. Couple sex therapy might have provided the support and information her husband required, but he refused to participate in any form of therapy.

I am continually amazed to find how easy it is for many couples to carry out this exercise. Perhaps hearing about the woman's masturbation homework throughout the process is adequate partner preparation in most cases.

One fairly devastating experience, however, taught me to be somewhat cautious. June, a competent, energetic, and enthusiastic group member, had been progressing beautifully. She experienced her first orgasm by the fifth session, had taken on a leadership role early in the group and was clearly respected and admired by the other members. She had been widowed at a very young age and had been living with a man for three years in a very unsatisfactory relationship. She mentioned the problems they were having a number of times in the group and although she was very aware of her dissatisfaction, she had been unable to end the relationship on three occasions over the years. When another group member was assigned the exercise to masturbate with a partner, June decided she would like to try it as well.

I was uneasy about this decision but trusted June's ability to handle the assignment. June did not show up for the following session. When I called her, she apologized and asked me not to tell the other group members what had happened because she felt so embarrassed. Her partner had agreed to the exercise on the condition that a friend of hers also be included. She agreed with interest and enthusiasm but in the actual situation allowed herself to be excluded and was left to observe her partner and good friend together. Although the experience had been painful, she could see how she had undermined herself. However, the incident resulted in her discontinuing the partner homework. (June separated from her partner a few months later and she has since involved herself in more successful emotional and sexual relationships.) The episode reinforced my conviction that adequate partner preparation for this assignment is essential, particularly in relationships that have serious problems.

The masturbating with a partner exercise can be carried out in a number of ways depending upon the feelings of the woman and her partner. If either of them express concern, it is necessary to identify the areas of concern explicitly so that appropriate safety precautions can be employed. The following cases illustrate some areas of concern and the solutions that were arrived at.

Barbara was concerned that she would look unattractive or ugly when she had an orgasm and would disgust her partner. We further isolated the ugliness to her face (she was not concerned about other parts of her body looking ugly). Barbara said she would feel safest masturbating with her partner if he could not see her face, so the exercise was to take place with them lying on their sides with his front flush against her back. He could touch her breasts, legs, and stomach while she stroked her genitals but he could not see her face when she had an orgasm. This arrangement was Barbara's creation. She could have decided to masturbate while sitting between her partner's legs, back to front, as in Masters and Johnson's (1970) nondemand position for female stimulation; with him reading or sitting at the foot of the bed, back turned to her; or in the dark. The best alternative is generally the one the woman designs for herself.

Jean tried to masturbate with her partner present but felt too anxious and embarrassed to continue. At the following group session she decided that he should stay outside the room but know that she was inside masturbating. The next time he stayed in the room but read a newspaper while she masturbated. Following that they masturbated together, side by side.

Diane tried masturbating a number of times with her partner present but had no success. She had learned to masturbate alone quite easily and was unprepared for encountering difficulty with the exercise. We spent considerable time in the group trying to isolate exactly when she became anxious or lost the feeling of arousal. Finally,

Diane realized that although she liked to have her partner stimulate her breasts and legs while she masturbated, she was always afraid that he would take over the genital stimulation even though he never did. To create the sense of safety she required, she explained to her partner that he was not to touch her in the area below the waist and above the knees. With this understanding acknowledged, Diane was able to relax enough the next time to experience orgasm.

Ann did not trust her partner sufficiently and consequently felt too vulnerable to have an orgasm with him. She thought that if he would masturbate in front of her first she would feel secure enough to do it in front of him afterward. Her partner reluctantly agreed, and Ann was so surprised and relieved to find that he, too, felt uncomfortable and awkward that she was able to carry out the exercise with less self-consciousness than she had anticipated.

Since masturbating with a partner present is generally an anxiety-producing exercise, I always state explicitly that it is unusual for a woman to experience orgasm the first time she tries this assignment and that the group members should not expect or try to do so. This caution helps to ease performance pressure. In one group, the first woman who masturbated in front of her partner had an orgasm on the first attempt. I explained how unusual she was and that it typically took most women a few times before they felt relaxed enough to have an orgasm this way. A couple of sessions later another woman, given the same assignment, reported to the group that although she had not experienced orgasm the first time, she remembered what I had said and was not concerned. The next time she did succeed and felt terrific because it took only two attempts. Had her expectations been different, she might not have repeated the exercise.

An Hour of Sexual Pleasuring

An hour of sexual pleasuring gives the couple an opportunity to practice initiating and responding, being active and passive, in a circumscribed sexual situation. It is also designed to lengthen the couple's lovemaking experience. Gebhard's (1966:95) analysis of Kinsey's (1953) data showed that if marital coitus was preceded by over 20 minutes of foreplay, only 7.7 percent of the wives did not experience orgasm.

For this exercise, the couple is asked to set aside an hour to experiment with new techniques of sexual stimulation and to elaborate on or just to enjoy old ones. Intercourse is banned during this exercise, but all other forms of verbal or nonverbal sexual interaction such as oral sex, manual clitoral stimulation, and fantasy sharing are encouraged. The period of an hour is chosen to provide adequate time for sexual arousal, stopping, resting, and communicating about feelings and preferences in a non–goal oriented atmosphere. This assignment differs from the sensate focus massages in that it emphasizes sexual arousal and techniques of genital stimulation.

Intercourse with Clitoral Stimulation

Once a heterosexual woman is orgasmic masturbating with her partner as well as masturbating alone with a phallic object inside the vagina in positions resembling those used during intercourse, it is appropriate to assign Lobitz and LoPiccolo's ninth step, intercourse with clitoral stimulation.

This exercise combines the hour of sexual pleasuring, using various stimulation techniques and lengthy foreplay, with intercourse. Intercourse is not to be initiated until the woman feels sufficiently aroused. At that point, she is to assume a position for intercourse that will allow her to stimulate her clitoris manually or mechanically, with a vibrator, while at the same time remaining in control of the thrusting; for example, the woman in the superior position kneeling over her partner, who is lying on his back, the woman in a kneeling position with her partner entering her from behind, or the couple at right angles, with the man on his side and the woman on her back with one of her legs under and the other over her partner's top leg. In these positions most women can maintain control over both the thrusting and the clitoral stimulation while the partner remains relatively passive. Once the woman can have orgasms this way, her partner can become more active. She can also experiment with other positions that provide access to the clitoris during intercourse.

Partner Manual Stimulation

If the woman wishes to do so, she can teach her partner to apply effective stimulation manually. Although this is Lobitz and LoPiccolo's eighth step, I generally have found it more difficult to accomplish than their ninth step, intercourse with the woman providing clitoral stimulation. The woman can teach her partner stimulation techniques through either verbal or nonverbal instructions. During the initial period, if these new ways do not work, the woman will still be able to provide the effective stimulation when she wants to experience orgasm.

Intercourse

Kaplan (1974) described a program for teaching women to experience orgasm as a result of penile thrusting by decreasing manual clitoral stimulation just prior to orgasm. However, she acknowledged that women fall along a spectrum of responsiveness ranging from those who have orgasms through fantasy alone to those who require lengthy and intense clitoral stimulation to reach orgasm. She noted that intercourse alone may provide insufficient stimulation for many perfectly normal women to attain orgasm. Consequently, some women can use Kaplan's bridging techniques to permit orgasm during intercourse in certain positions. The therapist must be careful not to reinforce the implied message that the "look, Ma, no hands" orgasm is somehow superior. Because all women differ in respect to the sexual manipulations that produce orgasm, it is important to remove the expectation that there is one right way for a woman to respond sexually.

EROTIC ENHANCEMENTS

Doing anything repeatedly can result in its becoming mundane or mechanical. Sexual activities are no exception, particularly in long-term monogamous relationships. However, couples can spice up their sex lives if they are willing to try something new, to risk the possibility that it may be a flop, and to persevere through awkward or uncomfortable initial trials.

Fantasy and other erotic enhancements can help keep a sexual relationship vital. Fantasy can be particularly enjoyable for some women. Hariton and Singer studied women's fantasies during marital intercourse and noted that

> perhaps the major outcome of this investigation is the evidence that in a sample of reasonably normal married women the occurrence of daydreams during sexual relations is quite common and not generally related to interpersonal disturbances, adjustment problems, or lack of fulfillment in the sexual area. It seems likely that fantasy is a general phenomenon, accepted and indulged in more by some wom-

en than others. Its occurrence during the sex act probably reflects a stylistic variation rather than a withdrawal, defense, or alienation [1974:322].

Fantasy can be enjoyed silently without the partner's knowledge. It can be shared with a partner verbally or acted out together. Milonas's *Fantasex* (1975) is filled with ideas for fantasy sex games that couples can play. Some couples enjoy making love while reading pornography aloud or silently together. Erotic talk during sex arouses some people.

ORAL SEX

Oral sex can provide very effective stimulation for the woman and for the man as well. Many men and women find that performing oral sex is as exciting as experiencing it. For most women the natural lubrication provided by oral sex makes this form of genital stimulation more pleasurable than manual stimulation. If the issue of oral sex does not emerge during the 10 sessions, it almost always is brought up in the follow-up.

Some rapid desensitization methods are effective in lowering anxiety and in overcoming feelings of disgust in regard to oral sex for both men and women. The principles of small steps and safety apply here. It is often helpful for the couple first to imagine, while making love or masturbating, that they are licking their partner's genitals or that their genitals are being licked. Some people are uncomfortable performing oral sex; others are uncomfortable receiving it. Once oral stimulation is attempted, the couple is to return to more familiar forms of lovemaking at any point if either person becomes very uncomfortable.

Fellatio

Fears of gagging or of receiving the ejaculate in the mouth are common among women reluctant to perform fellatio. The desensitization can begin by having the women spend time kissing the penis before inserting it in her mouth. The first time she decides to put the penis in her mouth the penis should be flaccid, which generally reduces both fear and the tendency to gag. When the penis is erect, positions that allow the woman to be on top and control the thrusting help reduce her concern about gagging, especially if she places her hand around the base of the penis. In this way, her hand prevents the penis from going too far into her mouth.

Shari Shultz (1977) designed an effective technique for the woman who does not want the man to ejaculate in her mouth. The couple can use a condom over the penis until the woman gains trust in her partner's ability to signal when he is about to ejaculate. Once trust has been established the condom can be removed. The woman may never want to receive the ejaculate in her mouth, but if she does, the desensitization process can begin with both people tasting the ejaculate. Then the woman can be taught to close off her throat by placing her tongue against the back part of the roof of her mouth. She can then swallow the ejaculate if she wants to.

Cunnilingus

The man can be desensitized to cunnilingus by having both partners smell and taste the woman's lubrication. Love oils, or lickables,* flavored and scented oils specifically for use on the genitals, can be licked off nongenital areas of the body as a preliminary step. Once the couple is ready to use the oil on the genitals, they should be instructed to progress by small steps to prevent anxiety. Taking a shower or bath together can alleviate concern about odor. Then, after the couple is aroused using their familiar techniques, the partner's lips can be briefly brushed over the woman's genitals. With each successive trial the time spent on oral stimulation can be increased slowly.

Often, women are as uncomfortable with cunnilingus as with fellatio. They fear that their genitals are dirty and that the smell might be offensive to a partner. Some women find unmanly the partner's physical position while performing oral sex. These problems can be overcome if a woman feels sufficiently motivated. Motivation generally arises out of her partner's enjoyment of cunnilingus or out of her expectation of pleasure, which enables her to endure the initial discomfort. Bathing before oral sex and asking her partner as often as necessary if he finds the experience distasteful can help allay the woman's fears; choosing positions that do not make her partner seem unmanly also may be appropriate.

---

*These products are available in many places that sell massage oil. They can also be ordered from Eve's Garden, 119 West Fifty-seventh Street, New York, New York 10019, and Sensory Research, 2424 Morris Avenue, Union, New Jersey 07083.

Couple Progress

The exact exercises done are not as important to a successful out-come as is the couple's ability openly to discuss their sexual situation—their feelings about sex, their preferences, and of course their attitudes toward new behaviors. The risk taking that is necessary to participate in discussions and exercises is often great. The willing-ness of a couple to experiment with new sexual interactions instead of repeating familiar unsatisfactory patterns is most crucial to the development of a rewarding sexual relationship. When anger is great and more satisfaction is gained by thwarting the needs and desires of the other than by enjoying sex together, the prognosis for the sexual relationship is poor.

CHAPTER 8

The Final Sessions and Follow-up

Termination Plans

PREPARATION FOR TERMINATION should be started by the eighth session. Most group members voice a wish to continue after the ten sessions when the subject of termination first arises. The women are generally very invested in the group and quite unhappy about the end coming so soon. However, after preparing themselves for the end of the group and the homework progression to follow afterward, the women feel less dependent on the group process and look forward to spending time working on their own.

Even the women who have not yet experienced orgasm with a partner are usually much less worried about this aspect of their sexuality than they were when they began the group. They no longer feel abnormal and they generally understand the importance of sexual communication and the steps they need to take in order to be orgasmic with a partner. The knowledge that they can join another group to assist them in continuing the process is comforting. However, most women opt to work on their own for a period of time before deciding to join another group. Some groups do continue to meet regularly with or without the leader, but usually most of the women prefer a hiatus. A few may decide individually either to begin another form of therapy or to wait until the follow-up session to determine how best to proceed.

The Final Sessions

The eighth, ninth, and tenth sessions resemble the preceding sessions. However, by this time, the women's homework assignments are quite diversified. Some are doing partner exercises; others may be focusing on changing masturbatory positions and stroking techniques; still others may be beginning to use vaginal inserts and carrying out the initial partner assignments in fantasy during masturbation. Perhaps one woman has not yet experienced her first orgasm and is concentrating on the appropriate exercises to attain this goal.

By the ninth session the women are sufficiently skilled in using the tools they have acquired through participating in the group to begin planning a homework exercise progression to help them reach any additional sexual goals they may have. They are now realistic about their sexual objectives, knowledgeable about the ways to attain them, and familiar with the key principle of small steps under conditions that minimize risk and reduce the pressure to perform. Therefore, I instruct them to write out a series of homework assignments that they can work on until the follow-up session. The exercises are to be made explicit, with the understanding that for every goal set, the next assignment in the progression is not to be undertaken until success has been experienced with its predecessor.

The tenth session is devoted partly to reviewing the women's future sexual goals and planning the course of action to be taken after the group has ended. It is not uncommon for group members to experience a setback around the ninth or tenth session. Anxious about termination, women who were reliably orgasmic may abruptly lose this ability, and procedures that worked before may suddenly fail. Predicting this possibility in the ninth session can reduce its likelihood. If there are setbacks, however, simple reassurance can relieve the anxiety, freeing the natural sexual responses once again.

THERAPIST: You're upset. Miraculously, on the last session, your orgasms have stopped.

JOSEPHINE: I do everything more intensely, but nothing happens.

ABBY: I have the same thing. I made love yesterday and I could have been doing something else. And I masturbated this week and old *Fanny Hill* didn't even do it. And I would sit there and masturbate and it felt good and I thought, "Oh, Jesus." And I wasn't getting anywhere. And I was doing it longer, too.

B.J.: Is this common?

THERAPIST: Unfortunately, yes. Very common. I don't know what's going on with you, but all I know is that in many groups a couple of things happen. One is the sixth session slump, which you all had in the fifth session. But there tends to be a session right around there where everybody gets really depressed. And then around the ninth or tenth session, people will come in and all of a sudden their successes will have all turned into total failures. Orgasms have stopped and everything.

B.J.: But why?

THERAPIST: Well, all I know is that there is frequently that response when the group is about to end, a feeling that it's been a good experience but, nobody's in a situation where everything is so solid that they feel 100 percent absolutely certain, because it's a short group. And everybody's anxieties come out at the end, like, "Oh, my God, the group's not going to be here. Now what? I've lost everything." It's very common.

B.J.: Well, what should I do? Something's happening, but I don't climax.

THERAPIST: But you always have climaxed even if they were small. Now, you're not having anything, right? That's got to be related to the group. Orgasms don't stop just like that. I'm not really worried about it in the long term. I've just never known anybody to get to a place and all of a sudden totally lose it. I'm not worried about it coming back.

B.J.: What do I do in the meantime?

THERAPIST: Take a vacation. Don't push it.

ABBY: Just because for a week you can't have an orgasm does not mean that you're not going to have another one. Just flip-flop your thinking around to say you can have an orgasm and just take a little vacation. I started thinking, "I'm never going to have another orgasm." I could get myself in such a state doing this if I let myself. And I just thought, "I'm under so much pressure right now, about everything else that has nothing to do with sex." I know what to do. We all know what to do now.

207

We have all the tools. You know what to do for yourself. You just have to have a little faith.

THERAPIST: But there is that real concern. Sometimes for six months following the group everyone does just fine, and then there may be a decline for some. And then, some of the people go right back up again. Some people go up and down. If they expect to have some downs and realize that downs are part of the ball game, then as soon as they go down, they say, "Oh, I'm down here. Now, let's see, what are the things I can do to feel better again." Then they can get back up out of it.

JENNY: I see a lot of things that are ups and downs, so why should sex be any different?

THERAPIST: Exactly.

Progress after termination of the group is highly dependent upon the expectations created by the leaders. Throughout the group the leaders have stressed the importance of reducing performance pressure and tuning in to bodily processes. For example, if a woman does her homework on a day when she has no interest in sex, she probably will not experience orgasm. Consequently, the women are encouraged to listen to their bodies and act accordingly. As the last part of the previous transcript illustrates, the leaders prepare the group members for reality. They let them know that women frequently experience a lessening of sexual interest after the group terminates due to fatigue resulting from the concentrated emphasis on sex during this period. Likewise, the women can expect to experience a lack of sexual interest during other periods in their lives.

Sexual problems arise most commonly during times of personal and interpersonal stress. Even though the feelings experienced during such times will be reminiscent of feelings experienced before the group began, they are not the same because the women have developed the necessary skills to deal with the sexual difficulties. Once they realize that a sexual problem exists, they can again utilize the tools acquired in the group. If they lose perspective during particularly difficult times, they can return to therapy for some additional sessions.

Referrals

Many women in preorgasmic groups make too much progress too rapidly to integrate fully all the changes they have experienced in ten sessions and further therapy—group, individual, or couple—may be required to solidify the integration process. I always make certain that each woman has an appropriate referral if the need is indicated. Less than 5 percent of the women decide to participate in a second group. Less than 15 percent desire individual or couple therapy for nonsexual issues. However, approximately 40 percent of the women in committed relationships seek a few sessions of conjoint or group sex therapy with their partners.

Women's Group Follow-up

I have a follow-up session for all of my groups. The postgroup meeting serves as a reunion: the women get together again and see how their lives have progressed since the group ended. They can share the problems they have encountered, as well as any techniques they have learned or developed; discussion in this session generally extends beyond sexuality to other issues of personal and relationship growth.

The group reunion can be a powerful therapy session. The sense of positive competition serves as an incentive to the women to persist in their own sexual pursuits. Those who have fallen behind often feel renewed hope as the result of hearing about the progress of others; whereas those who are moving ahead at a reasonable pace are reinforced for their continued growth.

The impact of the follow-up session depends upon the amount of time that has elapsed since the conclusion of the group. As has been noted, most of the women experience a lessening of interest in working on their sexuality in the four to six weeks immediately following the tenth group session. Although the women continue to feel pleased about being able to masturbate to orgasm, the frequency with which they masturbate generally has declined. Consequently, if the follow-up is scheduled for less than two months after the tenth session, many of the women will still be in the midst of a postgroup slump and a reunion will serve only to generate a sense of hopelessness among the members. However, by two months postgroup, the women's natural interest in sexuality usually has returned. A reunion at this time encourages the women to continue working on the homework exercises in a more diligent and aware fashion.

For the therapists, the group follow-up is an opportunity to appraise the women's progress after termination of treatment. In general, the women not only maintain the changes but continue to increase their sexual satisfaction long after the tenth session. This extra meeting also enables the therapists to provide the information, guidance, support, or therapeutic intervention needed by women who are having problems with their sexuality. The follow-up is often the best point at which to make an appropriate referral. The woman has had the opportunity to work on her own and, if she has had difficulty, she may be more receptive to seeking additional therapy than she was at the tenth session.

Couples' Group Follow-up

If the women and their partners so desire, a two- to four-session couples' group can begin either after the tenth group session or after the follow-up. I have tried both schedules and prefer to run the couples' group immediately after the women's group since there is less time for problems to develop and solidify.

For the most part, the concerns of the male partners occupy the couples' group sessions. Most of the men have been keeping their own concerns private in an attempt to be helpful to their partners; thus, they may be somewhat resentful. Reopening direct communication by having the partners check out their assumptions is a primary aim of the couples' sessions.

Bruce had not been initiating sex because he did not want to impose on his wife, Alice. Alice had not minded this situation since she had been concentrating on sex so intently during the previous two months. When Bruce voiced his needs, Alice was happy to accommodate. Although she had not felt like initiating sex, she was receptive to his suggestion. She had been operating under the misconception that work stress and other problems were causing Bruce's apparent lack of sexual interest. The simple discussion that took place in the group clarified the issue.

Another topic dominating the couple sessions is the worry the men have about their own sexuality—for example, occasional experiences of being unable to ejaculate or of ejaculating too rapidly. Generally, the men also desire more explicit information regarding the sexual preferences of their partners to enable them to become more proficient lovers.

For the most part, the men enjoy meeting the other men and their partners and give support when it seems to be needed, usually by sharing common concerns. I am always surprised by the relative ease with which the men discuss their intimate sexual problems and feelings. This openness may occur so readily because the women kept the men apprised of the content of the group sessions throughout the group process. Even though the men were not physically present, they felt emotionally involved. In any case, the sessions are attended with interest and generally are sufficient to meet the couples' needs. (However, conjoint sessions may also be necessary when changes in the sexual relationship have created an extensive disequilibrium in a couple's system.)

CHAPTER 9

Ethical Issues in the Group Treatment of Sexual Dysfunctions

Confidentiality and Right to Privacy

IN ANY THERAPEUTIC RELATIONSHIP, issues of confidentiality and right to privacy arise. In sex therapy these issues are complicated by the highly private nature of sexuality, around which many personal and cultural taboos exist. Sex therapy in a group setting, where participants are required to share highly personal information with other clients, presents unique problems in this area.

In individual or couple sex therapy, the therapist is ethically obliged to guard the clients' confidentiality. Yet in group treatment, the group members are not bound to maintain confidentiality in the same way that therapists are, and although the importance of confidentiality must be stressed, there is no guarantee that one group member will not tell her partner or friends the details of a sexual problem revealed by another group member. To some extent, the women can protect themselves from unwanted exposure by withholding information they do not wish others to have, but withholding can prove detrimental to treatment.

Another serious issue is the right to privacy of partners of participants in group sex therapy programs that do not involve partners directly. A partner in this situation has no control over the information supplied or withheld. This lack of input is of special concern in cases where the partner is not aware of the client's involvement in sex therapy. Frequently, women in preorgasmic groups do not feel comfortable informing a casual partner of their sexual problems, particularly if they have been faking orgasm. Yet relevant details of such relationships must be revealed in the group in order for the women to gain the necessary skills to derive greater satisfaction from sex.

In general, clients and their partners should be forewarned about the problems involved in maintaining total confidentiality in a group treatment program. It is also helpful to disclose only the first names of clients and partners and to instruct group members to disguise the identity of uninformed partners. These precautions can help but they do not totally protect confidentiality and the right to privacy in any group therapy program.

Welfare of the Client

The safeguarding of a client's values is critical in any area of psychotherapy; however, it is a particularly sensitive issue in regard to sexuality. Clients seeking assistance with sexual dysfunctions come from a variety of religious and cultural backgrounds, most of which define acceptable and unacceptable sexual practices. Remember that clients are seeking help for their particular sexual dysfunction as they experience it and not for their sexual lifestyles—although at times there may be a relationship between these areas that must be explored.

Sometimes the sex therapist must expand the client's list of permissible sexual activities in order to relieve a dysfunction. Permission giving is a fundamental therapeutic factor in the treatment of sexual problems. However, permission can easily turn into coercion, especially when backed by peer pressure, and the therapist must carefully guard against this possibility.

Peer support and peer permission make the group treatment approach especially powerful. As I have frequently noted, being in a group with people who have similar problems works quickly to alleviate a sense of alienation and abnormality and to facilitate behavioral change by removing inhibitions. One woman, for example, had had a strict Catholic upbringing, which initially kept her from masturbating. However, when other group members reported success with the masturbation homework, she decided it might be all right for her to do it for "training" purposes. In this sense, the group forms a mini-society to counteract the negative sexual messages of the society at large.

But the same process that enhances change has potential drawbacks. Some members may inadvertently impose their sexual values on other group members, or group support may have a restricting rather than a liberating effect on a given client. For example, if a woman feels morally indignant about the sexual attitudes of other group members she may not express her views for fear of being ridiculed or excluded from the group. In this case, the client may leave the group feeling more sexually inadequate than she did when therapy began.

It is up to the therapist to be aware of differences in values among group members and to acknowledge individual uniqueness so that negative peer pressure is kept to a minimum. (The equally relevant concern of therapist imposed sexual values is discussed in the section on therapist competence.)

All group treatment programs run the risk of not supplying sufficient individual attention, particularly to the more quiet members. In these cases, some individual sessions during the course of the group may be required. In some cases, the group situation may benefit shy members. In one preorgasmic group, a woman was so embarrassed about sex that she talked very little during the meetings. Meanwhile, her attention during the groups was riveted on the other members and she completed all her homework assignments, allowing her to become orgasmic. Possibly, for this client the intensity and personal focus of individual or couple therapy would have been overwhelming.

The goal orientation of any behavior therapy, but particularly sex therapy, can present some drawbacks in a group setting. Since the members' goals are often similar, every member is acutely aware of the progress of the others. Some clients may get discouraged when they compare other group members' successes with their own lack of progress. In these cases, the therapist must maintain the focus on an individualized process, emphasizing that each person's situation is unique and that each will move through the process at her own speed. Ultimate satisfaction rather than speed must be constantly re-affirmed as the objective of the program.

The therapist's decision to terminate treatment when the therapy is not benefiting a client is a difficult one to implement in a group treatment situation. In a group, the therapeutic relationship extends beyond the client and the therapist to the client and the other group members. If, once the group commences, the therapist decides that individual therapy would be more beneficial to one member than group therapy, the issue can become a very complex and uncomfortable one for everyone involved. Asking the woman to leave the group could exacerbate her existing feelings of failure as she compares her progress with that of other group members; in addition, feelings of rejection and exclusion might be engendered.

As previously mentioned, the short-term nature of group sex therapy gives the issues of follow-up and referral greater significance than they have in long-term treatment. A person who successfully completes a sex therapy program frequently finds that a good deal more than her sexual responsiveness has changed as the result of the therapy. Particularly in the preorgasmic women's groups, positive changes in body image, self-esteem, partner communication and interaction, and sense of control over life may not be fully integrated within the brief treatment period. Consequently, the therapist is ethically bound to insure that adequate follow-up supervision or treatment is available to enable clients to integrate the changes brought about during treatment.

Therapist Competence

The therapist directing group treatment of sexual dysfunctions not only must be competent in general psychotherapy and specifically in the behavioral treatment of sexual dysfunctions but also must understand group process and have adequate group treatment skills. Every group is different and each develops a process or sense of group that is unique. Within this idiosyncratic group sense negative group norms often develop, which can interfere with the treatment of the entire group (see pp. 166–170).

An issue previously discussed concerns the treatment of only one partner in a relationship. A competent therapist must have knowledge of the couple's relationship and interaction in order to understand the absent partner and to aid with interventions that will not worsen the couple's system but work to improve it. Taking a one-sided view may result in the breakup of a relationship, with the excluded partner feeling angry, confused, hurt, and abandoned. I do not suggest that termination of a relationship is necessarily a negative outcome: it may be the most beneficial solution for both parties. However, the therapist should be sensitive to the relationship and cognizant of the therapy's effects on it. Accordingly, some clients should be encouraged to participate in conjoint sex therapy.

A third issue related to therapist competence again, previously mentioned—has to do with personal disclosure on the part of the therapist. In sex therapy, appropriate disclosure can be a highly effective therapeutic technique. Not only does it provide good modeling, but it enables the client to see that it is possible to overcome sexual problems. In a group situation, the therapist's personal disclosure promotes sharing among the members. However, the therapist must appreciate the limits of self-disclosure: she must be careful not to impose her own problems on group members and to avoid offering "liberated" sexual values as the standard for the clients to live up to, thereby replacing one sexual value system with another equally restrictive one. For example, we used to expect people over a certain age to cease being sexual. Now that we know it is possible to remain sexual until an advanced age, we are in danger of giving people the coercive message that they *must* remain sexually active in their later years. (Some people welcome this time as a respite from sex, which perhaps they never enjoyed or which has ceased to be enjoyable.)

I hope the reader recognizes that in any treatment of sexual problems it is of the utmost importance to treat each individual's sexual attitudes and values with respect. The more free people are to pick sexual behaviors that coincide with their unique preferences, the more likely they are to experience a satisfying sexual relationship. Treating sexual dysfunctions is often more than merely reversing a symptom. Particularly with women who are not orgasmic, it entails restructuring a sexual encounter to meet each woman's sexual needs. The harder a woman tries to fit into another's framework, the more awkward and strained her sexual encounters are likely to be. Breaking in a partner, like a new pair of shoes, may be uncomfortable in the beginning, but it will create a situation where comfort can exist from that point on.

Dr. Lonnie Barbach is continuing to conduct workshops throughout the country for properly credentialed therapists who desire further training in running women's sex therapy groups. She can be contacted directly at Nexus: 1968 Green Street, San Francisco, California 94123.

Bibliography

ANNON, JACK. *The Behavioral Treatment of Sexual Problems.* Vols. 1 and 2. Honolulu: Enabling Systems, 1974, 1975.

ANONYMOUS. *The Pearl.* New York: Grove Press, 1968.

AYRES, T.; RUBENSTEIN, M.; AND SMITH, C. *The Yes Book of Sex: Masturbation Techniques for Women.* San Francisco: Multi-Media Resource Center, 1972.

BACH, GEORGE, AND DEUTSCH, RONALD. *Pairing.* New York: Avon, 1970.

BACH, GEORGE, AND GOLDBERG, HERB. *Creative Aggression.* New York: Avon, 1974

BACH, GEORGE, AND WYDEN, PETER. *The Intimate Enemy.* New York: Avon, 1968.

BANDURA, A. *Principles of Behavior Modification.* New York: Holt, Rinehart & Winston, 1969.

BARBACH, LONNIE G. "Group Treatment of Preorgasmic Women." *Journal of Sex and Marital Therapy*, V. 1 (Winter 1974): 139–145.

_____. *For Yourself: The Fulfillment of Female Sexuality.* New York: Doubleday, 1975.

_____, AND AYRES, TONI. "Group Process for Women with Orgasmic Concerns." *Personnel and Guidance Journal*, V. 54 (March 1976): 389–391.

_____, AND FLAHERTY, MARIA. "Group Treatment of Situationally Orgasmic Women." *Journal of Sex and Marital Therapy*, to be published Spring 1980.

BARDWICK, JUDITH M. *Psychology of Women: A Study of Bio-Cultural Conflict*. New York: Harper & Row, 1971.

BEAUVOIR, SIMONE DE. *The Second Sex*. New York: Bantam, 1952.

BELLIVEAU, FRED, AND RICHTER, LIN. *Understanding Human Sexual Inadequacy*. Boston: Little, Brown, 1970.

BENEDEK, T. "Sexual Functions in Women and Their Disturbance." *American Handbook of Psychiatry*, ed. S. Arieti. New York: Basic Books, 1959. Vol. 1, pp. 569–591.

BERGER, M.M. "The Function of the Leader in Developing and Maintaining a Working Therapeutic Group." Unpublished manuscript, 1967.

BERGLER, E. "The Problem of Frigidity." *Psychiatric Quarterly*, V. 18, 3 (1944): 374–390.

_____. "Frigidity in the Female: Misconceptions and Facts." *Marriage and Hygiene*, V. 1 (1947): 16–21.

BERNSTEIN, DOUGLAS A., AND BORKOVEC, THOMAS D. *Progressive Relaxation Training: A Manual for the Helping Professions*. Champaign: Research Press, 1973.

BERZON, B.; PIOUS, G.; AND PARSON, R. "The Therapeutic Event in Group Psychotherapy: A Study of Subjective Reports by Group Members." *Journal of Individual Psychology*, V. 19 (1963): 204–212.

BLANK, JOANI. *My Playbook for Women: About Sex*. Burlingame: Down There Press, 1975.

_____. *Good Vibrations: The Complete Woman's Guide to Vibrators*. Burlingame: Down There Press, 1976.

_____. *I Am My Lover*. Burlingame: Down There Press, 1978.

BONAPARTE, M. *Female Sexuality*. New York: International Universities Press, 1953.

BOSTON WOMEN'S HEALTH BOOK COLLECTIVE. *Our Bodies, Ourselves: A Book by and for Women*. New York: Simon & Schuster, 1973.

BRADY, J. P. "Brevital Relaxation Treatment of Frigidity." *Behavior Research and Therapy*, V. 4 (1966): 71–77.

BRECHER, EDWARD. *The Sex Researchers*. London: Deutsch, 1969.

BRECHER, RUTH, AND BRECHER, EDWARD. "Sex during and after Pregnancy." *An Analysis of Human Sexual Response*, ed. Ruth Brecher and Edward Brecher. New York: New American Library, Signet Books, 1966. Pp. 88–95.

BRECHER, RUTH, AND BRECHER, EDWARD (eds.). *An Analysis of Human Sexual Response*. New York: New American Library, Signet Books, 1966.

BROWN, D.G. "Female Orgasm and Sexual Inadequacy." *An Analysis of Human Sexual Response*, ed. Ruth Brecher and Edward Brecher. New York: New American Library, Signet Books, 1966. Pp. 125–174.

BULLOUGH, VERN, AND BULLOUGH, BONNIE. *Sin, Sickness, and Sanity: A History of Sexual Attitudes*. New York: New American Library, 1977.

CAPRIO, F. *The Sexually Adequate Female*. New York: Citadel, 1953.

CARTWRIGHT, D. AND ZANDER, A. (eds.). *Group Dynamics: Research and Theory*. Evanston: Row, Peterson, 1962.

CHESLER, PHYLLIS. "Patient and Patriarch: Women in the Psychotherapeutic Relationship." *Woman in Sexist Society: Studies in Power and Powerlessness*, ed. Vivian Gornick and Barbara K. Moran. New York: New American Library, Signet Books, 1972. Pp. 362–392.

CLARK, ALEXANDER L., AND WALLIN, PAUL. "Women's Sexual Responsiveness and the Duration and Quality of Their Marriages." *American Journal of Sociology*, V. 71, 2 (1965): 187–196.

CLELAND, JOHN. *Fanny Hill: Memoirs of a Woman of Pleasure*. North Hollywood: Brandon House, 1963.

COMFORT, ALEX (ed.). *The Joy of Sex*. New York: Crown, 1972.

CORINNE, TEE. *Cunt Coloring Book*. San Francisco: Pearlchild Productions, 1975.

DeLORA, JOANN, AND WARREN, CAROL. *Understanding Sexual Interaction*. Boston: Houghton Mifflin, 1976.

DEUTSCH, H. *The Psychology of Women*. Vols. 1 and 2. New York: Grune & Stratton, 1945.

DICKENSON, ROBERT LATOU. *Atlas of Human Sex Anatomy*, second ed. Baltimore: Williams and Wilkins, 1949.

DICKOFF, H., AND LAKIN, M. "Patient's Views of Group Psychotherapy: Retrospections and Interpretations." *International Journal of Group Psychotherapy*, V. 13, 1 (1963): 61–73.

DODSON, BETTY. *Liberating Masturbation*. New York: Bodysex Designs, 1974.

DOWNING, GEORGE. *The Massage Book*. New York: Random House; Berkeley: Bookworks, 1972.

DREIFUS, CLAUDIA. *Woman's Fate: Raps from a Feminist Consciousness-Raising Group*. New York: Bantam, 1973.

ELLIS, HAVELOCK. *Studies in the Psychology of Sex*. New York: Random House, 1936.

ENGEL, LEWIS. Personal communication. 1977.

ERON, LEONARD D. "Responses of Women to the Thematic Apperception Test." *Journal of Consulting Psychology*, V. 17, 4 (1953): 269–282.

ERSNER—HERSCHFIELD, ROBIN. "Evaluation of Two Components of Group Treatment for Preorgasmic Women: Couple vs. Women Format and Massed vs. Distributed Spacing." Ph.D. diss., Rutgers University, 1978.

FALK, RUTH. *Women Loving*. New York: Random House; Berkeley: Bookworks, 1975.

FARBER, LESLIE H. "I'm Sorry, Dear." *An Analysis of Human Sexual Response*, ed. Ruth Brecher and Edward Brecher. New York: New American Library, Signet Books, 1966. Pp. 291–312.

FARNHAM, M., AND LUNDBERG, F. *Modern Woman: The Lost Sex*. New York: Harper, 1947.

FAULK, MALCOLM. "Frigidity: A Critical Review." *Archives of Sexual Behavior*, V. 2, 3 (1973): 257–266.

FENICHEL, O. *The Psychoanalytic Theory of Neurosis*. New York: Norton, 1945.

FIEDLER, L. "Factor Analysis of Psychoanalytic, Non-Directive, and Adlerian Therapeutic Relationships." *Journal of Consulting Psychology*, V. 15, 1 (1951): 32–38.

FISHER, SEYMOUR. *The Female Orgasm*. New York: Basic Books, 1973.

FITHIAN, MARILYN; HARTMAN, WILLIAM; AND CAMPBELL, BARRY. "The Treatment of Female Orgasmic Dysfunction in the Laboratory Utilizing Polygraphic Readings." Paper presented at the International Congress of Sexology, Rome, October, 1978.

FORD, CLELLANS, AND BEACH, FRANK A. *Patterns of Sexual Behavior*. New York: Harper, 1951.

FRANK, J.D. "Some Determinants, Manifestations, and Effects of Cohesion in Therapy Groups." *International Journal of Group Psychotherapy*, V. 7, 1 (1957): 53–62.

FRANKFORT, ELLEN. *Vaginal Politics*. New York: Bantam, 1972.

FREUD, SIGMUND. *Three Contributions to the Theory of Sex*, Fourth ed., trans. A.A. Brill. New York: Nervous and Mental Disease Publishing, 1930.

————. *New Introductory Lectures on Psychoanalysis*, trans. and ed. James Strachey. New York: W.W. Norton, 1965.

————. "Female Sexuality." *Psychoanalysis and Female Sexuality*, ed. H. Ruitenbeek. New Haven: College & University Press, 1966. Pp. 88–105.

FRIDAY, NANCY. *Forbidden Flowers*. New York: Simon & Schuster, Pocket Books, 1975.

GEBHARD, P.H. "Factors in Marital Orgasm." *The Journal of Social Issues*, V. 22, 2 (1966): 88–95.

GODIVA. *What Lesbians Do*. Eugene: Amazon Reality Collective, 1975.

GORDON, DAVID COLE. *Self Love*. Baltimore: Penguin, 1968.

GORDON, THOMAS. *P.E.T.: Parent Effectiveness Training*. New York: Wyden, 1960.

GORNICK, VIVIAN, AND MORAN, BARBARA K. (eds.). *Women in Sexist Society: Studies in power and Powerlessness*. New York: New American Library, Signet Books, 1971.

GREENBERG, JEROLD S., AND ARCHAMBAULT, FRANCIS X. "Masturbation, Self-Esteem, and Other Variables." *Journal of Sex Research*, V. 9, 1 (1973): 41–51.

GREER, GERMAINE. *The Female Eunuch*. New York: Bantam, 1970.

HALEY, JAY. *Strategies of Psychotherapy*. New York: Grune & Stratton, 1963.

_____. *Uncommon Therapy*. New York: W.W. Norton, 1973.

HAMBURG, D.A. "Emotions in Perspective of Human Evolution." *Expressions of the Emotions of Man*, ed. P. Knapp. New York: International Universities Press, 1963. Pp. 300–317.

HARITON, E. BARBARA, AND SINGER, JEROME L. "Women's Fantasies during Marital Intercourse: Normative and Theoretical Implications." *Journal of Consulting and Clinical Psychology*, V. 42, 3 (1974): 313–322.

HARTMAN, WILLIAM, AND FITHIAN, MARILYN. *Treatment of Sexual Dysfunction*. Long Beach: Center for Marital and Sexual Studies, 1972.

HARTMAN, WILLIAM; FITHIAN, MARILYN; AND CAMPBELL, BARRY. "The Polygraphic Survey of the Human Sexual Response." Paper presented at the International Congress of Sexology, Rome, October, 1978.

HEIMAN, JULIA. "Physiology of Erotica: Women's Sexual Arousal." *Psychology Today*, V. 8, 4 (1975): 91–92.

HEIMAN, JULIA; LOPICCOLO, LESLIE; AND LOPICCOLO, JOSEPH. *Becoming Orgasmic: A Sexual Growth Program for Women*. Englewood Cliffs: Prentice-Hall, 1974.

HEINE, R.W. "A Comparison of Patients' Reports on Psychotherapeutic Experience with Psychoanalytic, Non-Directive, and Adlerian Therapists." *American Journal of Psychotherapy*, V. 7, 1 (1953): 16–23.

HEINRICH, ANNA GEYER. "The Effect of Group and Self-Directed Behavioral-Educational Treatment of Primary Orgasmic Dysfunction in Females Treated without Their Partners." Ph.D. diss., University of Minnesota, Department of Psychology, 1976.

HERSCHBERGER, RUTH. *Adam's Rib*. New York: Pellegrini & Cudahy, 1948.

HITE, SHERE. *The Hite Report*. New York: Macmillan, 1976.

HOMANS, GEORGE C. "Group Factors in Worker Productivity." *Readings in Social Psychology*, ed. T. Newcomb and E. Hartley. New York: Holt, 1947. Pp. 448–460.

HORNEY, KAREN. "The Denial of the Vagina." *International Journal of Psychoanalysis*, V. 14 (1933): 57–70.

_____. *Feminine Psychology*. New York: Norton, 1967.

HUELSMAN, BEN R. "An Anthropological View of Clitoral and Other Female Genital Mutilations." *The Clitoris*, ed. Thomas Lowry and Thea S. Lowry. St. Louis: Warren Green, 1976. Pp. 111–161.

HUNT, MORTON. *Sexual Behavior in the 1970's*. Chicago: Playboy Press, 1974.

JORGENSEN, VALERIE. "The Gynecologist and the Sexually Liberated Woman." *Obstetrics and Gynecology*, V. 42, 4 (1973): 607-612.

KAPLAN, HELEN SINGER. *The New Sex Therapy*. New York: Brunner/Mazel, 1974.

KEGEL, A.H. "Sexual Functions of the Pubococcygens Muscle." *Western Journal of Surgery*, V. 60, 10 (1952): 521-524.

KINSEY, ALFRED C.; POMEROY, WARDELL B.; AND MARTIN, CLYDE E. *Sexual Behavior in the Human Male*. Philadelphia: Saunders, 1948.

KINSEY, ALFRED C.; POMEROY, WARDELL B.; MARTIN, CLYDE E.; AND GEBHARD, PAUL H. *Sexual Behavior in the Human Female*. New York: Simon & Schuster, Pocket Books, 1953.

KLEEGMAN, SOPHIA. "Frigidity in Women." *Quarterly Review of Surgery, Obstetrics, and Gynecology*, V. 16 (1959): 243-248.

KLINE-GRABER, GEORGE, AND GRABER, BENJAMIN. *Women's Orgasm: A Guide to Sexual Satisfaction*. Indianapolis: Bobbs-Merrill, 1975.

KOEDT, ANN. "The Myth of the Vaginal Orgasm." *Liberation Now*. ed. Deborah Babcox and Madeline Belkin. New York: Dell, 1971. Pp. 311-320.

KRAFFT-EBING, RICHARD VON. *Psychopathia Sexualis*, trans. F.J. Rebman. New York: Physicians & Surgeons Book Co., 1922.

KRONHAUSEN, PHYLLIS, AND KRONHAUSEN, EBERHARD. *The Sexually Responsive Woman*. New York: Ballantine, 1964.

KURIANSKY, JUDITH; SHARP, LAWRENCE; AND O'CONNOR, DAGMAR. "Group Treatment for Women: The Quest for Orgasm." Paper presented at the American Public Health Association of Washington, D.C., October, 1976.

LAZARUS, A.A. "The Treatment of Chronic Frigidity by Systematic Desensitization." *Journal of Nervous and Mental Disease*, V. 136, 3 (1963): 272-278.

_____. *Behavior Therapy and Beyond*. New York: McGraw-Hill, 1971.

LEIBLUM, SANDRA, AND ERSNER-HERSHFIELD, ROBIN. "Sexual Enhancement Groups for Dysfunctional Women: An Evaluation." *Journal of Sex and Marital Therapy*, V. 3, 2 (1977): 139-152.

LEVINE, LINDA. Personal communication. 1976.

LIEBERMAN, M. "Behavior and Impact of Leaders." *New Perspectives on Encounter Groups*, ed. L.N. Solomon and B. Berzon. San Francisco: Jossey-Bass, 1972. Pp. 135-170.

LIEBERMAN, M.; YALOM, I.; AND MILES, M. *Encounter Groups: First Facts*. New York: Basic Books, 1973.

LOBITZ, W. CHARLES, AND LOPICCOLO, JOSEPH. "The Role of Masturbation in the Treatment of Orgasmic Dysfunction." *Archives of Sexual Behavior*, V. 2, 2 (1972): 163-171.

LOCKE, H., AND WALLACE, K. "Short Marital and Adjustment Tests: Their Reliability and Validity." *Marriage and Family Living*, V. 21 (1959): 251-255

LORAND, S. "Contribution to the Problem of Vaginal Orgasm." *International Journal of Psychoanalysis*, V. 20 (1939): 432-438.

LOWEN, A. *Love and Orgasm*. New York: New American Library, 1965.

LOWRY, THEA. Personal communication. 1975.

LYDON, SUSAN. "The Politics of Orgasm." *Sisterhood Is Powerful: An Anthology of Writings from the Women's Liberation Movement*, ed. Robin Morgan. New York: Random House, Vintage Books, 1970. Pp. 197-204.

MADSEN, C.H., JR., AND ULLMAN, L.P. "Innovations in the Desensitization of Frigidity." *Behavior Research and Therapy*, V. 5, 1 (1967): 67-68.

MARMOR, J. "Some Considerations Concerning Orgasm in the Female." *Psychoanalysis and Female Sexuality*, ed. H. Ruitenbeek. New Haven: College & University Press, 1966. Pp. 198-207.

_____. "Changing Patterns of Femininity: Pschoanalytic Implications." *Psychoanalysis and Women*, ed. Jean Baker Miller. Baltimore: Penguin, 1973. Pp. 221-238.

MARTIN, DEL, AND LYON, PHYLLIS. *Lesbian Women*. New York: Bantam, 1972.

MASTERS, WILLIAM H., AND JOHNSON, VIRGINIA E. *Human Sexual Response*. Boston: Little, Brown, 1966.

_____. *Human Sexual Inadequacy*. Boston: Little, Brown, 1970.

MEAD, MARGARET. *Male and Female: A Study of the Sexes in a Changing World*. New York: Dell, Laurel Editions, 1949.

MEADOR, BETTY; SOLOMON, EVELYN: AND BOWEN, MARIA. "Encounter Groups for Women Only." *New Perspectives on Encounter Groups*, ed.

N. Solomon and B. Berzon. San Francisco: Jossey-Bass, 1972. Pp. 335–348.

MILLER, JEAN BAKER (ed.). *Psychoanalysis and Women*. Baltimore: Penguin, 1973.

MILLET, KATE. *Sexual Politics*. New York: Doubleday, 1970.

MILONAS, ROLF. *Fantasex: A Book of Erotic Games for the Adult Couple*. New York: Grosset & Dunlap, 1975.

MORGAN, ROBIN (ed.). *Sisterhood Is Powerful: An Anthology of Writings from the Women's Liberation Movement*. New York: Random House, Vintage Books, 1970.

MOULTON, RUTH. "A Survey and Reevaluation of the Concept of Penis Envy." *Psychoanalysis and Women*, ed. Jean Baker Miller. Baltimore: Penguin, 1973. Pp. 239–258.

NELSON, ARVALEA. "Personality Attributes of Female Orgasmic Consistency (Or, Romance Makes You Frigid)." M.A. thesis, University of California, Berkeley, 1974.

NETTER, FRANK H. *The CIBA Collection of Medical Illustrations*, Vol. 2, second ed. Summit: CIBA Corporation, 1965.

NIN, ANAÏS. *Delta of Venus*. New York: Harcourt, Brace, 1977.

NOMADIC SISTERS. *Loving Women*. P.O. Box 793, Sonora, California 95370, 1976.

O'CONNOR, JOHN F., AND STERN, LENORE O. "Results of Treatment in Functional Sexual Disorders." *New York State Journal of Medicine*, V. 72, 15 (1972): 1927–1934.

OTTO, HERBERT A., AND OTTO, ROBERTA. *Total Sex*. New York: New American Library, Signet Books, 1972.

PAYN, NADINE. "Beyond Orgasm: A Study of the Effect on Couple Systems of Group Treatment for Preorgasmic Women." Ph.D. diss., Wright Institute, 1976.

POMEROY, WARDELL. *Dr. Kinsey and the Institute for Sex Research*. New York: New American Library, Signet Books, 1973.

PRICE, SUSAN, AND HEINRICH, ANNA GEYER. "Group Treatment of Secondary Orgasmic Dysfunction." Paper presented at the American Psychological Association, San Francisco, August, 1977.

REICH, W. *The Function of the Orgasm*. New York: Orgone Institute Press, 1942.

RIBBLE, M. "The Infantile Experience in Relation to Personality Development." *Personality and the Behavior Disorders*, ed. J.M. Hunt. New York: Ronald, 1944, Pp. 621–651.

ROBINSON, PAUL. *The Modernization of Sex*. New York: Harper & Row, 1976.

ROGERS, CARL. *Becoming Partners: Marriage and Its Alternatives.* New York: Dell, 1972.

ROSEN, L., AND ROSEN, R. *Human Sexuality Today.* New York: Random House, 1980.

ROSENBERG, JACK LEE. *Total Orgasm.* New York: Random House; Berkeley: Bookworks, 1973.

ROSENBERG, M. "Self-Esteem Scale." *Measures of Social Psychological Attitudes*, ed. John P. Robinson and Phillip R. Shaver. Ann Arbor: Institute for Social Research, 1969. Pp. 98–101.

ROTTER, J. "Generalized Expectancies for Internal versus External Control of Reinforcement." *Psychological Monographs*, V. 80, 609 (entire issue), 1966.

RUBIN, I. "Sex after Forty—and after Seventy." *An Analysis of Human Sexual Response*, ed. Ruth Brecher and Edward Brecher. New York: New American Library, Signet Books, 1966. Pp. 251–266.

RUITENBEEK, H. (ed.). *Psychoanalysis and Female Sexuality.* New Haven: College & University Press, 1966.

SCHMIDT, GUNTER, AND SIGUSCH, VOLKMAR. "Women's Sexual Arousal." *Contemporary Sexual Behavior: Critical Issues in the 1970's*, ed. Joseph Zubin and John Money. Baltimore: Johns Hopkins Press, 1973. Pp. 117–144.

SECORD, P.F., AND JOURARD, S.M. "The Appraisal of Body Cathexis: Body Cathexis and the Self." *Journal of Consulting Psychology*, V. 17 (1953): 343–347.

SHEEHY, GAIL. *Passages.* New York: Dutton, 1974.

SHERIF, M.; HARVEY, O.J.; WHITE, E.J.; HOOD, W.R.; AND SHERIF, W.C. *Intergroup Conflict and Cooperation: The Robbers Cave Experiment.* Norman: University Book Exchange, 1961.

SHERFEY, MARY JANE. "A Theory of Female Sexuality." *Sisterhood Is Powerful: An Anthology of Writings from the Women's Liberation Movement*, ed. Robin Morgan. New York: Random House, Vintage Books, 1970. Pp. 220–229.

_____. *The Nature and Evolution of Female Sexuality.* New York: Random House, Vintage Books, 1972.

_____. "On the Nature of Female Sexuality." *Psychoanalysis and Women*, ed. Jean Baker Miller. Baltimore: Penguin, 1973. Pp. 135–154.

SHOPE, D. "A Comparison of Orgastic and Nonorgastic Girls." *Journal of Sex Research*, V. 4, 3 (1968): 206–219.

SHULMAN, ALIX. "Organs and Orgasms." *Woman in Sexist Society: Studies in Power and Powerlessness*, ed. Vivian Gornick and Barbara K. Moran. New York: New American Library, Signet Books, 1971. Pp. 292–303.

SHULTZ, SHARI. Personal Communication. 1977.

SKLAR, ALAN D.; YALOM, IRVING D.; ZIMMERBERG, ALYOSHA; AND NEWELL, GEARY L. "Time Extended Therapy: A Controlled Study." *Comparative Group Studies*, V. 1, 4 (1970): 373–386.

SLATER, PHILIP E. "Sexual Adequacy in America." *Intellectual Digest*, November 1973, pp. 17–20.

SOLOMAN, N., AND BERZON, B. (eds.). *New Perspectives on Encounter Groups*. San Francisco: Jossey-Bass, 1972.

STEGER, J. "A Time Series Analysis of the Covariation between Measures of Marital and Sexual Satisfaction." Paper presented at the Western Psychological Association, San Francisco, April, 1974.

STONE, ABRAHAM, AND LEVINE, LENA. "Group Therapy in Sexual Maladjustment." *American Journal of Psychiatry*, V. 107, 3 (1950): 195–202.

SULLIVAN, H.S. *The Interpersonal Theory of Psychiatry*. New York: Norton, 1953.

_____. *Conceptions of Modern Psychiatry*. London: Tavistock, 1955.

TALLAND, G., AND CLARK, D. "Evaluation of topics in Therapy Group Discussions." *Journal of Clinical Psychology*, V. 10, 2 (1954): 131–137.

THOMPSON, CLARA M. *On Women*. New York: New American Library, Mentor Books, 1971.

_____. *Psychoanalysis: Evolution and Development*. New York: Hermitage House, 1950.

TRUAX, C., AND CARKHUFF, R. *Toward Effective Counseling and Psychotherapy*. Chicago: Aldine, 1967.

VELDE, H. VAN DE. *Ideal Marriage: Its Physiology and Technique*. New York: Ballantine, 1926.

WALLACE, DOUG, AND BARBACH, LONNIE. "Preorgasmic Group Treatment." *Journal of Sex and Marital Therapy*, V. 1 (Winter 1974): 146–154.

WALLACH, LEAH. "Vaginal vs. Clitoral Orgasm." *Forum*, September 1973, pp. 44–47.

WALLIN, PAUL, AND CLARK, ALEXANDER L. "A Study of Orgasm as a Condition of Woman's Enjoyment of Coitus in the Middle Years of Marriage." *Human Biology*, V. 35 (May 1963): 131–139.

WATZLAWICK, PAUL; BEAVIN, JANET; AND JACKSON, DON. *Pragmatics of Human Communication*. New York: Norton, 1967.

WATZLAWICK, P.; WEAKLAND, J.; AND FISH, R. *Changes*. New York: W.W. Norton, 1974.

WEISSTEIN, NAOMI. "Kinder, Küche, Kirche as Scientific Law: Psychology Constructs the Female." *Sisterhood Is Powerful: An Anthology of*

Writings from the Women's Liberation Movement, ed. Robin Morgan. New York: Random House, Vintage Books, 1970. Pp. 205–219.

WOLPE, J. *Psychotherapy by Reciprocal Inhibition.* Stanford: Stanford University Press, 1958.

_____. "The Systematic Desensitization Treatment of Neurosis." *Journal of Nervous and Mental Disease*, V. 132, 3 (1961): 189–203.

_____. *Behavior Therapy Techniques.* New York: Pergamon, 1966.

_____. *The Practice of Behavior Therapy.* New York: Pergamon, 1969.

WRIGHT, HELENA. *More about the Sex Factor in Marriage*, second ed. London: Williams and Norgate, 1959.

YALOM, I.D. "A Study of Group Therapy Dropouts." *Archives of General Psychiatry*, V. 14, 4 (1966): 393–414.

_____. *The Theory and Practice of Group Psychotherapy.* New York: Basic Books, 1970.

YALOM, I.D.; HOUTS, P.S.; NEWELL, G.; AND RAND, K.H. "Preparation of Patients for Group Therapy." *Archives of General Psychiatry*, V. 17, 4 (1967): 416–427.

YALOM, I.D., AND RAND, K.H. "Compatibility and Cohesiveness in Therapy Groups." *Archives of General Psychiatry*, V. 13, 2 (1966): 269–276.

YOUNG, WAYLAND. *Eros Denied.* New York: Grove Press, 1964.

ZILBERGELD, BERNIE. *Male Sexuality.* Boston: Little, Brown, 1978.

ZUBIN, JOSEPH, AND MONEY, JOHN (eds.) *Contemporary Sexual Behavior: Critical Issues in the 1970's.* Baltimore: Johns Hopkins Press, 1973.

Index

F

Facilitation, leader and, 51
Failure, learning from, 146
Faking orgasm, 46–47, 81, 82
Fanny Hill (Cleland), 121
Fantasex (Milonas), 202
Fantasy, 35–36, 114, 119–121, 147,
  181, 201–202
Fears, confronting, 144
Fee collection, 74
Fellatio, 202–203
Fenichel, O., 2, 4
Fiedler, L., 47
Films of female masturbation, 111–116
Fisch, R., 140
Fisher, Seymour, 13
Fithian, Marilyn, 101, 192
Flaherty, Maria, 24, 27, 182
Focusing, 49, 83
Follow-up session, 209–211
For Yourself (Barbach), 43, 74, 85, 99
Forbidden Flowers (Friday), 121
Ford, Clellans, 12
Foreplay, 199–200
Freud, Sigmund, 3, 16
Friday, Nancy, 121

G

Gebhard, P.H., 199
General sexual dysfunction, defined,
  59
Genital looking exercise, 99, 102–105
Genital modeling exercise, 109
Genital touching exercise, 104–105
Genitals
  female, 99–100, 192–193
  male, 100, 192–193
Goal setting, 60–61, 109
Goldberg, Herb, 185, 187
Gordon, Thomas, 186
Graber, Benjamin, 172
Group conflicts, 53
Group norms, 39, 77, 166–170
Group pressure, 32–33
Group size, 65–66
Guilt, 62

H

Hariton, E. Barbara, 120, 201–202
Hartman, William, 101, 192
Heiman, Julia, 121
Heine, R.W., 47
Heinrich, Anna Geyer, 11, 22–23, 24
Hite, Shere, 4, 5, 15, 60, 100, 110
Home sexological exam, 192–193
Homework assignments, 38, 41
  ban on orgasm, 92–93
  body looking, 45, 88–91, 95–96
  body touching, 42, 45, 91–92, 95–98
  breast examination, 105
  completing, 66
  couples: *see* Partner sex
  exaggeration exercise, 90–91, 97
  feedback from, 94–98
  genital looking, 99, 102–105
  genital touching, 104–105
  individualizing, 144–166
  Kegel exercises, 85–87, 94–95, 104,
    105
  leader's evaluation of, 49, 51–52
  luxuriating, 105–106
  masturbation: *see* Masturbation
  mothers, talking to, 106–108
  reading, 85
  relaxation and private time, 87–88
  resistance to, 93–94
Homogeneous versus mixed groups,
  63–65
Horney, Karen, 4
Human Sexual Response (Masters and
  Johnson), 43
Humor, 45
Hunt, Morton, 15, 110

I

I Am My Lover (Blank), 99
Imaginal desensitization, 17
In vivo desensitization, 17
Inadequacy, feelings of, 34
Individualizing therapeutic approach,
  135–144
Information, lack of, 2, 7
Initial interview, 67–70
Injury, fear of, 12